'This marvelous [illegible] thas: wise, humane, and tho[illegible]tful teaching, an inspiring [illegible]candalous amount of word[illegible] political theory and politics, and suggestive about the place of both in the good life. Most of all, it models productive dialogue on some of the most divisive and polarizing issues today, while exploring the best versions of what there is to be said on many sides.'

Jacob T. Levy, *Tomlinson Professor of Political Theory and Professor of Political Science at McGill University, Canada*

'Resurrecting the Platonic tradition of dialogue, Kukathas engages one of the most urgent questions of our time—freedom of movement—with depth, nuance, and Socratic irony. Through sharp yet open-ended exchanges, this beautifully written book invites readers to confront their own assumptions and wrestle with the complexities of migration, identity, refugees, justice, the state, and the ideal of an open society. A much needed philosophical exercise in an age where only dogmas about immigration seem to surround us.'

Lea Ypi, *Professor of Political Theory at the London School of Economics and Political Science, UK*

Dialogues on Immigration and the Open Society

After some friendly pestering from six of his students curious about his thinking about immigration, a philosophy professor invites them to present their own ideas to him over a series of meetings throughout the term. This book is about their conversations.

These dialogues introduce the reader to the most important ethical and political questions about immigration. They begin by considering the claim that significant levels of immigration pose a threat to the very civilization of the West, where the immigration issue is a particularly vexed one. The chapters that follow consider the economics of immigration, whether or not the state is justified in its efforts—or even obliged—to control immigration, and whether everyone has a right to move or if only refugees can make so strong a claim. The final chapter considers the implications of a philosophy of immigration on the ideal of an open society. Throughout the book, there is a strong emphasis on addressing the conceptual questions that are vital for making any headway in understanding practical issues. What is a refugee? What are rights? What is an open society? Indeed, what is immigration?

Chandran Kukathas is Professor of Political Science at Singapore Management University. He is the author of *Immigration and Freedom* (2021), *The Liberal Archipelago* (2003), and *Hayek and Modern Liberalism* (1989).

Philosophical Dialogues on Contemporary Problems

Philosophical Dialogues on Contemporary Problems uses a well-known form—at least as old as Socrates and his interlocutors—to deepen understanding of a range of today's widely deliberated issues. Each volume includes an open dialogue between two or more fictional characters as they discuss and debate the empirical data and philosophical ideas underlying a problem in contemporary society. Students and other readers gain valuable, multiple perspectives on the problem at hand.

Each volume includes a foreword by a well-known philosopher, topic markers in the page margins, and an annotated bibliography.

Dialogues on Climate Justice
Stephen M. Gardiner and Arthur R. Obst

Dialogues on Gun Control
David DeGrazia

Dialogues on Human Enhancement
Nicholas Agar

Dialogues on Democracy
Julia Maskivker

Dialogues on Ethical Vegetarianism, 2nd Edition
Michael Huemer

Dialogues on Immigration and the Open Society
Chandran Kukathas

For more information about this series, please visit: www.routledge.com/Philosophical-Dialogues-on-Contemporary-Problems/book-series/PDCP

Dialogues on Immigration and the Open Society

Chandran Kukathas

Routledge
Taylor & Francis Group
NEW YORK AND LONDON

Designed cover image: Getty Images / Krimzoya

First published 2025
by Routledge
605 Third Avenue, New York, NY 10158

and by Routledge
4 Park Square, Milton Park, Abingdon, Oxon, OX14 4RN

Routledge is an imprint of the Taylor & Francis Group, an informa business

Library of Congress Cataloging-in-Publication Data
Names: Kukathas, Chandran author
Title: Dialogues on immigration and the open society / Chandran Kukathas.
Description: New York, NY : Routledge, 2025. | Includes bibliographical references and index. | Provided by publisher.
Identifiers: LCCN 2024060970 (print) | LCCN 2024060971 (ebook) | ISBN 9781041047377 hbk | ISBN 9781032996028 pbk | ISBN 9781003629641 ebk
Subjects: LCSH: Emigration and immigration–Moral and ethical aspects | Emigration and immigration–Political aspects | Emigration and immigration–Economic aspects | Emigration and immigration–Government policy | Emigration and immigration–Social aspects
Classification: LCC JV6035 .K85 2025 (print) | LCC JV6035 (ebook) | DDC 304.8–dc23/eng/20250326
LC record available at https://lccn.loc.gov/2024060970
LC ebook record available at https://lccn.loc.gov/2024060971

ISBN: 978-1-041-04737-7 (hbk)
ISBN: 978-1-032-99602-8 (pbk)
ISBN: 978-1-003-62964-1 (ebk)

DOI: 10.4324/9781003629641

Typeset in Sabon
by SPi Technologies India Pvt Ltd (Straive)

For William "Bill" Maley

Contents

Foreword

Robert E. Goodin

Chandran and I are both immigrants, several times over. Most academics I know are. When universities hire someone from abroad, no one bats an eyelid (except the poor secretary who is put to the trouble of getting them a work permit). Academics are by nature itinerants. A famous sociologist writes, only half in jest, of ours as 'The Class Consciousness of Frequent Travellers'.[1]

Academics' allegiance is to a profession that straddles the globe, and a great many of us have spent large chunks of time studying, teaching or researching in countries not our own. When we do, we often remain outsiders rather than sinking deep roots in those other places, taking up new citizenships and the like. I spent fully a third of my own academic career in the UK as a 'permanent resident' but never as a 'citizen'. My line always was, 'I prefer being an object rather than a subject of the Crown'. If all that makes us sound untethered, well, maybe we are—but not in a way that I, or I think Chandran, find in the least bit unsettling.

'But academics are not your typical migrants!' I hear you exclaim. Academics are highly educated, well paid and securely tenured in their jobs. They are in demand elsewhere, should things turn sour where they currently are. They do not fear for their lives (any more than everyone rightly does, from climate change).

1 Craig Calhoun, 'The class consciousness of frequent travellers: towards a critique of actually existing cosmopolitanism,' *Conceiving Cosmopolitanism*, ed. Steven Vertovec and Robin Cohen (Oxford: Oxford University Press, 2002), 86–109.

And of course academics all speak good(ish) English, the *lingua franca* of virtually all academic disciplines.

All that is true, but it is hardly unique to academics. Many other migrants are highly educated professionals, even if their qualifications are not recognized in their new host country. Many other of them bring useful skills to their new country. (To Brexiteers complaining of the much maligned 'Polish plumber', I always replied: 'Have you ever tried to get a *British* plumber?') Migrants, in general, have 'get up and go'—obviously, so, because they got up and went. So while there may be special reasons that academic migrants have it easy, there seems to be no obvious reason that non-academic migrants usually have it so hard.

Except maybe for one thing: culture. Academics belong everywhere and nowhere—with the emphasis on 'nowhere'. They are not 'cultural carriers', or if they carry a culture it is a peculiar one that no one else much cares about one way or the other. The fear of being 'swamped' by carriers of a foreign culture drives much of the animus against 'excessive' immigration. I won't say that that has never happened. Native Americans have legitimate grounds for complaint. But mostly the addition of new elements of culture enriches rather than erases the existing national culture. To those who complain about 'multiculturalism', I always say: 'Did you ever get a good meal in Australia before the White Australia policy ended and Asian immigrants flooded in?'

These are the sorts of issues that Chandran Kukathas explores in these charming dialogues with his students. These are dialogues, not of the brow-beating, Socratic form. Instead they are free-flowing discussions, exploratory rather than hectoring, light-touch, often funny, albeit with a serious point. They invite you to 'ponder some puzzles together'—even if (as the 'reveal' in the final chapters makes clear) the author does indeed have some firm views on the controversial matters previously under such free-and-easy discussion.

Preface and Acknowledgements

This work is written primarily for students, though I hope it will also reach a wider audience. The dialogue format is particularly well suited to making ideas accessible to non-specialists, and I have tried to make the text as readable as possible. The footnotes supply references to readings that treat in greater depth the various topics covered here. Overall, I have aimed to present a balanced view of the ethics of immigration, but my own views come out more plainly in the final chapter and epilogue. The literature on immigration is vast, and there are more questions to be examined than can be considered in a short work. This is, in the end, an introduction rather than a definitive statement.

Some of the names of the characters in the dialogue are those of my former graduate students at the London School of Economics and Political Science, but the characters themselves are drawn entirely from the imagination. They are purely fictitious and, now, fictional.

For helpful advice in the preparation of this book, I would like to thank the anonymous referees of earlier drafts of the manuscript. My greatest debt is to Christine Henderson, who read and re-read the work and offered her usual insightful suggestions for improvement.

'I dedicate this book to my dear friend, sometime co-author, and erstwhile colleague, Bill Maley. He has taught me more about immigration policy and refugee issues, particularly in Australia, than anyone else. His work both as a scholar and as a refugee advocate has always been an inspiration.'

Chandran Kukathas
Agia Marina, Crete
October 2024

1 Immigration and Civilization

Heading home early after the morning's classes, I went down to pick up a snack at *Pies R Us*—the most popular of the eateries on campus. This was a Friday after all, and it being Diwali, there would be festival events to attend all evening. The college prided itself on its diversity and made a point of celebrating every tradition it could. But I was hungry, and I also knew I wouldn't get a chance for a little quiet time later in the day.

As luck would have it, however, no sooner had I reached the Union Building than I found myself mobbed by a group of my students, along with one fellow I didn't recognize. Antoine, Astrid, Diana, Kaveh, Temi, and Tracy were soon to graduate and full of enthusiasm on seeing me. I could tell that they were in the mood to chat. Tracy did not look so happy, but then she rarely did, perhaps because she was the odd one out in that group as the only conservative among them. The fellow I didn't know, Stephan, was not from the university and did not have the demeanour of a student, though he looked cheerful enough when introduced. He seemed particularly interested in Diana (and unaware that she was married—to someone named Alex, I recalled).

'Let's find a table, Xandros,' said **Temi**. 'There are some things we want to ask you—if you wouldn't mind.'

'Yes, yes,' they all said, not quite in unison but with equal delight.

'Oh, but Stephan won't be able to come,' said **Diana**. 'He's not a student.'

Stephan beamed at this. He was clearly rather taken with Diana.

DOI: 10.4324/9781003629641-1

'Oh, don't worry about that,' said **Astrid**. 'No one will notice. It's a silly policy anyway. I don't see why he can't come with us.'

'Yes,' said **Antoine**. 'In France, the student unions are always open to everyone.'

'Well, they're not open here,' said **Kaveh**, 'and it looks like they're monitoring all the entrances. I think there've been too many people coming in for cheap, student grub.'

'They're not that strict,' said **Diana**, 'and besides, people come in illegally all the time. I think the monitors just stop the people they don't look the like of. I'd bet if you offered one a couple of dollars to look the other way, he would.'

'Maybe,' said **Antoine**, 'but I don't think that's right either. The doors should be open to everyone.'

'Well,' said **Temi**, 'I do see the union's point if we consider that we've all paid dues for membership. Though I think they could give us a bit more freedom to bring in guests.'

'I haven't paid any dues,' **I** said. 'Does that mean I can't enter?'

'Oh no,' **Diana** said. 'There's an exemption for faculty. I guess it's a bit of a perk for you.'

'I guess it is,' **I** said, laughing, and rolling my eyes.

'Come on, Stephan,' they started to say, 'we'll smuggle you in—like, like… like an asylum-seeker!'

The one person not laughing, however, was **Tracy**, who was looking increasingly uncomfortable before she burst out: 'No, the rules are the rules. We can't just smuggle Stephan in. He doesn't have a right to enter. And we don't have the right to make an exception.'

'We don't, but we should have,' said **Astrid**. 'It's a silly rule.'

'Students have paid to have exclusive use of this facility,' **Tracy** continued, 'and we have to respect these rules. It's our union, they're our rules.'

'They're not rules I agreed to,' said **Kaveh** drily. 'I didn't want to join the union, but the university made me and forced me to pay dues. I don't even come here that much.'

'That makes no difference,' said **Tracy**. 'We can't just go around deciding what rules we will and won't respect whenever it suits us.

If you want to change this rule, go to the union meetings and make a case.'

'Really, Ms Rand?' said **Kaveh**, grinning. 'I thought you said the union was just a bunch of lefties playing politics.'

'Maybe not the union, then, but take it up with the university,' **Tracy** answered, slightly flustered. 'And please don't associate me with Ayn Rand. I've avoided reading her and plan to continue avoiding.'

At that point, **Stephan** put up his hand a little sheepishly and said: 'Sorry guys, sorry to cause all this fuss, but actually I have to go. I start work soon. But I appreciate how many of you are willing to break the law and risk imprisonment, or maybe torture, to get me into this wonderful building. The coffee must be great! Another time? Bye, everyone. Bye, Diana.'

Everyone, including Tracy, started to giggle.

'Okay,' said **Temi**. 'Let's buy our esteemed professor some coffee.'

'I really should go too,' **I** said. 'All this chatter has taken up a lot of time.'

'Oh no, you're not getting away yet, Xandros,' said **Diana**, putting her hand on my shoulder. 'We do need to ask you a few things before you slip on your invisibility cloak. Actually, we also wanted to make sure we saw you properly before the end of the year. Everyone disappears so fast at the end of term, and we won't be back for any of your classes. One last dose of wisdom from the philosopher?'

'Alright,' **I** said, 'let's go in.'

We made our way to *Pies*, where we found a large comfortable table in the corner. It was a quiet time for business, and we were virtually the only ones there. The students were in a light-hearted mood, possibly because they'd completed most of their credits and were anticipating an easy ride to the end of their undergraduate careers.

'So, what is it you want to ask me?' **I** said.

'Well,' said **Temi**, 'there's nothing really. We just wanted to make sure we got a chance to hang out with you one last time. It's our final year, and someone said you were going on sabbatical next year, so we might not see you again.'

'Yes,' said **Astrid**. 'Where are you going on your sabbatical? And what are you going to do? Are you writing a book?'

'No, I'm not going anywhere,' **I** replied, 'but I am writing a book.'

'On what?' asked **Tracy**. 'Let me guess... something only philosophers would read ... something like, uh, *the concept of intuition*... or *the meaning of meaning*...'

Everyone chuckled, and before **I** knew it, there were a dozen more imaginary titles proposed, all beginning *the concept* or *the meaning*.

'Laugh if you will,' **I** said, 'but I make no apology for being interested in conceptual questions. Someone should be asking what we mean when we say certain things—doing the necessary work of clearing away a little rubbish if it obscures our understanding.'

'Yeah, well, fine,' said **Antoine**. 'It's all very well to do that, but surely there's more to philosophy than just being a janitor. Don't you want to address some real questions? Some problems? Philosophers have only interpreted the world; the point is to...'

'Change it,' **I** said, finishing his sentence. 'Thank you, comrade. Perhaps after the revolution, we can do away with all this conceptual analysis. Still, you'll be pleased to know that I'll be both doing some conceptual analysis and addressing a "real" question. My book is about immigration.'

'What made you decide to write about that?' asked **Diana**. 'It doesn't seem like your thing.'

'It wasn't,' **I** said. 'But I was in a meeting with our department chair, and he started grumbling about how everything was changing too fast, and the old order was breaking down. He surprised me, but it really wasn't so surprising in one way, since he comes from a very prominent family that's been quite vocal about how America is not what it used to be. Anyway, Professor Keffler started saying that there was too much immigration and we needed to rethink public policy, and it got me thinking. It's about the fate of civilization, he said.'

'What was his view? Did he have an argument?' asked **Temi**.

'No,' **I** said. 'I tried to press him, but he said he had a meeting to go to and muttered something about it all having gotten a bit too much for him. Surprising, really, since he's only a year or two older than I am. He just left, saying we've all got to pay our debts.'

'We know all about that,' said **Kaveh**. 'Our student loans will turn from in-comings to out-goings pretty soon.'

Everyone nodded solemnly.

'But what's your view, Xandros?' said **Diana**. 'We did a whole term with you on justice and never found out what you thought. We know what Rawls[1] thought, well, sort of… And we know what Nozick[2] thought, and Hayek[3] and Walzer,[4] and all those crazy, mixed-up communitarians.[5] But what do *you* think? Do *you* have any opinions?'

'I don't have opinions, I have knowledge,' **I** said smiling quietly, prompting a series of giggles, groans, and bows of mock respect until I couldn't help laughing out loud.

1 John Rawls (1921–2002) was the author of *A Theory of Justice* ([1971], Revised Edition, Cambridge, MA: Belknap Harvard University Press, 1999). His other notable works include *Political Liberalism* ([1993], Revised Edition, New York: Columbia University Press, 1999); *Justice as Fairness: A Restatement* (edited by Erin Kelly, Cambridge, MA: Belknap Press of Harvard University Press, 2001); and *The Law of Peoples with 'The Idea of Public Reason Revisited'* (Cambridge, MA: Harvard University Press, 2002). His views on immigration are discussed in later chapters.

2 Robert Nozick (1940–2002) was the author of *Anarchy, State and Utopia* (Oxford: Blackwell, 1974). It presented a libertarian challenge to Rawls's theory of justice.

3 F.A. Hayek (1899–1992) was a Nobel laureate in Economics whose major works include *The Constitution of Liberty* (London: Routledge, 1960) and *Law, Legislation and Liberty* (London: Routledge, 1979).

4 Michael Walzer is an American political theorist who presented an alternative view of justice that was critical of both Rawls and Nozick, notably in *Spheres of Justice: A Defense of Pluralism and Equality* (New York: Basic Books, 1983). His discussion of immigration in Chapter 2 of *Spheres of Justice* has been influential and will be considered in later chapters.

5 Writers described as 'communitarians' were critics of liberal theories of justice, particularly of Rawls's views. For an analysis, see Stephen Mulhall and Adam Swift, *Liberals and Communitarians* (revised edition, Oxford: Wiley, 1996).

'Epic!' said **Kaveh**. 'Totally epic!'

'And that, Professor Prakash, is why we call you Xandros!' said **Diana**. 'You needed a proper Greek name as a philosopher. Socrates or Plato or Aristotle sounded too cheesy, but something starting with "X" sounded right because you, good professor, have the "X" factor! Even if you don't have any views of your own.'

'He doesn't have any views,' said **Kaveh**. 'We should really call him Skepticurus or something like that.'

'Okay,' **I** said, 'I do have some views, even if to some extent I'm still trying to work out exactly where I stand. I can say, though, that I've started out with a puzzle: why do we have borders and, for that matter, nations, in the first place? And what makes *these* particular borders the right ones? And I do rather like Skepticurus, Kaveh.'

'Forget it,' said **Diana**. 'Xandros you are and Xandros you shall remain!'

'If you mean to ask why we don't have a borderless world, I think it's pretty obvious,' said **Tracy**. 'It's progress. We live in an ordered world—well, mostly ordered, but we're getting there. You can't have civilization without order, and that means laws, and laws mean jurisdictions and boundaries, and to enforce them you need governments.'

'What if we had a world government?' said **Kaveh**. 'One government, one jurisdiction, no boundaries, everyone following the same rules. Democratically elected, of course.'[6]

'That's ridiculous,' **Tracy** replied almost before Kaveh had finished speaking. 'No one would agree to it. Can you imagine the Chinese letting Americans make laws for them or having a say in what laws they live under? Or vice versa? People are too different and used to their own ways. Countries should sort themselves out internally, and we can try to make international law to regulate relations between them.'

6 For a defence of the idea of a world state, see Luis Cabrera, *A Political Theory of Global Justice: A Cosmopolitan Case for the World State* (London: Routledge, 2004).

'What are you suggesting, Tracy?' **I** said. 'I've been thinking about the civilization question quite a bit of late, but I don't know that I've got completely clear what it means or what I think about it. But you seem to have a considered view. It sounded almost as if you were suggesting that protecting civilization might require closing off immigration or even closing off societies more broadly. Is that what you're suggesting?

'Yes,' **Astrid** chimed in, 'it sounds very authoritarian. I mean, I know you're a bit of a conservative, but that seems rather extreme.'

Tracy was clearly getting flustered and responded sharply while trying unsuccessfully to conceal her annoyance.

'Extreme? You mean like calling for world government?'

'I was just joking,' said **Kaveh**, grinning.

'Oh, I took you quite seriously,' **I** said, 'but we can come back to that. Right now, I'm more interested in what Tracy has to say, since she's advanced a position she genuinely holds—and not as a joke. Should we be more closed, and how closed? Assuming that we can give a useful answer to such a question.'

'I don't know if I have an answer to that question,' **Tracy** said, 'but I think it's absolutely right to put the fate of civilization front and centre of the debate about immigration.'

'Okay,' **I** said, 'but what do you mean by civilization? Do you mean all civilizations, or just ours—if we have more than one today?'[7]

'Well, I believe it's both, now that I come to think of it,' **Tracy** replied a little tentatively, 'because, of course, we need to acknowledge that there are different civilizations, but we also have a world

7 According to Josephine Quinn, the idea of 'civilization' or 'civilizational thinking' is a relatively recent European invention, developed in the Victorian period, when the world was divided into civilizations that were separate and mutually opposed. See Quinn, *How the World Made the West: A 4,000-Year History* (London: Bloomsbury, 2024). She writes (p. 18): 'there has never been a single, pure Western or European culture. What are called Western values – freedom, rationality, justice and tolerance – are not only or originally western, and the West itself is in large part a product of long-standing links with a much larger network of societies, to south and north as well as east.'

in which we've got order in the relationships between different countries. We have international law, international institutions, international regimes, all designed—perhaps imperfectly—to manage our financial transactions, our trade, our health, the development of poorer regions. Managing movement has to be part of that. But at the same time, we have to protect our own civilization from being undermined or destroyed.'

'Who's "we"?' said Diana.

'Yes, who?' **Astrid** jumped in. 'Do you mean America?[8] Or the West? Or white people?'

'No, I don't mean white people,' said **Tracy**, now visibly annoyed. 'But I'm not sure exactly where to draw the line. The West—maybe. America—maybe that too, but I know America is full of a range of people. Still, I'm pretty sure it's different from China, or Africa, or India, or the Middle East. People there have their own ways of life that they want to preserve and protect. We should too.'

'Do you mean we should limit immigration by taking only the right people, or are you worried about taking too many?' **I** asked.

'Both, I think,' **Tracy** replied. 'We have to consider everything if we don't want society to collapse. And maybe we're just full, or close to full. Maybe there's no room for any more people. But surely we ought to be thinking about this, not just assume we can open the borders to everyone and as many as want to come and that everything will be alright.'

'You make it sound like we face an existential crisis,' **I** said.

'Perhaps we do,' **Tracy** replied.

'So, it's us or them,' said **Temi** grimly.

'That makes it sound like I'm being melodramatic,' **Tracy** said, 'but okay, if you want to force me to be ridiculously simplistic, yes: it's us or them, and I vote for us. Happy?'

8 See, for example, Samuel P. Huntington, *Who Are We? The Challenges to American National Identity* (New York: Simon and Schuster, 2005), which argues that the United States faces a civilizational threat as its Protestant identity is at risk of being undermined by Hispanic immigration.

'Are you some kind of "America First" person?' **Temi** shot back, 'because if you are, then no, I'm not happy. I actually think "America First" is not very American. I know I'm from Britain, and my parents were from Africa, but from everything I've read about the US, the whole American nationalist turn is really new.'

'Well, not entirely,' **I** said. 'The history is a more complicated one than we can get into right now. Maybe we can talk about that sometime, but I'd like to get back to Tracy's idea that immigration poses an existential threat and that what's at stake is civilization. Much as you all like to tease me about being obsessed with conceptual niceties, I really do want to get clearer about what Tracy means because there may be something interesting and important here.'

'But who really thinks there's an existential crisis?' said **Diana**. 'I mean, apart from a few right-wing radio talk show hosts, no one seriously believes civilization is under threat. I think it's a bit of a beat-up.'

'I'm not so sure,' **I** replied. 'Consider Douglas Murray's book, *The Strange Death of Europe*, which is a pretty sustained argument about the threat immigration poses to a continent and, indeed, a way of life.[9] Or David Goodhart's books.[10] Or consider those in the United States who worry that immigration will transform—or has transformed—America as well as Europe for the worse. This includes not only anti-immigrant advocates like Peter Brimelow,[11] who make disparaging comments about non-whites, but even figures like Hillary Clinton,[12] who not so long ago

9 Douglas Murray, *The Strange Death of Europe: Immigration, Identity, Islam* (London: Bloomsbury, 2017).

10 David Goodhart, *The British Dream: Successes and Failures of Postwar Immigration* (London: Atlantic Books, 2013); *The Road to Somewhere* (Harmondsworth: Penguin, 2017).

11 Peter Brimelow, *Alien Nation: Common Sense About America's Immigration Disaster* (New York: Random House, 1995).

12 Quoted in David Frum, 'If Liberals Don't Enforce Borders, Fascists Will', *The Atlantic Monthly*, April 2019, https://www.theatlantic.com/magazine/archive/2019/04/david-frum-how-much-immigration-is-too-much/583252/.

advised Angela Merkel to be more cautious about admitting immigrants because of the threat this posed to democratic institutions. Remember Barack Obama saying how he felt a bit of 'patriotic resentment' on seeing Mexican flags waving at pro-immigration demonstrations?[13] And Bernie Sanders did not want a lot of immigration, largely because of its impact on that part of America he wants to preserve—though he has changed his mind and now says he is on the side of immigrant workers. American scholars and commentators are worried about the fate of the white working class, British ones fear the transformation of Britain into something unfamiliar, and critics of immigration more generally worry that the movement of people will see the West overrun by an alien religion—Islam—even as its democratic institutions are undermined by the sheer number of culturally, or politically, different people.'

'Yes, yes,' said **Tracy** eagerly, 'exactly, exactly!'

'You've said there are all these people who are worried about the decline of civilization, Xandros,' said **Temi**, 'but is that what you think? Do you believe it? Are *you* worried?'

'Ah,' **I** replied, 'I said there was a question worth considering, not that I accepted all the claims I've described. Don't you agree that they're worth a closer look? After all, they're not trivial claims, and what's at stake is the question of how we ought to live, no?'

'Okay, then,' said **Astrid**, 'where should we start?'

'We should probably begin with where we want to end, though it will be only when we reach the end that we'll really understand where we were when we began,' **I** said.

'That's a little obscure, professor,' said **Kaveh**, 'if you don't mind my saying so.'

'Not at all,' **I** said, 'not at all. So, let's start by considering Tracy's claim more closely, beginning with the question of what we mean by "civilization". How hard can that be?'

13 Barack Obama, *Audacity of Hope* (New York: Crown Publishing, 2006), 263.

'I'm sticking to what I said before,' said **Tracy**. 'At the heart of civilization is order. Without order, nothing is possible—or at least, nothing lasts for long. I think order means law, boundaries—literal as well as metaphorical—and citizens who understand the need to respect the law, to respect limits, to respect others.'

'So, the citizens, as you call them, must be educated?' **I** asked.

'Yes,' **Tracy** replied, 'they've got to be in sync with their societies, to understand their own countries, to internalize the norms that make peaceful co-existence possible.'

'You could say that if you look into the soul of the citizen, then, you'd see the soul of their own country, perhaps. Is that what you're getting at?' **I** asked.

'I hadn't thought of it that way,' **Tracy** answered, 'but that seems right. If I were suddenly dropped into Mongolia as an American, even if I knew the language well enough to get by, I wouldn't fit in, I wouldn't know how to be a citizen, I wouldn't be part of the country, because I'm not cut from the same cloth as everyone else. I'd be a stranger.'

'But what about taking in refugees?' said **Temi**. 'Are they a danger to civilization, too? Should Angela Merkel not have allowed in all those Syrians?'[14]

'Sadly, yes,' **Tracy** answered defiantly.

'Well, I do recall reading that Henry Kissinger told Mrs Merkel as much,' **I** said.

'What did he say to her?' **Antoine** asked.

'He said something like, to shelter a single refugee is a humanitarian act, but to allow one million strangers in is to endanger German civilization,' **I** explained.

'Wow!' **Antoine** exclaimed. 'But wasn't he a refugee himself?'

14 Civil war in Syria led to an outflow of people seeking asylum, and in 2015 Angela Merkel, the German Chancellor, announced that the country would welcome refugees, saying 'Wir schaffen das' (we will manage). Over 500,000 Syrians moved into Germany over a short period afterwards. By 2020, about 40% of all refugees seeking asylum in the European Union were in Germany.

'No,' **I** said, 'not strictly speaking. There was no Refugee Convention[15] then, of course, so there were no official definitions, but by the terms of that Convention, he did not qualify, even though he left Germany because of the growing mistreatment he and his family suffered as Jews. He was what's since been called an "anticipatory refugee," meaning someone who flees because he expects, correctly, that he's about to become a victim.[16] But all this is distracting us from the original question. I'm really still interested in the whole idea that immigration is an existential threat—a danger to civilization. I want to know what the thing is that's being threatened.'

'I sounds to me like it's a threat to a country—if it's a threat at all, which I'm not so sure about,' said **Astrid**.

'No, it's broader than that,' said **Tracy**. 'It's a danger to the world, because if international order breaks down, we'll be heading down the road to geopolitical conflict.'

'That sounds overstated to me,' said **Diana**. 'I don't think Germany letting in refugees is going to destabilize Brazil.'

'No, but it will destabilize Europe,' said **Kaveh**, 'or at least that's what Douglas Murray seems to be saying.'

'Maybe now we're getting somewhere,' **I** said, 'since we finally have some options on the table. It appears that there are three contenders for what needs protection from an existential catastrophe of the kind immigration might bring: the world, the state or nation, and something in between, like a continent. Is that right?'

'I don't think it can be a continent,' said **Diana**, 'because that's not a real thing. Asia is a continent, but it has had at least three civilizations, namely Chinese, Indian, and Islamic civilization. Besides, that doesn't include Russia, which is partly in Asia and

15 The International Refugee Convention of 1951 provides the foundation of the legal framework governing the treatment of refugees in international law. See the United Nations High Commissioner for Refugees website for the text: https://www.unhcr.org/sites/default/files/legacy-pdf/4ca34be29.pdf.

16 The term was coined by E.F. Kunz, 'The Refugee in Flight: Kinetic Models and Forms of Displacement', *International Migration Review*, 7 Summer 1977, 125–146.

partly in Europe. And there's Southeast Asia and Japan, now that I come to think of it, but I don't know much about their histories.'

'That's true,' said **Astrid**, 'and Turkey sees itself as part of Europe, but the EU thinks of Turkey as Asian.'

'What is it, then, that exists between world civilization and national civilization?' **I** asked. 'It looks like the second category exists within fixed boundaries, and the first without boundaries altogether, while the middle category straddles national boundaries but still somehow requires boundaries.'

'Aren't we complicating things needlessly?' said **Tracy** impatiently. 'I'm sure we're making more of this than necessary. After all, we know Lex Luthor is bald because he has no hair, and we know Superman is not, and just because we can't say exactly when someone has lost enough hair to qualify as bald doesn't mean we can't make the distinction. There are always grey areas.'

'Not if you're totally bald,' said **Kaveh**, grinning.

'Very funny,' **Tracy** snapped, struggling not to smile, 'but you know what I mean.'

'Okay, Tracy,' **I** said, 'I think you make a reasonable point. So perhaps we should begin by trying to tackle the middle category first. I think a good way to approach it would be by trying to define Europe, since we have a thesis that immigration is an existential threat to European civilization and indeed that Europe is about to die a strange death. But I think it's going to be tricky.'

'I think it should include all the countries we can identify between and including Iceland in the west and Russia in the east and Greece in the south,' said **Astrid** decisively, 'and all of Scandinavia in the north if you think we need to complete the picture.'

'Does that mean you're including Turkey?' asked **Kaveh**.

'No,' **Astrid** replied firmly.

'Well, Turkey is a candidate for admission to the EU,' **Kaveh** said slowly.

'Makes no difference, they'll never let them in because the EU doesn't think they're European because they're Muslim,' **Astrid** replied. 'I'm not saying it's right, but that's just the way it is.'

'What about Israel?' **Temi** asked.

'Asia,' **Astrid** said.

'Then how come Israeli football teams have played in the European Champions' League?' **Temi** shot back. 'In fact, Turkish teams have too.'

'Teams from Kazakhstan, which some say is a part of central Asia, have played in the qualifying rounds for the Champions' League,' **I** pointed out. 'That makes me wonder whether different people, or organizations, have different views about what qualifies one as European. I was a bit surprised to find Kazakhstan on the list of UEFA [Union of European Football Associations] teams, I have to admit. Does that mean Tajikistan, and Kyrgyzstan, and Uzbekistan and even Afghanistan might qualify? The EU might decide who can be admitted into the European Union, but who decides who is European?'

'Maybe Europe is held together by the fact that it is a Christian civilization,' said **Tracy** hopefully.

'I don't know about that,' said **Antoine**. 'I may be French, but I'm also Jewish.'

'And I may be an atheist, but I was born in Iran, and I'm supposed to be a Muslim and definitely not Christian,' said **Kaveh**.

'I think you're all missing the point,' said **Astrid** with a hint of irritation. 'The point is not that we're all Christian now but that the culture that's evolved is a Christian culture. Sure, it's one that's welcomed Muslims and Jews, and also Hindus and Ba'hais and Buddhists, and a host of other religious believers, but the whole tradition has been shaped by Christianity. Just look at the British houses of Parliament, with its history of representing the clergy as well as the aristocracy. Look at all the cathedrals and the little country churches. It's a Christian continent.'[17]

'I'm not so sure,' said **Diana**. 'It appears to me that what we're calling Europe has had a pretty mixed history, and all the more mixed the further back in history you go. The ancient Greeks

17 On the ways in which Christianity has shaped the world, see Catherine Nixey, *Heresy: Jesus Christ and Other Sons of God* (New York: Picador, 2024).

weren't Christians, and the Romans weren't until centuries after Christ. In fact, wasn't St Augustine, who was the first to really develop a philosophical account of Christian belief, an African? Wasn't north Africa the hotbed of Christian controversy in the 4th century when the Romans were starting to have doubts?'[18]

'Yes,' said **Temi** enthusiastically, 'all my family in Africa are Christian, though they didn't really convert until the British colonised Ghana a hundred and fifty years ago. But most of north Africa is now Muslim, isn't it?'

'That's true enough,' **I** said, 'as was much of Europe until the 15th century. But then there wasn't always a Europe that saw itself as Europe. Until the rise of Islam, the heart of Christian civilization was along the coastal regions of the Mediterranean Sea. Islam pushed Christianity north, and while it did move back south, North Africa is now predominantly Muslim, and the Levant is more mixed, as are countries like Albania, Bosnia, and Kosovo. Of course, none of this takes into account the divisions within Christianity since the separation between the eastern and western churches in the East–West Schism of 1054, which reflected not only deep differences of doctrine but also political disagreements. The pope in Rome may have claimed universal jurisdiction, but the patriarch in Constantinople did not recognize even his spiritual authority over all Christians—and this was nearly 500 years before Martin Luther nailed his 95 Theses to the door, repudiating the authority of the pope over anyone. The Wars of Religion, as they're called nowadays, weren't just a feature of the 16th century but a notable part of Christianity's earlier history too. The fourth Crusade saw an assault not just on Muslim regions in the Middle East but also on Constantinople itself, with the victorious crusaders destroying eastern churches and turning Orthodox holy sites into centres for Latin Catholic worship. The Orthodox returned

18 See St Augustine of Hippo, *City of God* (translated by Henry Bettenson, with an introduction by R.G. Evans, London: Penguin Classics, 2003). On Christianity in Africa in the 5th century CE, see Peter Brown, *St Augustine of Hippo: A Biography* (Los Angeles: University of California Press, 2013).

the favour in the massacre of the city's Roman Catholic inhabitants in 1182. If we're going to say that what makes Europe *Europe* is its Christian character, I think we'll need to finesse this argument before it will work. What exactly is Europe?'

'I can't believe how you turn everything into a conceptual question!' said **Diana**. 'Just when I thought you were going to give us a history lesson, there you go making it a philosophical one.'

'I don't think historians can escape the conceptual questions,' **I** said, 'and I think on the whole they're pretty careful to get them clear. They just don't show their working. Philosophers, on the other hand, are interested in the conceptual questions for their own sake. Though on this occasion, I'll admit, I'm very interested in the normative issue. I do want to know what to think about immigration.'

'Well, if we want to figure out the answer, aren't we starting to wander off the point?' said **Astrid**. 'Perhaps you could just tell us what you think.'

'I wish I could,' **I** replied, 'but I genuinely am puzzled about a few things and feel more confident about what arguments or explanations don't work than about which ones do.'

'And you don't think the argument that there's an existential crisis—a crisis of civilization—is one that works,' said **Antoine**, 'am I right? Maybe you could say a bit more about why.'

'Okay,' **I** said, 'I'll try to say a little more, but please remember that I'm not entirely sure of myself here. Treat what I have to say with a little indulgence.'

'Yeah, like you showed our essays,' said **Diana** drily.

'Fair point,' **I** replied, 'but there's nothing at stake here—no degrees, no best performance prizes, no GPAs…'

'Yes, nothing at stake, nothing important, except understanding how we are to live,' said **Temi**, to uproarious laughter at my expense.

'Okay, you got me twice,' **I** conceded, 'so I agree, no excuses, and anything I say is fair game. A bad argument is a bad argument, no matter how innocent or worthy the proponent. So… First off, let me say that I recognize that many people have advanced arguments in the language of civilizational imperatives and not just when talking about immigration. Even Gandhi, defending the idea of home rule, presents his case in terms of the need to defend Indian civilization from corruption by Western, and especially English, influences. Just as some Europeans want to preserve something called Europe, so did Gandhi want to preserve India and not have the British bequeath something called Englistan.[19] Candidly, I find both propositions—that there's an India or a Europe, or a China for that matter—highly dubious.[20] These entities may now have a political reality, but the identity follows the political construction, and imperfectly at that, because boundaries are fuzzy, permeable, and liable to change.'

'You don't think there's any India?' said **Astrid**, sounding a little incredulous. 'That's crazy! Don't you have Indian ancestors? They must be turning over in their graves.'

'No, they were all cremated,' **I** said. 'But hear me out. I'm not denying the existence of a country called India or doubting that we can speak, for example, about Indian movies, or Indian food, or Indian literature, or Indian languages, without falling into incoherence. Yet, even these categories begin to look a little fuzzy once you start asking for a bit more precision or accuracy. Indian cuisine for many is the food found or originating anywhere on the Indian subcontinent but does not stop being prepared abruptly at the external borders of Afghanistan or Bangladesh, any more than the different styles stay within Bengal or Tamil Nadu or Punjab. As for literature, is Tagore, to take just one example, an Indian writer, or a Bengali one, or a poet of Bangladeshi origin?[21] To put it another way, where does India begin or end? There are political boundaries,

19 See M.K. Gandhi, *Hind Swaraj and Other Writings* (edited by Anthony J. Parel, Cambridge, UK: Cambridge University Press, 2010).

20 See Bill Hayton, *The Invention of China* (New Haven and London: Yale University Press, 2020).

21 Rabindranath Tagore (1861–1941), who was awarded the Nobel Prize for Literature in 1913, was born in Calcutta, close to India's eastern border, but is a descendant of a family with earlier origins in what is now Bangladesh. He lived in 'British India'.

to be sure, but those lines on the map have their origins in political conflicts and don't track some kind of antecedent reality on the ground.'

'I'm not really getting this,' said **Kaveh**. 'You make it sound like we can't distinguish India from China or India from Europe or India from Africa. That doesn't sound right. I understand that boundaries are always fuzzy, and I accept that political boundaries may not track social reality, but there is a social reality. No one mistakes me for an Indian or an African.'

'Perhaps,' **I** said, 'although that might depend a bit on which part of the subcontinent you wander into. Or which part of Europe or America. On my first day at school in Australia in 1969, the other children thought the Chinese boy I arrived with was my brother, even though no one from Sri Lanka or China would ever make that mistake. More to the point, however, there's nothing that allows us to group people together biologically in any meaningful way, any more than you could, say, group them by height and claim this to be significant.'

'Okay,' said **Antoine**, 'I accept that biological markers of identity are problematic, even before we consider people of mixed descent.'

'Even, then,' **I** said, 'it's not clear what it means to say someone is mixed, unless you mean that everyone is mixed as the offspring of people who are themselves mixed. Still, let's leave that aside for the moment. You were about to add a "but" to the end of that sentence!'

'I was,' said **Antoine**, 'because while I'm persuaded that human biological variation is continuous and any lines distinguishing colour, or demarcating one "race" from another, is arbitrary and probably the result of some political preference, I don't think that means we can't distinguish civilizations—or cultures or traditions, or languages, or in the end, political identities.'

'I agree we can distinguish all these things,' **I** said, 'but I'm not convinced that the distinctions we draw are anything more than, at best, ways of making rough generalizations to try to communicate something or, at worst, tools to enforce separations that serve particular interests that have somehow managed to convince us that the distinctions identify something that's somehow *there*.'

'I disagree,' said **Tracy**. 'Europe is made up of different languages, and peoples can be distinguished according to their mother tongues—granting that some people have second languages and that there are all kinds of dialects that reflect regional variations. You can't deny the existence of French, German, Spanish, Portuguese, Italian, Serbo-Croat, Greek, Czech, Hungarian, Polish, Swedish, Danish, Norwegian, Romanian, Bulgarian, Albanian, Icelandic, and English.'

'I don't deny the existence of these languages,' **I** said, 'but I do question your analysis and what you propose to make of all this. If you want to suggest that language supplies the natural basis of identity, I think you're going to have a hard time. Imagine you were to walk from, say, Lisbon in Portugal all the way along the coast to Durres in Albania. Were you to stop every few miles you would detect a slight difference in the language spoken by the locals, though they would understand those with whom they conversed in the village before and the one on the next leg of your journey. But by the time you reached, say, Barcelona, the distance between the language spoken at your point of departure and the language spoken at this point would be as great as the distance you travelled. Yet along the way, everybody was able to understand their neighbours. By the time you reach Juan Les-Pins, the language will have changed again, and even more by the time you get to Genoa, or to Rijeka, and finally Durres. Of course, we have to recognize that with the creation of national boundaries came state education that required people to learn the national language and much variation was lost as linguistic usage was standardised, but before that, variety and continuity were more securely entrenched—though *entrenched* might not be the best word to use, if you see what I mean.'

'Do you mean that there are, or used to be, lots of dialects that have now been lost?' asked **Diana**.

'It's true enough that many languages have been lost,' **I** said, 'but it's a mistake to think of these variations as dialects, as though there were a way of distinguishing them from "proper" languages. Just because some languages have become dominant—whether for political or other reasons—does not make them more real, as languages, than others.[22] My broader point, however, is that human society, like language, is continuous. We draw boundaries, and make distinctions between some clusters and others, but do so in the service of narratives or explanations we want to offer to make sense of the world. That is fine as long as we recognize that these just-so stories are nothing more than that. Some are more useful than others, but they are as real as constellations in the sky. Recognizing Orion or the Big Dipper may be helpful to someone navigating by the stars, but it would be a mistake to think there is any relationship among these stars separated by thousands or millions of light years of space, even if they are united in our imaginations.'

'Are you saying there's no such thing as society?' asked **Temi**, sounding a little troubled, 'because that just sounds like Margaret Thatcher.'

'In a way, I am,' **I** said, 'though my inspiration is not Baroness Thatcher so much as the sociologist Michael Mann.[23] I don't deny the reality of social relations but, like Mann, I question our tendency to draw boundaries and then invest them with more significance than they warrant. Before you know it, you end up reifying things that have what unity they possess only in the imagination. And so we get Indian civilization and European civilization and Chinese civilization, and then social and political movements to uphold, protect, glorify, and fix something that is continuously changing, evolving, transforming, because the unceasing interaction of human beings with each other and with the natural world recreates the world anew day by day.'

22 See David Shariatmadari, *Don't Believe a Word: The Surprising Truth About Language* (London: Weidenfield and Nicholson, 2020).

23 Michael Mann, *The Sources of Social Power, Volume 1: A History of Power from the Beginning to AD 1760* (Cambridge, UK: Cambridge University Press, 2012).

'You make it sound like we're living inside a whirlwind,' said **Antoine**, 'and that nothing is stable. If that's the case, maybe what we need is a little stability, and that's why we need boundaries. But it feels to me that you're overstating matters, Xandros. The world is more stable than you make out, though, granted, some parts are more so than others that are in turmoil.'

'Perhaps we need a closer look at the notion of stability,' **I** said.

'Oh, no,' said **Astrid**, 'more conceptual analysis!'

'I'm afraid so,' **I** answered, to a chorus of groans, with everyone pretending to commit suicide, whether by blowing out their brains with finger guns, or self-garrotting, or slitting their own throats with imaginary knives.

'I can see I've whetted your appetites,' **I** said. 'You're all just begging for more. Happily, you're in luck. More distinctions are coming your way!'

'Gosh, is that the time?' said **Diana**, 'I think I have an appointment to watch paint dry.'

'Yeah,' said **Antoine**, 'I think I'm due to be somewhere, too. I think I have to rearrange my sock drawer.'

'I'll help,' said **Temi**. 'You have a lot of socks.'

'Three,' said **Antoine**, 'three!'

'Wow,' said **Temi**, 'I think we'd all better go help Antoine.'

'Very funny,' I said, laughing, 'but I'm happy to explain what I mean by stability to anyone who cares to stay.'

'More distinctions?' **Antoine** asked.

'More than you have socks,' **I** said, 'and better arranged, I'm guessing.'

'Okay, okay,' said **Astrid**. 'We're listening.'

'Good,' **I** said. 'Then let me begin by making clear that nothing I'm about to say presumes a kind of individualism that some of you may have been tempted to attribute to me—at least, gauging from your remarks about Margaret Thatcher. We exist as individuals in a world of social relations. Those relations create individuals just as much as individuals create society. Indeed, in today's world, we are more interdependent than ever, and our actions can sometimes affect people halfway around the world more readily than they affect our immediate neighbours. If Jennifer Aniston throws a party and sports a new hairstyle, or Gong Li gets married in a pink wedding gown, suddenly hairstylists in London and dressmakers in Hong Kong will find people clamouring for imitations.'

'Yeah,' said **Temi**, 'like a social butterfly effect.'

The group fell about laughing, and I smiled, even as I fought to retain my composure.

'Try to be serious, people,' **I** said finally. 'These insights I'm about to offer won't travel around the world in a hurry, and you're the first to hear them. You can all be early adopters.'

'Yes, boss,' said **Temi**, pretending to zip his mouth shut.

'But we will get back to the immigration question, won't we?' said **Diana**. 'Eventually, and before too long, I hope.'

'We will,' **I** said, 'we will. But first there is the question of stability, which is an issue you aren't the only ones to have raised. Antoine, you said we need boundaries to maintain stability, right? Could you elaborate before I go on?'

'I'll try,' said **Antoine**, 'though I've not thought things through. It seems to me that if we are to survive, and ultimately to prosper, we have to have order.'

'You're sounding like Tracy,' **I** said, 'though she's been rather quiet for a while.'

'Maybe I am,' said **Antoine**, 'but be that as it may. The thing is, if the world is as changeable as you, say, with everything we do reshaping it all the time, then what we also need is to ensure that change is not so rapid that we can't keep up or can't predict what will happen next. We need some part of the world—our own little world, perhaps—not to change so fast and maybe to change really slowly in some respects. We need stability in this regard. We want there to be laws, and to know how and where they apply, and to be sure the framework doesn't change even as the laws themselves change. I think we also need to know the people around us won't suddenly become different people, with different ideas or values or understandings of the rules, or different attitudes to the rules, so we can count on them. Finally, we need political stability, so we aren't living in a world where there is no peace because political succession is uncertain. We want peaceful transitions of power. If we are to have that, however, we need boundaries that establish the jurisdictions within which political power operates. If we don't have that, what we will have, at worst, is civil war. And people will leave.'

'They'll emigrate!' said **Kaveh** brightly. 'Problem solved!'

'Can I ask how this bears on the question of whether the world is rightly divided into civilizations,' **I** said, ignoring Kaveh, who looked a little crestfallen.

'I don't think I have an answer to that yet, I have to admit,' said **Antoine**, 'but maybe it will come to me.'

'No matter,' **I** said, 'I thought you offered a very cogent explanation as to why you think we need to be more concerned about stability. Let me try to respond—not so much to try to refute you as to find a way of better understanding your concern and then to figure out how it might best be addressed.'

'We're all ears,' said **Diana**. 'Don't stop now. You're on a roll!'

'Well, to begin with, I think Antoine has focussed on what looks like legal stability,' **I** said, 'though his references to transitions of power suggest that he also has political stability in mind. So I'm going to take the hypothesis to be that immigration—of either a certain type or a certain amount or some combination of numbers and type—poses a threat to legal and political stability. If this happened, it would be because too many migrants would be difficult to assimilate, and too many types of people who are different would be less likely to adapt to a society's norms and more likely to make it harder for people to get along. Let's go further and hypothesise that too much of the wrong kind of immigration would provoke a backlash from people who were hostile to foreigners and who would most likely draw support from people who were more moderate when immigration was low. Neo-fascism flourishes when foreign populations swell. So far, so good?'

'Yes,' said **Tracy** enthusiastically, 'that's the argument, and a pretty convincing one. I'm actually a little surprised you started it off, Antoine. I thought you were more of a leftie.'

'I am,' **Antoine** replied, 'so I guess I'm a bit surprised myself. Sometimes, when you're on the spot, you start saying something you believe, and before you know it, your premises take you somewhere you didn't think you wanted to go. Maybe Xandros will save me.'

'Xandros to the rescue!' **I** said. 'So back we go into battle. But before I begin to tackle your argument, let me try to make sure we have the strongest version of it we can find. My sense is that the kind of stability you're interested in is not something fleeting but, rather, a feature of society that will endure.'

'Yes, yes,' said **Tracy** enthusiastically.

'That may be taken to mean that, to be truly stable, a society has to be stable for the right reasons,' **I** continued, 'for a mere *modus vivendi* is not a stable form of order.[24] It's no more a stable order than a truce is during battle. So the most stable arrangement would have to be one in which the relations holding between people were not of the sort we find among adversaries, wary of one another and tempted to play for advantage in case the other strikes first.'

'That sounds reasonable,' said **Diana**. 'A truce between enemies would last only as long as neither side felt it was strong enough to win.'

'I'm not so sure,' **Temi** jumped in, 'not if society is made up of not two warring parties but a lot of different people who are wary of each other. Once you had a truce, each individual group would still feel too vulnerable to break the peace even if it felt it had gotten a lot stronger because it would need to be powerful enough to dominate everyone else—or at least a good part of the rest. I think a truce could be pretty stable. And what would be wrong with that? After all, getting a lot of people to live together peaceably for any reason is not an insignificant achievement.'[25]

24 This is a view advanced by John Rawls in *Political Liberalism*. For a discussion of the idea of a modus vivendi, see David McCabe, *Modus Vivendi Liberalism: Theory and Practice* (Cambridge, UK: Cambridge University Press, 2010).

25 This an argument advanced by Robert Sugden, *The Community of Advantage: A Behavioural Economist's Defence of the Market* (Oxford: Oxford University Press, 2018).

'That's a very good point, Temi,' **I** said. 'The ideal of a *modus vivendi* is very much under-appreciated in my view. But even *modi vivendi* never operate in pure form, as outcomes delivered after agreements are reached among self-interested actors with symmetrical information. At the very least, people would have to accept the idea that agreements should be kept: *pacta sunt servanda*! If they didn't, there couldn't be a truce, for a professed commitment not to strike unless one had an advantage is a commitment that's of no use at all to the other party—it you could call it a commitment at all. So, yes, I think Temi is right not to discount the idea of a stable society as one in which a kind of implicit agreement to abide by existing norms prevails, even when the motives are a mixture of fear, self-interest, and a desire for approval. But this third motive is useful only if it leads people to internalize the norms of the society in which they live. If they don't, I think you're more likely to see order break down—though, to be sure, there are many other sources of instability?'

'Like what?' **Tracy** said, looking puzzled.

'Well, Aristotle suggests that an unhappy middle class is a sure predictor of political instability,'[26] **I** said, 'but there are other factors too. Some bring trouble indirectly, by creating the disaffection that manifests itself in the condition of the middle class, but sometimes the rise of great men—and I do mean *men*—anxious to pursue power can lead whole nations astray, as can the rise of regions within political society that want independence from the centre. And social movements born of ideas can bring about social change, both for better and for worse.'[27]

'I'm starting to see what you're getting at, I think,' said **Tracy**, 'but that makes me even more convinced that we need better control over immigration and that we should have less immigration overall.'

26 Aristotle, *Politics* (translated by T.A. Sinclair, revised and edited by Trevor J Saunders, London: Penguin, 1981), 1295b.

27 See Thomas Hobbes, *Leviathan* (edited by Richard Tuck, New York: Cambridge University Press, 1991), Chapter 29 on the causes of the dissolution of a commonwealth.

'Could you explain?' **I** asked.

'If social stability requires that people internalize the norms of their society, that means both the norms and the population itself need to remain stable,' **Tracy** replied. 'If people move in and out too quickly, there's no way they can all come to believe the same things, let alone develop a real commitment to the legal order. They'll just see the rules in transactional terms, as part of a system to game, and their fellow citizens as just a bunch of strangers with whom they have no relations of reciprocity. It would be just like one big, open, market. It seems to me that if we want a stable society, we need a more closed society. That doesn't mean people couldn't come and go at all, but we'd need to regulate that to make sure our society was made up of people who belonged—who felt they belonged—and shared some deep beliefs.'

'If people keep moving in and out, they wouldn't be around enough to make trouble,' said **Kaveh**. 'So who cares what they believe?'

'Are you serious?' said **Tracy**. 'Really?'

'I think it is a serious point,' **I** said, 'but let's put that aside for the time being. Beliefs about what, Tracy? A religion, perhaps? And how would we ensure that they all shared the same beliefs?'

'We'd need a system of education,' **Tracy** said, a little hesitantly, 'though I'm not sure it could be a religious education if we have different religious believers in a country. We've become diverse on that score, and that genie can't be put back in the bottle.'

'So, what kind of education,' I asked, 'if not a religious one?'

'A national one, I guess,' **Tracy** answered after a little reflection. 'We'd have to have some kind of focal point for their attention.'[28]

'That sounds a bit manipulative,' said **Kaveh**, 'and a little disturbing, to be quite frank. It doesn't sound like there'd be much room for the freedom to be different.'

28 On this, see Eamonn Callan, *Creating Citizens: Political Education and Liberal Democracy* (Oxford: Oxford University Press, 2004). See also Stephen Macedo, *Diversity and Distrust: Civic Education in a Multicultural Democracy* (Cambridge, MA: Harvard University Press, 2000).

'There would,' said **Tracy**, 'because people would be free to worship as they liked and have the right to be part of the whole process of governing themselves.'

'But not the freedom not to be part of it, because they'd all be educated to believe the same things,' **Kaveh** replied.

'That's true,' said **Tracy**, 'but it's not as sinister as you make it sound. There's a certain amount of compulsion that's inevitable in any society, but in this case the aim is to make everyone free.'

'I don't like it,' **Kaveh** said. 'It just doesn't feel right. Forcing people to be "free" in the name of stability is not something you do if you care about freedom. In your society, you're relieving people of the need to think. They'd be like robots, just going through the motions.'

'Freedom's just another word for nothing left to do,' **Diana** chimed in.

'No, not at all,' said **Tracy** impatiently. 'You're just making it sound more invasive than it is. We aren't talking about re-education camps and making people dress the same and wave little red books ...'

'Or take pledges of allegiance, or sing national anthems, or celebrate national days...' **Kaveh** said, his voice dripping with sarcasm.

'There's a difference when communists do it,' said **Tracy**, sounding a little hurt.

'This is taking an unexpected turn,' **I** said, 'because it looks like the whole question of civilization is receding into the background. We started off trying to understand how immigration posed an existential threat to a way of life that transcended national boundaries, but we seem to have ended up arguing about the merits of preserving national stability. What is it that needs to be stable—though we haven't quite finished figuring out what stability means—and how stable does it need to be? And if education is key, shouldn't it be organized across Europe and shaped by European values rather than by national ones.'

'I still think the civilizational crisis is real, and important,' said **Tracy**, 'at least in Europe. You can't have national stability if your civilization is being undermined in the countries all around you. Even if our borders have to be kept closed to some degree, we still belong to the same family, and we're joined together by our common defence agreements, our Christian heritage, our history, our trading relations.'

'And in America?' said **Astrid.** 'Is there an American civilization that needs to be protected from immigrants from Mexico and Honduras and Guatemala?'

'That's different,' **Tracy** replied. 'There are different reasons for limiting immigration at America's southern borders.'

'Not to do with stability?' **I** asked.

'Stability is still an issue,' **Tracy** answered, 'but for different reasons. I don't think people from Latin America are so different from us in the US, but if they come over in such large numbers and quickly, that could be destabilizing too—for the economy in particular.'

'Xandros, you seem to be up to your old tricks, asking a lot of questions but not offering a lot of answers,' said **Antoine** mischievously. 'Is this book of yours going to actually say something, or will it be written as a dialogue?'

'Okay, okay,' **I** said, 'I accept that we've been circling around the topic without really settling on anything, but at least we've come to see how many awkward questions the issue of immigration raises. And the big question is: what is the ultimate concern?'

'That seems a little vague,' said **Antoine,** 'I'm not sure what you mean by that.'

'Fair enough,' **I** said. 'So let me try to make things a little clearer—with some distinctions, naturally.'

'Oh dear,' said **Diana,** 'oh dear, oh dear, oh dear.'

'Thank you for the vote of confidence,' **I** said, 'but here it is all the same. The three questions I want to ask are: What is civilization? Is it under threat? And why do we care? And these are the three answers I want to offer. To the first, I would say that there is no such thing as civilization if we mean to identify something that is any more real than a constellation. Whether we speak of Indian, or European, or Chinese, civilization, what we're doing is drawing boundaries around more or less random groupings and giving them an identity by ignoring, suppressing, or explaining away differences and diversities that would otherwise make the category meaningless. When Gandhi writes of Indian civilization, or even just India, he is appealing to a fiction, which is given an identity or a coherence only by contrasting it with British or European civilization.'

'I thought you'd like Gandhi,' said **Antoine**. 'After all, he was quite inclusive in his attitudes, even to the British.'

'Not so much to the Africans,' said **Temi**.

'There are things to admire in his thinking,' **I** said, 'but on the question of civilization, I don't find him philosophically convincing. It may have been politically expedient to appeal to claims about a superior Indian civilization to draw attention to the ways in which the imposition of imperial demands on an unsuspecting population was damaging to local traditions and destructive of forms of knowledge, but that doesn't make the theory any more plausible. The same goes for Europe, which, no less than India, has seen the movement of people and ruling powers shape and re-shape that part of the world—and re-shape other parts of the world too as ideas and technologies emanating from this little corner of the world have spread through trade, religious proselytization, and conquest. Is Russia European or Asian, or does it depend on where in Russia you sit? And is America—whether North or South—European, or is there a separate civilization we can distinguish here—one that's under threat in the north from the peoples of the south?'

'I can see you don't think much of the idea of civilization,' said **Astrid**, 'but what of the next two questions?'

'I don't think much of civilization as a concept by which we might demarcate or distinguish one part of the world from another,' **I** said, 'but it's not that I want to disparage the idea of culture or refinement—which is a topic for another day. On the other two points, however, I do doubt that civilizations like those attributed to Europe or India are under threat, if only because ways of living are always being transformed, whether through the rise of new technologies, or the emergence of ideas that originate in religious doctrines or the new-found convictions of political elites, or the movement of people that leads to the adoption or rejection of new and old practices. Things will change—sometimes slowly and at other times quite quickly. There's not a lot we can do to control that.'

'What about the third question,' said **Antoine**, 'why should we care?'

'I want to say that we should not,' **I** said, 'largely because I'm dubious about the very idea that we can distinguish civilizations, but also because there isn't anything we can do about the ways in which they evolve.'

'So it's the idea that immigration poses an existential threat that you doubt,' said **Diana**, 'and you're saying we shouldn't worry about it.'

'Yes,' **I** said, 'but perhaps I should say a little more about the general orientation of my thinking. As I see it, philosophers in particular, but also people in general, have been too ready to divide up the world into categories. There may be some warrant for it to the extent that we need to find concepts to deploy in order to make sense of our surroundings and communicate with others, but we are all too often misled into thinking that they have a significance or a reality that warrants treating them as somehow fixed parts of the world and even in need of preservation or perpetuation. Existence is continuous, and the human world is too, even if parts of the world can sometimes end up being cut off from others and developing in ways that reflect the divisions and barriers that have emerged. It may be too much to insist that these be eliminated, since they may serve some useful purpose, and their destruction could be harmful to some, even if only in the short run. But in time, everything will be transformed, even as life goes on.'

'But doesn't it trouble you that identities might be destroyed,' said **Temi**, 'or at least disappear? That would be a loss, wouldn't it? People need to belong.'

'Would it?' **I** asked. 'I'm not so sure.'

'I'm starting to find all this a bit disturbing,' said **Temi**, 'and I'm not sure how this helps us understand the whole immigration question. When you said you were writing a philosophical book, I thought you'd be discussing whether we had the right to exclude people and whether everyone had the right to move.'[29]

'Yes,' said **Antoine**, 'I thought you were going to talk about the costs and benefits of immigration and whether consequentialist considerations could trump principles of free movement.'

'I was hoping you'd say something about refugees,' said **Astrid**, 'because it seems to me there are special cases, whatever one's theory. Yours seems to be operating at a level of abstraction that's just too removed from reality.'

'Your view also seems to be very unhistorical,' said **Diana**, 'and not to take account of the fact that countries are independent, self-determining nations and that they deserve some respect.'

'Well,' **I** said, 'I had the impression that when we started you were all—except, perhaps, for Tracy—going to turn out to be advocates of open borders. Suddenly, you all seem to be in favour of a much greater degree of control.'

'No, no,' came protests from **Temi**, **Diana**, **Astrid**, and **Antoine**, 'we aren't saying that.'

'I think it's hard to see where you're coming from,' said **Diana**, 'even if we're sympathetic to more open immigration.'

'I think you're all being a bit wishy-washy,' said **Tracy** firmly, 'and are trying to have it both ways. I just can't agree with Xandros, because he's not simply questioning immigration control. I think he's calling into question far too much. Though I agree that we can't discuss immigration without talking about all the other issues you've all raised.'

29 Wellman, Christopher Heath, and Phillip Cole, *Debating the Ethics of Immigration: Is There a Right to Exclude?* (New York: Oxford University Press, 2011). See also Christopher Heath Wellman, 'Immigration and Freedom of Association,' *Ethics* 2008, 119 (1): 109–141; Sarah Fine, 'Freedom of Association is not the Answer', *Ethics*, 2010, 120 (1): 338–256.

'Very well,' **I** said. 'You've all made a fair point about how I've approached the immigration question, though to be clear, at this stage all I've responded to is the challenge that immigration might prove to be an existential threat and that this is reason enough to restrict it. I've tried to call this idea into question. Still, there's much more to be said.'

'What are we going to do, then?' asked **Temi**. 'I don't think we can settle this here.'

'The only thing to do is to work through this systematically,' **I** said, 'but if you're really that interested, we could take this question on as a matter for personal study.'

'For credit?' asked **Astrid**.

'That I can't tell you,' **I** replied, 'so you'll have to ask your course advisors. But for credit or not, we could meet for a number of sessions next term—if you're prepared to do some real work.'

'How so?' asked **Astrid**, 'and how many sessions?'

'Well,' **I** said, 'you've all raised some interesting questions. Why don't you go away and research those topics and come back prepared to defend yourselves on the subject? This will help me with my book as it should enable me to see how people might react to it. Let's meet, say, four more times, the first three to tackle some particular problems, and the final one to try to wrap things up by coming back to the beginning where all this started.'

'That's fine,' said **Kaveh**, 'but where do we begin?'

'I suggest that we begin with the economic question,' **I** said, 'since some of you wanted us to get back to the real world and away from all this abstract philosophising. Though I warn you, don't blame me if we find ourselves coming back to deal with conceptual matters more quickly than you anticipate.'

'Okay,' said **Diana**, 'I'm up for that. I volunteer to look into the *economics* of immigration and return with the reasons why economic considerations mean we should have some controls—to protect the poor, obviously.'

'Which poor?' **I** said, a little mischievously.

'All of them!' said **Diana** without hesitation, before starting to laugh.

'Okay,' **I** said, 'we shall see. After that, perhaps we should consider the *rights* issue. It may be all very well to figure out what are the economic pros and cons of immigration, but we will need to ask who gets to decide what to do, particularly given that there is no shortage of controversy when it comes to the economics.'

'I'll look into that,' said **Antoine**. 'I think I have an idea for an argument I want to make, but I'll have to research it first. I think there may be a right to immigrate.'

'Fine,' **I** said, 'and we should follow that up with a look at how that fits with the idea of the nation or state, since that may have a bearing on the workability of the idea of a right to immigrate.'

'I'll do that,' said **Tracy**. 'I think this is the heart of the issue. If we care about protecting the institutions that make modern life possible, then this is where the rubber meets the road. I know I haven't explained it fully, but I'm pretty sure I can do this if I have a bit more time to think things through.'

'Very well, Tracy,' **I** said. 'Good luck on that score.'

'I think we should also consider whether refugees or forced migration makes a difference,' said **Astrid**, 'and whether our past affects matters. Shouldn't our colonial history change things? Aren't there special cases? Maybe we shouldn't be thinking in such general terms because in political life there are always exceptions.'

'Then do it,' **I** said, 'and good luck with that one too!'

'Is that it?' asked **Kaveh**. 'I think I'd like to contribute something.'

'Yeah,' said **Temi**, 'me too.'

'What would you two like to do?' **I** said.

'I'd quite like to have another go at you, Xandros,' said **Temi**, smiling.

'Ooh, that sounds good,' said **Kaveh**. 'I'll be in that!'

'Well, gentlemen,' **I** said, 'I was thinking that in our last session we'd try to put it all together and ask what kind of society we were imagining and how that affected the way in which we think about immigration. My intention had been to advance a defence of the open society.'

'Perfect,' said **Temi**, 'Kaveh and I can have a go at that. I'm not sure what we think, but if that's what you're going to defend, that's what we're going to come ready to challenge.'

'Okay then,' **I** said, 'let's see how we go. I think this is going to work out very well. Very, very well.'

2 The Economics of Immigration

After such a spirited first conversation, I was looking forward to seeing the students again, curious as to what conclusions they might try to advance about immigration. There was something of the contrarian spirit about them, and it was abundantly clear that the struggle mattered as much as, if not more than, the outcome. Which is as it should be in any serious inquiry.

I'd offered to host our little symposium at my home, and to this everyone agreed enthusiastically. I would supply the wine, they the pizza. Diana and Antoine were the first to arrive, the former bearing a thick-crust pie with every conceivable topping, and the latter, as a vegetarian, a plain cheese pizza loaded with extra cheese.

'This is going to be amazing,' said **Antoine**.

'Or frightening,' said **Diana**.

'How are you two?' **I** said, waving a bottle of wine and a glass to signal that I was ready to pour.

'Good, good, Xandros,' said **Antoine**, nodding eagerly, 'and yes to some red wine!'

'I'm okay,' said **Diana**, 'though I've been getting quite a bit of correspondence from Stephan, who's discovered I'm researching the economics of immigration and keeps asking questions or offering help.'

A knock on the door stopped me from answering, and within moments Astrid, Temi, and Kaveh were making their way noisily to the living room.

DOI: 10.4324/9781003629641-2

'It's good to see you guys,' said **Temi**, smiling broadly, 'though it looks like you all spent the holidays eating!'

'I think the word you're searching for is "working",' said **Kaveh**, 'though I realize that you may not be familiar with the concept.'

'Well, I think that I struck the right balance,' said **Astrid**, 'just the right amount of work but plenty of festive socializing.'

'I'd expect nothing less,' **I** said, 'but where's Tracy?'

'She said she'd be late,' said **Diana**, 'and told me it's fine to go ahead before she gets here. But she'll bring dessert.'

'That alright,' **I** said, 'but we haven't time to waste, so grab some pizza and a glass of whatever makes you happy and find a comfortable place to sit so we can hear what Diana has to tell us about the economics of immigration.'

'I'm ready when you're all ready to learn,' said **Diana** with a giggle.

'I believe that's your cue, Diana,' **I** said. 'So take it away.'

'Suddenly, I'm feeling a bit nervous,' said **Diana** slowly, 'so maybe I should start by saying that I don't have a fully developed view to defend. I think I have a good sense now of the issues we need to consider, and maybe even a sense of where I see the fault lines in the debate over immigration, but I have to admit that the economic literature is confusing. It seems like economists have reasons to justify every available alternative. I'm starting to realize that it's not just philosophical questions that are intractable.'[1]

'I think that's a good start,' **I** said. 'Coming to agreement on the facts, so called, can be as tricky as settling on solutions or coming

1 For some general works on the economics of immigration, see Cynthia Bansak, Nicole B. Simpson, and Madeleine Zavodny, *The Economics of Immigration* (second edition, New York: Routledge, 2021); George Borjas, *Immigration Economics* (Cambridge, MA: Harvard University Press, 2014); David Lebland and Benjamin Helms, *The Ties that Bind: Immigration and the Global Political Economy* (Cambridge, UK: Cambridge University Press, 2023). A particularly accessible and informative work is Helen de Haas, *How Immigration Really Works: The Facts About the Most Divisive Issue in Politics* (New York: Basic Books, 2023).

to a mind on questions of value. But go on, tell us where you want to take us.'

'Okay,' **Diana** began, 'so the first thing we need to settle in considering the economics of immigration is whose economy we're talking about. I'm going to say that we should focus on the economic impact of immigration on the receiving society.'

'That seems odd,' **Astrid** said at once. 'Surely, we should consider the impact on everyone.'

'We could,' **Diana** replied, 'but I don't think we need to, because it's pretty clear that immigrants benefit from migrating. I'm leaving out refugees, obviously, since they may not have a choice, but those people aside, immigrants gain from moving—why else would they move? The real issue is the effect on receiving countries—the consequences for third parties.'

'What about the brain drain?' **Temi** said. 'Emigrants affect the societies they leave if they take with them their skills and talents.'

'Sure,' said **Diana**, 'but that's a minor consideration in most of the cases I think you're imagining since immigrants tend to leave because they have few or no opportunities where they are and also send home remittances that make them more significant contributors than they could be if they stayed.'[2]

'This is a complicated issue,' **I** said, 'and maybe we'll come back to it. In the meantime, let's allow Diana to proceed.'

'Thank you,' **Diana** replied. 'Now where was I? Oh yes, the impact of immigration on domestic society. There are two issues here: does immigration make the society as a whole better off, economically speaking, and does immigration make some parts of society better off at the expense of other parts? I think only the second part is worth considering in detail because it's pretty clear that immigration increases a society's wealth and income. The real issue is the distributional one.'

2 See Kieran Oberman, 'Can Brain Drain Justify Immigration Restrictions', *Ethics*, 123 (3), 2013, 427–455.

'Hang on a second,' said **Antoine**. 'That's a very arrogant-sounding claim. You make it seem so obvious, but there must be a lot of people who doubt what you're claiming. Is there no disagreement about this among economists, let alone real people?'

'Sorry, I wasn't intending to come across as arrogant,' said **Diana**, sounding a little hurt or pretending to be (I couldn't tell). 'I'm a very nice person. I just wanted to get to what I think is the main point. You're right that not all economists agree on this, though I have to say that after reading all the immigration economics I ever want to, I'm surprised that economists agree on anything. They're always saying: "on the one hand" or "it all depends" or "compared to what." It's infuriating!'

'You're right,' **I** said, 'but it's what I love about economists: they ask: "compared to what?" We philosophers could learn a lot from them on this score. Still, Antoine has a point. Perhaps you could give us a sketch of the reasons why you don't want to spend too much time on the first question and intend to talk about distribution.'

'I don't wish to overstate things,' **Diana** said, 'but to some extent it's quite straightforward. If you want economic growth, then the free movement of capital and labour is the way to go. Goods go to those who want and are willing to pay for them, and workers go to where they are most wanted. If you stop people exchanging for any reason, you force them to go to the next best option, which in the labour market means hiring not the person who's most suited but the person you are allowed to—or not hiring anyone at all.'

'It's a pity Tracy isn't here,' said **Kaveh**. 'She'd love all this free market worship!'

'Hey!' said **Diana**, now genuinely cross. 'I said I wouldn't overstate things and I haven't. I've just started. I'm not saying there's never a case for preventing market exchange, only that if the goal is economic growth, then I can see why, in principle, the free movement of labour is a positive. It's hard to find economists who disagree. They only quarrel over how much growth and whether it's worth it. You don't have to accept that world GDP would go up by trillions of dollars a year, as some argue. It's enough that hundreds of billions are created in value.'[3]

'Yes, but who's getting the benefit?' said **Astrid**.

'That's my point,' said **Diana**, now a little exasperated. 'That's my point! The economic issue is distribution, not production. The real worry about the free movement of labour is the impact on the poor and maybe even on the middle classes of any society. Capitalism is great for winners but maybe not for the losers.'

'What do you mean by "capitalism"?' **I** asked, provoking groans and cries of mock despair.

'You just can't resist using that phrase, can you, Xandros?' said **Antoine**. '"What do you mean?" is your all-purpose catchphrase. Did you ever manage to get a second date?'

'Of course,' **I** said. 'Though I wouldn't date someone who didn't understand some basic concepts that are relevant—like the concept of a "date", for example. But we're not here to discuss my personal life, we're here to talk about the economics of immigration. What I'd really like to find out more about from Diana is why we're approaching the matter in this way? Why are we beginning with the matter of wealth and economic growth? Is that what really matters? Isn't this a very limited standard we're setting, as if human beings are no better than satisfaction-seeking machines? Is that what we're concerned about, ultimately? Is consumption the point of it all?'

'Better Socrates dissatisfied than a pig satisfied,' said **Astrid** in a triumphant voice.

3 See Michael A. Clemens, 'Economics and Emigration: Trillion-dollar Bills on the Sidewalk', *Journal of Economic Perspectives*, 25 (3), 2011, 83–106, who claims constraints on emigration from poor countries distort the global economy to such an extent that the world forgoes trillions of dollars in income as measured by lower global gross domestic product. See also his discussion paper: *Migration on the Rise, a Paradigm in Decline: the Last Half-Century of Global Mobility* (Centre for Research and Analysis of Migration, London, 2022). https://www.cream-migration.org/publ_uploads/CDP_02_22_1.pdf. And see Michael A. Clemens and Lant Pritchett, 'The new economic case for migration restrictions: An assessment', *Journal of Development Economics*, 138, 2019, 153–164.

'Precisely,' **I** said. 'Are we talking about how we are to live in Porcinopolis, or do we have something nobler in mind?'

'Would that make us students of oinkonomics?' said **Kaveh** with a broad a grin—to groans from everyone else.

'Give me a chance,' said **Diana**, 'I'm not a barbarian! Of course, I think there are higher things to consider than the mere satisfaction of our desires, but for a lot of people, having their basic needs met is more of a struggle than it is for us. That's why we have to address the first question, because some think immigration makes us poorer. I don't think it does globally, or even nationally, but it may make some poorer even as it makes others a lot richer. That's how capitalism—however you want to define it—works.'

'Conan the Barbarian says that the best thing in life is to crush your enemies, see them driven before you, and to hear the lamentations of their women,' said **Kaveh** brightly.

'Thanks, Kaveh,' said **Diana**. 'I'll keep that in mind for when I transition from being a woman.'

'Actually, it was Genghis Khan who first expressed that sentiment, Kaveh,' **I** said, 'and, yes, people do have different ideas about the good.'

'Oh,' said **Kaveh**, sounding a little deflated.

'But you're absolutely right, Diana,' **I** continued. 'I've been a bit unfair in pushing you in this direction, though it's partly because I think we need to get clearer about what we're considering when we talk about the economics of immigration. You're quite correct in distinguishing the two different ways in which we might examine the impact of immigration, but there's also a larger issue at stake. What is the value in question when we ask whether immigration is going to make us better or worse off? Is it just the satisfaction of our desires? And if so, what desires are these—the desire to be well fed, comfortable, and suitably amused?'

'It's about happiness,' said **Astrid**, 'obviously! Some would say "utility", but I really don't see what's gained by using that vulgar term. People want to be happy, and the aim of public policy and political institutions more generally is to make us happy—or at least enable us to find happiness. A big part of that means making sure we aren't prevented from achieving it because we're too poor to live comfortably.'

'Food first, then morality,' said **Antoine**, as if to underline Astrid's point.

'Thank you, Herr Brecht,'[4] **I** said, 'but are you all quite sure that this is what is most important? The last time we met, I recall, some of you were quite worried about the fate of civilization. Now you seem to be more interested in making sure there's enough wine and pizza to go around. Oinkonomics indeed!'

'Am I ever going to get to finish my presentation?' said **Diana** plaintively. 'If we keep going back to first principles with every statement I make, we'll never get anywhere.'

'Fair enough,' **I** said. 'Let's press ahead. But don't think these questions we've raised will go away. They'll be back.'

'Yeah,' said **Kaveh**, 'like the Terminator—with an indestructible skeleton and a bad accent.'

'Kaveh! Enough with the Arnold Schwarzenegger references already!' said **Diana**.

'You're just jealous,' **Kaveh** answered, trying to look solemn.

'As I was saying,' **Diana** continued, 'we can take it as a given that freedom of movement is economically advantageous at the global level because, as almost all economists agree, a flexible labour market will enable us to be more productive and to create greater total wealth. The question is, who gets that wealth? Moreover, does some people getting more wealth mean at least some others ending up not only without any gains but with actual losses. A move towards freer immigration may not be pareto optimal. If it were, perhaps there'd be less of an issue—other than an increase in inequality between the gainers and those just left behind. But the worry is that some will be left behind and some will find themselves falling below where they once were.'

'Let's leave the pareto optimality standard aside,' **I** said. 'It's of limited use to us because we're not operating in circumstances in

4 Bertolt Brecht (1898–1956) was a German playwright whose *Threepenny Opera* included the line: 'first comes food, then morality.'

which we can simply opt for the status quo. Decisions are taken every day by civil servants, and leaders, in a variety of different states, so standing still is just not an option. We can increase or decrease immigration; we can make immigration easier or harder; we can give people who are already here as residents—legal aliens—more or fewer rights; but we can't stand still, not least because every decision has ripple effects that would require other decisions to bring us back to the status quo. Every decision that benefits someone could also disadvantage another. The idea that we move forward only with changes that leave no one worse off is just not plausible.'

'Lampedusa[5] said that if we want to keep things as they are, we are going to have to change,' said **Astrid**, looking very pleased with herself.

'Indeed,' **I** said. 'And there's no way of doing that without advantaging some and disadvantaging others.'

'What does this imply? What does it mean?' asked **Diana**.

'It means that we have to consider the harm caused by the reduction of immigration no less than the harm caused by immigration itself if we are to assess the impact of immigration,' **I** said. 'If you're worried about the people who are among the worst off, you'll have to accept that immigration policies that improve the lot of some of them may worsen the economic circumstances of others. We live in a world of trade-offs.'[6]

'The simplest thing to do would be to make an overall calculation of what leads to the best results for society as a whole,' said **Temi**.

'Maybe,' **I** said, 'but does that mean making a judgment about total benefit in terms of well-being—regardless of how it's

5 Giuseppe Tomasi, the 11th Prince of Lampedusa (1896–1957) was a Sicilian nobleman and author of *The Leopard*, a novel whose most famous line is: 'If we want things to stay as they are, things will have to change.'

6 This is the nub of the argument advanced in Chandran Kukathas, *Immigration and Freedom* (Princeton: Princeton University Press, 2021). See also Tara Watson and Kalee Thompson, *The Border Within: The Economics of Immigration in an Age of Fear* (Chicago: Chicago University Press, 2022).

distributed? Or average well-being—again, regardless of how it's distributed?'

'Couldn't we use Rawls's Difference Principle,' said **Antoine**. 'You know, the one where he says that, provided we respect liberty unconditionally, institutions should be arranged so that they are to the benefit of the least advantaged?'[7]

'That's fine,' **I** said, 'but there are a couple of things we need to consider in thinking about this as a principle to guide our approach to immigration. The first is that it's not obvious which understanding of "least advantaged" we should adopt. On one view, we mean the least advantaged right now. So, make no changes that might lower their standard of living. On another view, the "least advantaged" refers to whoever would occupy the bottom rung on the social ladder once whatever institutions are in place. In this case, if there are rules that make the living standard of the least advantaged higher than any alternative set of rules, those are the rules we should have. But changing institutions to make the lowest standard of living higher could mean not only that people who were at the bottom under the old rules are both better off and higher up the pecking order but that those who were higher up the order before could find themselves at the bottom—and possibly worse off than before, even if they're richer than the previous bottom-dwellers.'

'Perhaps we should just prioritise the well-being of the existing generation of least advantaged,' said **Diana**. 'After all, they're the ones who are actually here, alive, and not just hypothetical people.'

'I don't think it's going to be as easy as that,' **I** said. 'First, because future people are already with us, since society is always made up of several generations. Do we prioritise sixty-year-olds over six-year-olds—or vice versa? But even if we think we could exclude the yet-to-be-born from consideration, I'm not sure that's how

7 In his theory of justice, John Rawls presented two principles of justice, the second of which included the 'difference principle', which states that 'social and economic inequalities are to be arranged so that they are to the greatest benefit of the least advantaged.' See *A Theory of Justice*, 302.

parents and would-be parents think. So much of what we do makes sense only because we care about future people.'

'I didn't think it was going to get this complicated,' said **Diana**. 'I wanted to defend a more straightforward thesis. Immigration increases the size of the labour force and that would have two bad consequences. First, it would lower wages, since there'd be more people competing for fewer jobs and employers could afford to wait for wages to be bid downwards—or at least, not bid up. Second, it would lower employment if wages don't fall, or if there just aren't enough jobs to go round. The people who'd be most affected by this are the poorest, since they're more likely to face competition from mass migration. Rich people would be better off being able to employ cooks and gardeners; construction companies would have access to a lower-waged and more compliant labour pool; and existing low-skilled workers would be left out in the cold. None of this seems fair.'

'That seems right to me,' said **Antoine**, 'at least in the US and Europe. I think this is why everywhere we're seeing the rise of right-wing, populist, parties, like the Alternativ für Deutschland in Germany and the whole pro-Trump movement here. It's because a lot of people feel like they're being left behind. I'm not anti-immigrant, but I have to admit this is a worry. It's fine for me to welcome immigrants, but what about those who lose out as a result? I think they feel let down by their fellow citizens.'

'These all sound like legitimate concerns,' **I** said, 'and I don't want to dismiss them. I do, however, think we should dig a bit deeper and ask two sets of questions. First, have we got our explanations right? Second, is immigration control the right solution even if we have?'

'Do you think immigration doesn't have the economic impact I've described?' asked **Diana**, sounding slightly incredulous.

'I don't doubt for a moment that what you're describing is accurate,' **I** said. 'If we take the US case, for example, one obvious development that's hard to ignore is the rise in what have been called "deaths of despair". The rate of suicide is one indicator, but if one digs a bit deeper it also becomes apparent that for significant parts of the American population, there is a sense of being left behind as society—the world—changes faster than they have been able to adapt.[8] Many of the jobs they once did no longer exist, and where they do, such forms of work no longer come with the income or the prestige—or even the respect—they once did. Falling wage levels are definitely part of the story.'[9]

'Then you accept that immigration is a problem!' said **Diana**.

'I think immigration has had an impact,' **I** said, 'but I think we need to be a bit more careful before rushing to lay responsibility for so much of what goes wrong on one possible causal factor.'

'What else could it be?' said **Antoine**.

'It would be a mistake to look for a single cause,' **I** said, 'not just because mono-causal explanations cannot work, since any effect is always the product of the interaction of at least two variables. In social life, there are always many factors in play, and the task is to work out how they interact—and which are more important than others.'

'What other factors?' said **Antoine**.

'Well, let's take the question of falling wage levels and the loss of jobs,' **I** said. 'I'm sure you'll all agree that competition within a growing workforce for the same number of jobs is going to slow, or possibly reverse, a rise in real wages. It may even lead to job losses. But there are two sides to this equation. We need to ask why there hasn't been an increase in the number of jobs. After all, as the world has gotten richer, there are more people with money to

8 See Angus Deaton and Anne Case, *Deaths of Despair and the Future of Capitalism*, Princeton: Princeton University Press, 2021. But see also important critiques of the 'deaths of despair thesis', including Matthew Yglesias, 'The Deaths of Despair Narrative is Wrong', *Slow Boring* blog: https://www.slowboring.com/p/the-deaths-of-despair-narrative-is.

9 See Justin Gest, *The New Minority: White Working Class Politics in an Age of Immigration and Inequality* (Oxford: Oxford University Press, 2016); Arlie Hochschild, *Strangers in their own land: Anger and Mourning on the American Right* (New York: The New Press, 2016); Eric Kaufmann, *Whiteshift: Populism, Immigration and the Future of White Majorities* (London: Penguin, 2019).

spend, so the demand for consumer goods and services has only been going up.'

'That's the problem,' said **Astrid**. 'We're consuming too much, which is not good for the planet.'

'A topic for another day,' **I** said, 'but the point for now is that immigration may not be the explanation we need for any slowdown in industrial or manufacturing or service sector growth in America, or the West more generally. The world is changing, and other countries are producing goods that compete with ours—and not just in markets here but also in potential markets for US exporters. If foreign manufacturers are paying wages that outcompete workers' wages here, it doesn't matter whether those workers are here in our midst or halfway around the world.'[10]

'Are you saying it's globalization?' said **Temi**.

'Globalization is a term that covers a multitude of sins,' **I** said, 'but I'm not sure we can usefully offer it as an explanation without identifying the mechanisms that allow us to connect cause with effect. Still, if you're asking if the inter-connectedness of the world is something we need to acknowledge when trying to explain what we see and experience, the answer is yes.'

'Society is to blame,' said **Kaveh**, trying to sound solemn.

'Can you say something serious, Kaveh?' said **Diana**, who was clearly getting a little exasperated. Her presentation was not going the way she expected.

'While I suspect that Kaveh was being flippant,' **I** said, 'I think there is a serious point behind his quip. Society is to blame to the extent that we are victims of our interdependence. That is the point made by Jean-Jacques Rousseau (the greatest of all social theorists,

10 This is an important point but one often overlooked or misunderstood. The size of the labour pool can rise whether or not immigrant workers enter the domestic labour market. For example, if a company relocates abroad, perhaps because of rising domestic wages, the workers it hires there will compete with those it might have hired if it had not moved. Even if it does not relocate but a foreign competitor in the same industry starts hiring, those workers will contribute to the size of the pool of labour and put pressure on wages.

in my view), who wanted to show us that we are the products of our sociability. All the ills that befall us have their roots in our nature as a cooperative species. It's why we have inequality. It's why we have rank and status, wealth and poverty.'[11]

'Exactly what I was driving at,' said **Kaveh**.

'Yeah, right,' said **Temi**, rolling his eyes, even as the others giggled.

'We're indebted to you, Kaveh,' **I** said, 'and I hope you won't mind if I say a bit more to build on your insight.'

'Be my guest,' said **Kaveh**.

'This seems to be taking us away from the economics of immigration,' said **Diana** sullenly.

'It isn't,' **I** said, 'though it may be that we're being forced to consider the economic question more broadly than you'd anticipated. You've wanted to look at it from the perspective of the worst-off in society to ask how immigration might be managed so that the burden doesn't fall predominantly on their shoulders—correct?'

'In a nutshell, yes,' said **Diana** slowly.

'Then the first thing we need to consider,' **I** said, 'is how confident we are that this one variable supplies the explanation we're seeking for the problem of disadvantage you've identified. My guess is that immigration is just one factor and not the critical one—if there is indeed just one factor that is of decisive significance. The second thing we need to ask is whether we can in fact control immigration to give us the results we seek. Some are undoubtedly harmed if they are outcompeted by immigrants, but others gain when immigrants make some enterprises economically

11 Jean-Jacques Rousseau, 'Discourse on the Origin and Foundations of Inequality Among Mankind', in J.J. Rousseau, *The Social Contract and the First and Second Discourses* (edited by Susan Dunn, New Haven: Yale University Press, 2002). For discussion, see Arthur Melzer, *The Natural Goodness of Man: On the System of Rousseau's Thought* (Chicago: University of Chicago Press, 1990).

feasible.[12] For example, without immigrant labour, many farmers would never be able to bring in their harvests because there just aren't enough Americans interested in these jobs at any price. This would affect not only those farmers but also other Americans whose livelihoods depend on the viability of this industry. Then there are those who never appear in the statistics because the jobs they might have had never came into existence because industries or businesses closed or never got going.'

'That works both ways, surely,' said **Antoine**. 'There might be people who never appear in the labour market statistics because they despair of ever finding work—because immigration has led to fewer jobs and lower wages.'

'And we know that there have been times in American history when immigration was significantly reduced and employment was higher,'[13] said **Temi.**

'And better paid,' **Antoine** added.

'Also, although I'm still generally pro-immigration, couldn't it be that even if all the things you're saying are true, it wouldn't change the fact that if we increased the size of the workforce dramatically, we'd see many more visibly negative effects on employment and wages,' said **Astrid.** 'If things haven't been that bad, it may be because we've actually limited immigration. Were we to open the borders to a massive influx of people, I'd bet we'd get some pretty significant effects on jobs—particularly among the poor. After all, if you increase supply, the price goes down—and that holds as much for labour as for anything else for sale.'

12 For an argument that workers' wages are adversely affected by immigrant labour, see Phillip Cafaro, *How Many is Too Many: The Progressive Argument for Reducing Immigration to the United States* (Chicago: Chicago University Press, 2015); see also George Borjas, *We Wanted Workers: Unravelling the Immigration Narrative* (New York: Norton, 2016). For a critique of these views, see Chandran Kukathas, *Immigration and Freedom* (Princeton: Princeton University Press, 2021), Chapter 5.

13 This claim is made by Stephen Macedo, 'Why can't we all just move around? *Mind* (2023), volume 132, issue 526, 595–604.

'You all make some very good points,' **I** said. 'I can see I have my work cut out for me. Let's start with the last claim, that an increase in the supply of labour must lead to a decline in the price of labour and therefore to falling wages. As economists would put it, an increase in immigration means an exogenous supply effect, so the supply curve shifts outwards. With demand held constant, what you'd see is a decline in the price of labour. So far so good?'

'All correct,' said **Astrid**.

'But we also have to consider the fact that an influx of immigrants means an increase in demand for everything, including labour,' **I** said. 'The demand curve also shifts outwards. That makes it very hard to assess the actual impact of immigration.'

'All this talk of curves is making me dizzy,' said **Kaveh**, 'which makes me even more convinced that economists never give you a straight answer.'

'Well, to put it simply, Kaveh,' **I** said, 'immigration increases the number of people looking for work but also increases the number of people needing workers. Sometimes the increase will lead to more employment and higher wages, and other times less employment and lower wages. But the margins are small. So, if you're going to make the case for less immigration—or indeed, more—this is not the argument to use.'

At that point, there was a knock on the front door and the group shouted almost as one: 'Come in, Tracy!' There was now no prospect of continuing the discussion for a while, since Tracy had come bearing the dessert as promised. More to the point, she had outdone everyone else with the sheer quantity and quality of offerings: baba au rhum, marzipan mice, a yuletide chocolate log, mince pies (with brandy butter), and an unopened bottle of tawny port.

'Wow!' said **Kaveh**. 'If immigrants arrived with this sort of nosh, no one would turn them away!'

'This is a very generous spread you've set before us, Tracy,' **I** said.

'It's my pleasure,' **Tracy** said, blushing slightly, 'but to be honest, these are mostly leftovers from our family Christmas and since everyone's gone off skiing for two weeks, I'm left with all this stuff I can't possibly finish on my own. I'm sorry to be so late, but I've only just been released from duty now that the last houseguest has left.'

'Why don't you all go ahead and fill your dessert plates,' **I** said, 'and whoever is done first can start catching Tracy up on our discussion?'

'That's me,' said **Kaveh** with a grin, his plate crammed with a sample of each and every dessert, 'which is lucky since I'm the one most responsible for the progress we've made.'

'Really?' said **Tracy**, sounding unsure as to whether Kaveh was joking or serious.

'Yup,' **Kaveh** grinned, 'so listen closely. In a word, what we've realised is that it's all about justice.'

'What?!' **Diana** cried out. 'What? I mean, what?!'

'Whisky, Tango, Foxtrot!' said **Astrid**.

'Yes, Foxtrot, absolutely, totally!' **Antoine** chimed in.

'Perhaps you'd better explain, Kaveh,' **I** said, 'since Tracy looks a little puzzled, and the others seem to be struggling with your rather cryptic summation.'

'Sure,' **Kaveh** replied, quite undeterred and clearly enjoying himself. 'We've been more or less in agreement that the immigration question is all about how benefits and burdens are distributed. So, it's about social justice, right? We also seem to have accepted that what matters most is the distribution in our own country, and no one else's interests really matter—or at least, not a lot. Justice begins at home, you might say.'

'Oh,' said **Tracy**, 'wow! I mean, that sounds right to me. How did you guys manage to get to agree on this? And so fast? I thought you'd all be much more hesitant and maybe even argue for open borders or something like that.'

'Actually, I'm for open borders,' said **Kaveh**. 'I was simply relating where the discussion got to. Just sayin', okay?'

'You make us sound like a bunch of nationalists,' said **Antoine**, sounding a little troubled. 'I don't think we are.'

'I don't know whether you consider yourselves to be nationalists,' said **Tracy**, 'but surely you have to be to some extent. Don't you think your country, and your fellow citizens, matter more than other countries and people with whom you have no connection? I'm not saying we shouldn't care at all about the rest of the world, but justice does begin at home.[14] Yes, it's all about justice.'

'I'm feeling very uneasy about all this,' said **Antoine**. 'I think I'm on the wrong side. I want to be on the side of the poor and the oppressed, but I don't see how I can be if I'm in the nationalist camp.'

'Don't give in the dark side, Luke,' said **Kaveh**. 'The Force is strong within you.'

'Who's Luke?' said **Astrid**, looking very puzzled. 'Is that your middle name, Antoine?'

'He's a Jedi,' said **Kaveh**. 'Try to keep up.'

'Antoine's a Jedi?' said **Astrid**. 'What's that?'

'No, Luke's a Jedi,' said **Kaveh**. 'Antoine's French. There are no French Jedi. C'est pas possible.'

'Kaveh, can you be serious for just one minute,' said **Diana**, clearly exasperated.

'Sure,' said **Kaveh**. 'Starting the countdown now.'

'I don't think believing in justice is going over to the dark side,' said **Tracy**. 'Justice is about what is right.'

'Doesn't that mean it's universal?' said **Antoine**. 'I mean, can a nationalist believe in justice?'

'I think the ideal of justice is universal,' said **Tracy**, 'but I don't think you can have justice unless you have a community of people who belong together. Justice is about what we owe to other people, but not all other people, only our people.'

14 On this, see the papers in the 1988 *Ethics* symposium on 'Duties Beyond Borders', vol. 98 no. 4, notably the following papers: Onora O'Neill, 'Ethical Reasoning and Ideological Pluralism', *Ethics*, 98 (4), 1988, 705–722; Robert E. Goodin, 'What is So Special about Our Fellow Countrymen?', *Ethics*, 98 (4), 1988, 663–686; David Miller, 'The Ethical Significance of Nationality', *Ethics*, 98 (4), 1988, 647–662. A fuller statement of Miller's view can be found in his *Strangers in Our Midst: The Political Philosophy of Immigration* (Cambridge, MA: Harvard University Press, 2016). See also Margaret Moore, *A Political Theory of Territory* (Oxford: Oxford University Press, 2017). For a critique of nationalist theories of immigration, see Kukathas, *Immigration and Freedom*, Chapter 7.

'What about the global poor?' said **Astrid**. 'Do we owe them anything?'

'Not as much as we owe our domestic poor,' said **Tracy**. 'We can be benevolent or charitable towards the foreign poor, but our own poor come first.'

'Does that mean that we have no warrant for giving anything to the foreign poor until we've completely eliminated poverty in our own society?' **I** asked.

'Probably,' said **Tracy** a little hesitantly. 'I don't see how we can justify spending money on foreign aid when any of our own citizens are struggling. Our government's job is to look after our own first.'

'Does that hold for our actions as individuals?' **I** asked.

'What do you mean?' **Tracy** replied.

'I mean, does justice demand not only that governments not operate for the benefit of foreigners but also that individuals put their fellow citizens first?' **I** said.

'Individuals can spend their money however they like,' said **Tracy**, 'but their governments can't.'

'Any way they like?' **I** asked. 'Are you sure?'

'Okay, not *any* way,' **Tracy** said, 'because they can't spend it in ways that are harmful to their fellow citizens. I guess, they can't spend it on things that would be harmful to citizens in other countries either. It wouldn't be right to send money to a terrorist group or to enemy states.'

'I think I see what you're getting at,' **I** said. 'It would be fine for me, for example, to order wine from my favourite Italian vineyard or to support an orphanage in Kabul, but I couldn't use it to support the Mafia or help an Afghan citizen pay a people-smuggler. Right?'

'Yes, I think so,' said **Tracy**, a little warily, as if she suspected a trap.

'I think I see a picture emerging,' **I** said, 'so let me try to present it to see if I've understood you correctly, Tracy. If I have, I suspect that you're all in agreement to a substantial degree, with the possible exception of Kaveh.'

'Sounds good to me,' said **Diana**.

'Yes, it's about time you started contributing a bit more,' said **Temi**, unable to suppress a giggle, 'instead of just serving wine and nodding sagely.'

'I'm a sage, it's what I do,' **I** said, prompting a round of mock kow-towing.

'Okay, we're ready,' said **Antoine**.

'As much as you're not going to like this,' **I** said, 'Kaveh is right.'

'Yes!' said **Kaveh**, with an exaggerated fist-pump.

'The economics of immigration as you've presented it comes down to the question of social justice,' **I** continued. 'Diana has made clear, and the rest of you seem to have accepted, that the critical issue is the impact of immigration not on the generation of wealth but on the distribution of benefits and burdens in society. Now, one does have to be mindful of making a simple distinction between the production of goods and their distribution, since rules of distribution will surely affect what is produced, just as what is produced shapes what can be distributed. But any theory of social justice, rightly or wrongly, invariably looks at the matter through the lens of the distributive issue.'

'Exactly,' said **Kaveh**, to a mixture of groans and grimaces from the others.

'Thank you, Kaveh,' **I** said. 'Your endorsement means the world to me. But here's the problem that's about to make Antoine unhappy. Immigration is going to have an impact on distribution within society—as well as, of course, across the world more generally. Leaving the immigrants aside, some people will gain a great deal, some will gain a little, and some will lose—either because they get outcompeted by foreign candidates for jobs or because their wages fall relatively or even absolutely. Now, it won't do to exaggerate this. It's all going to depend on circumstances, on the kinds of immigrants who want to enter, and on the availability of workers in different fields and industries. Increased immigration may in many circumstances make most people better off economically, and some (including the poorest) much better off, but it's highly unlikely that no one would be made worse off. It could also exacerbate existing economic inequalities, particularly if more of the immigrants join the ranks of the poorest in society. That's going to leave a lot of people unhappy.'

'I don't understand,' said **Antoine**. 'Why should this analysis make me unhappy?'

'Because the implication I suspect most of you wish to draw from this is one that prioritises the principle of nationality,' **I** said, 'and you expressed your disdain for any kind of association with nationalist thinking.'

'I do,' said **Antoine**. 'I'm on the side of the oppressed.'

'Your tired, your poor, your huddled masses,' said **Kaveh** helpfully.

'Thank you, Lazarus,' **I** said, 'but which ones—foreign, domestic, or all the huddled?'[15]

'Well, justice can't be confined within boundaries,' said **Antoine**, sounding a little miserable.

'It has to be,' said **Tracy**. 'We have to be realistic. We can't be responsible for the whole world. We should take care of our own first. That's the way most people see matters. It's time we woke up to this!'

'I think that's a bit harsh, Tracy,' said **Antoine**. 'I'm just trying to see two very different points of view. I get what you're saying, I really do, but if we in the wealthy countries just ignore the interests of the worst-off in the rest of the world, aren't we simply doing so not because it's just but because we have the power to. That doesn't seem right.'

'It's the way of the world,' said **Tracy** grumpily. 'Get used to it.'

'Are you saying that we can't spend a penny helping anyone outside our country until we've solved poverty within?' asked **Temi**.

'I think I need to spend a penny,' said **Kaveh**, 'but not outside. Where's the toilet?'

15 Emma Lazarus (1849–1887) was an American poet. Her sonnet, 'The New Colossus', was cast in a bronze plate and set in the Statue of Liberty. Its most famous lines read:' Give me your tired, your poor, your huddled masses yearning to breathe free.' The poem expresses feeling for the plight of Jewish refugees fleeing the anti-Semitic pogroms in eastern Europe in the nineteenth century.

'Down the hall, Mr Segue,' **I** said, 'and the light switch is by the door before you enter.'

'Is that guy ever serious?' asked **Tracy**.

'He is,' **I** said, 'though he disguises it.'

'He's doing a good job,' said **Diana**.

'Well, he got us to see that when we talk economics and immigration we are really talking about social justice and nationality,' **I** said. 'But to go back to Temi's question, I don't think we can reasonably say that we can't spend a penny on outsiders until we've fully taken care of our own. Pareto optimality can't be a sensible principle to guide our thinking or decision-making.'

'Why not?' said **Tracy**.

'In part for reasons I gave earlier,' **I** said, 'though to be fair, Tracy, you weren't here. In a nutshell, with circumstances constantly changing, maintaining the status quo is a matter not of doing nothing but of taking deliberate action; but we have neither the wit nor the technology to take steps or devise institutions such that the status quo is in fact maintained or that no improvement worsens nobody's condition.'

'You did make that point,' said **Astrid**, looking at me and glancing anxiously at Tracy.

'But it gets more complicated still,' **I** said. 'It's not clear to me that we can take care of our own without doing so at the expense of some of our own. I don't see how that can be justified in any straightforward way—though I daresay clever politicians, and even cleverer philosophers, could find a way to spin any proposed solution.'

'Really, Xandros,' said **Diana**, 'are you actually equating philosophical argument with the work of spin doctors?'

'Fair enough,' **I** said. 'That was a bit of a cheap shot at my fellow philosophers, but my main point stands. Taking care of our own will involve taking some decisions that will constrain, or harm, some of our fellow citizens, who will have to forgo opportunities, or abandon plans, or take financial and other losses—whether or not they wish to do so.'

'That's social justice for you,' said **Kaveh**, now back in the room.

'You make social justice sound like something very harsh,' said **Antoine**.

'Not at all,' said **Kaveh**. 'Social justice means never having to say you're sorry.'

'I don't think so,' said **Temi**. 'It sounds like it means we'll have to be apologizing all the time to those of our fellow citizens who've been disadvantaged or made worse off by our policies or actions.'

'If we're going to have to apologize, I guess we'll need to figure out who we're going to disadvantage and who we're going to benefit—or at least, not hurt,' said **Diana**.

'Or at least tell them a story they'd buy,' said **Temi**.

'I don't think that's going to be so easy,' said **Astrid**. 'People don't take kindly to a decline in their fortunes.'

'You're all quite right,' **I** said, 'but there's another aspect to this that has to be considered, and that's the freedom of those who are restricted by our efforts to improve the welfare of others.'

'What do you mean, "freedom", Xandros?' said **Diana**, with a triumphant air, 'and now you know what it's like to be on the receiving end of one of your "what do you mean?" questions!'

'Well played, madam!', **I** said, 'well played! But I will answer you rather than just moan and grumble about the question. Because I do know what I mean. So, listen carefully and be prepared to be amazed.'

'I knew this wouldn't work,' said **Diana**, now a little crestfallen.

'By "freedom", in this context,' **I** continued, 'I mean the condition of not being controlled by others. At the very least, that would mean not being prevented or prohibited by others from acting, though there are other respects in which one might be controlled that I won't go into right now. To be sure, we need to refine this account, since the concept of control also needs to be elaborated, and in doing so we would need to understand what counts as being controlled, or prevented, or prohibited. But some examples might make things clearer while speaking to the substantive point I want to make.'

'That would be amazing,' said **Kaveh**, though I couldn't tell from his deadpan delivery whether he was being serious.

'Take the case of immigration restrictions designed to limit the employment of foreign workers,' **I** said, 'which prohibit some of our fellow citizens from hiring whomsoever they choose, whether because foreigners are cheaper, or better qualified, or more highly prized for some other reasons. Such prohibitions prevent them from doing as they wish and associating with whom they choose. They lose that freedom. Or take the case of someone who wants to bring her parents into the country to live with her to help with childcare but is prohibited because this is deemed to damage the employment prospects of citizens who might be hired instead. These citizens' interests are deemed worthy of protection, but the citizen now unable to host her parents loses some of her freedom. Aren't these losses of freedom part of the price paid for immigration control, and shouldn't they be put into the equation?'[16]

'I don't find this point amazing,' said **Tracy**. 'Sorry, but it seems just obvious that if you want to reduce unemployment among your own citizens, you have to require others to hire their own or not at all. These employers should just hire citizens instead or foreign workers. Same goes for mothers.'

'I accept that we can require employers to comply with such regulations,' **I** said, 'but what the examples emphasise is that doing so requires restricting the freedom of some citizens for the benefit of others. Is this not an important consideration? And the warrant for disadvantaging some citizens in this case, you seem to be implying, is that it advantages others, yet it's not obvious why some citizens are being preferred over others.'

'We're protecting the poor!' said **Tracy**. 'Our poor! That seems like a pretty good justification.'

'The poor are the master race, we must bow to their wishes,' said **Kaveh**, 'if they're the right nationality, of course.'

'Very funny,' said **Tracy**, 'but obviously the interests of the poor don't trump every consideration. Yet we do limit the freedom of

16 On this, see Kukathas, *Immigration and Freedom*. See also Chandran Kukathas, 'Immigration and Freedom', in Johannes Knolle and James Poskett (eds.), *Migration* (Cambridge, UK: Cambridge University Press, 2020), 18–49.

our citizens in the interests of the poor all the time, don't we? We tax the rich to help the poor. That's limiting the freedom of some citizens in the interests of others. I agree that the interests of the rich, and of employers, deserve some consideration. It's just that it's perfectly justifiable to restrict them a little for the benefit of others who are less well off or more vulnerable.'

'You're quite right,' **I** said. 'We do tax the rich, and also the not-so-rich, to help the poor, and restricting some for the good of others—like the poor—is pretty standard. I'm not sure this is obviously justifiable for a number of reasons, not least because it's not evident that the poor have always gained from this purported strategy. But even if it we accept that restricting some for the benefit of the poor is a good idea, the problem is that not all the poor benefit, and some will do worse. If the issue is one of distributive justice, what is the case for immigration controls that restrict the freedom of some citizens, make some poor citizens better off, and make other poor citizens worse off? And didn't you say earlier that citizens should be allowed to spend their money as they wish? Why are you making an exception for those who want to spend their money on hiring foreigners?'

'Perhaps immigration restrictions will make the very poorest of the poor better off,' said **Astrid**. 'That would make it justifiable, wouldn't it?'

'Perhaps,' **I** said, 'but I'd like to see the calculations. Are you suggesting that if we improved the lot of the ten poorest people by such restrictions, controls would be warranted even if we worsened the situations of the next ten thousand who are above them on the welfare scale? Would it not be both simpler and fairer to find a more precise policy tool to address the problem of poverty?'

'The bottom ten percent will always be with us,' said **Kaveh** solemnly.

'Indeed,' **I** said, 'but I'm not offering a counsel of despair, merely questioning the idea that immigration control is the right policy tool for the purpose Tracy has in mind, given the harmful effects it has on others of our fellow citizens.'

'I see your point,' said **Tracy**, 'though I'm still unamazed! Maybe it is the case that some poor do worse for restrictions on immigration, and perhaps that even means that we're taking in too few immigrants. But it could just mean we're accepting the wrong kinds of immigrants, and we need to tweak our policies rather than just open our borders. I bet if we simply let in anyone who wanted to move, that would be a disaster for our poor. I don't think it's unreasonable to stop people hiring foreigners if allowing them to hire whom they like would harm the poor.'

'I'm not sure this is enough of a justification,' **I** said. 'It sounds like this would give us reason to restrict citizens in many ways because of such third-party effects. It may be one thing to tax a broad range of people to protect the vulnerable, but quite another to further restrict their freedom to do business or do what's important to them in their personal lives. That line of reasoning might justify stopping people from traveling abroad because it harms the poor who depend on domestic tourism or preventing companies investing abroad because they could be investing at home.'

'We'll just have to draw a line,' said **Tracy** defiantly. 'Maybe a few lines. But we can't use the difficulty of making fine distinctions a reason for not making them at all.'

'We take in about a million people a year in the US,' said **Diana**, 'including about 20,000 refugees. That's been pretty steady since 2010, though the government plans to continue to reduce the refugee intake. We took in 85,000 refugees in 2016, but it's gone down a lot since then.'

'That's a rather depressing statistic,' said **Antoine**. 'I mean about the refugees.'

'I know,' said **Kaveh**, with a burst of enthusiasm. 'Open borders for refugees, the rest pay cash!'

'I think we're due to explore the refugee issue at a later date,' **I** said, 'so I don't want to pre-empt those discussions. But if we're thinking like economists, we might wish to consider the behavioural consequences of open borders for people in one category. I think you'll find many more people trying to show they're refugees.'

'Oh,' said **Kaveh**, sounding oddly deflated.

'We also take in about a million international students each year,' said **Diana**, 'and they don't count as immigrants in the official statistics. Though in some countries they do.'

'That's all quite useful to know,' **I** said, 'but I'd like to get back to Tracy's point. I think what she's getting at is that even if we're not harming our poor too much right now, it's because immigration controls are in fact offering them the protection they need, so we ought to refine our policies to reduce the harm to those affected badly and be wary of undoing what good we've achieved—which is just what we'd be doing by opening up our borders even further. Is that fair, Tracy?'

'Yes,' said **Tracy**, with a smile, 'that's a reasonable statement of my view. You've got me right. Now I am amazed!'

'You're welcome,' **I** said, 'but I'd like to add a more critical note. What I think is missing still is an explanation of why you think a substantial increase in immigration, particularly of the poor, is likely to have the negative consequences you fear. Where is the evidence for this? I accept that it's a not unreasonable hypothesis, but what reasons do we have for thinking it's right?'

'Surely, it stands to reason that if a billion people turned up overnight, we'd be in trouble,' said **Astrid**, 'even if that's a pretty unlikely scenario.'

'It is indeed unlikely, if not entirely impossible, practically speaking,' **I** said, 'which makes it odd that philosophers invoke this hypothetical. It's like saying "what if every American decided to move to New York tomorrow?" which right now they're fully entitled to do.'

'Yes,' said **Temi**, 'I imagine the second 160 million wanting to move might start having second thoughts once the first half got to the city.'

'Not to mention the nine million Americans who live abroad,' **I** added.

'It would be really hard to get a cab,' said **Kaveh**, 'even if you pre-booked.'

'Okay, I get it,' said **Tracy**, 'but is there no way of thinking through the question of limits?'

'Maybe we should think in terms of carrying capacity,' said **Astrid**. 'I mean, how many people can the United States accommodate?'

'Yes,' said **Antoine**, 'some think we've reached the limit, environmentally speaking.'

'There's also the issue of whether we want to have more people adopting the American lifestyle,' said **Temi**, 'which is way too carbon-positive. Do we want people moving from low-consumption to high-consumption economies? I don't know if we can do that without speeding up the destruction of the planet.'

'I wouldn't worry about the planet,' said **Kaveh**. 'It's been bombarded by asteroids for billions of years and the earth is still around. It turned the dinosaurs into birds, though. Hey, maybe another hit and we'd start to evolve into something cool, like a flying lion-goat.'

'Yeah,' said **Diana**, 'I can totally see you flying, Kaveh, though I'm not sure about the lion part.'

'Fair point, Kaveh,' **I** said, 'but let's get back to the matter of limits. The question is, what is it that's limited—or, for that matter, that we're trying to limit? If it's environmental damage caused by increased consumption, well, more people moving from Malawi to the US will mean an increase in each of those immigrant's carbon footprints, but they'll also have fewer children, so fewer consumers with any footprint. But the other implication of this view that we should try to reduce global consumption is that we should not be doing anything that might encourage the global poor to consume more. I'm not sure this is a view the global poor find compelling.'

'It's ironic,' said **Antoine**. 'If we stop the global poor from improving their standard of living, they'll have more incentive to move.'

'Either way, they're going to increase their living standards,' said **Astrid** flatly. 'It's ridiculous to think people are going to just stand still and accept their fates. No matter what we want them to do. They'll either find a way to improve their lot in life or they'll move. We could slow their progress, but we can't stop it.'

'It's all about the poor, isn't it?' said **Temi**.

'What do you mean?' said **Antoine**.

'I mean, that's what has dominated our discussion from the beginning,' **Temi** replied, 'and what we're trying to figure out is how to deal with them without giving anything up ourselves.'[17]

'Yup,' said **Kaveh**.

'I'm not so sure,' said **Diana**, 'especially since Kaveh seems to agree with you. I don't think we're that selfish!'

'I don't know if it's because we're selfish,' **Temi** continued, 'but it strikes me that we want the benefits that having cheap labour bring, except we also want a clear conscience, so we try to protect some of the poor to make us feel better while we leave the other poor—the foreign poor—to rot.'

'It's all about distribution, we were told from the beginning,' **I** said. 'Do you still hold to this, Diana?'

'It is about distribution,' **Tracy** blurted out, 'absolutely! But it's about distribution among ourselves, not across the world. We have to be realistic about this and not fall into some romantic view about the brotherhood of man.'

'Am I my brother's keeper?' said **Kaveh**, before answering himself. 'Nah, too many brothers.'

'It's about protecting ourselves,' **Tracy** continued, 'and our way of life.'

'The way of consumption,' said **Temi**.

'Yes, consumption,' said **Tracy**, 'which includes baba au rhum and marzipan mice and tawny port and pizza and wine.'

17 See Chandran Kukathas, 'The Case for Open Immigration', in Andrew I. Cohen and Christopher Heath Wellman, *Contemporary Debates in Applied Ethics* (Malden, MA: Wiley-Blackwell, 2005), 207–220. See also David Miller, 'Immigration: The Case for Limits', in Andrew I. Cohen and Christopher Heath Wellman, *Contemporary Debates in Applied Ethics* (Malden, MA: Wiley-Blackwell, 2005), 193–206.

'That's great,' said **Antoine**, 'but shouldn't we share all this bounty, the way you did, Tracy?'

'With our friends, our family, our compatriots,' **Tracy** replied in a flash. 'Not with anyone and everyone.'

'So, justice does begin at home,' **I** said.

'Yes,' said **Tracy**, 'and that's where it ends too.'

'And that's where we'll have to end,' **I** said, 'as it's getting late and I'm not sure we're going to get much further on the economic question. It seems clear, I hope you'll agree, that the issues we're going to have to confront are ones not of economic policy but rather of ethics more broadly understood.'

'Where to now, then?' said **Diana**.

'Well, the next move has to be Tracy's,' **I** said, 'don't you think? If we're agreed that we need to focus on the distributional question, then we have to ask who is to be included in the category or group who are to share the spoils, and why. I think Tracy has been clearest and most forthright about the idea that we owe our fellow citizens more than we owe outsiders and that this is what has to shape our thinking about immigration. What we need to do now is get a little clearer on what exactly all this means. Does that sound reasonable?'

'Yes,' said **Temi**, 'I think we all agree.'

'Then you're up next, Tracy,' **I** said, 'leading us on the question of country and political community and what it is and why it matters. Same place, same time, in a month?'

'Sure,' said **Tracy**.

'Go, Tracy,' said **Kaveh**. 'Good luck defending that coldest of all cold monsters—the state!'[18]

'No more dessert for you, Kaveh,' said **Tracy**, 'not even a morsel.'

18 'State is the name of the coldest of all cold monsters. It even lies coldly, and this lie crawls out of its mouth: "I, the state, am the people."' Friedrich Nietzsche, *Thus Spoke Zarathustra: A Book for All and None* (edited by Adrian Del Caro and Robert Pippin, translated by Adrian Del Caro, Cambridge, UK: Cambridge University Press, [1883–85] 2006), 34.

3 Immigration and the State

I must confess to being a little anxious about this next meeting with the students. Underneath the friendly banter, I thought I detected a harder—and sharper—edge that had begun to make itself felt in the last conversation. It wasn't clear to me whether they were tiptoeing around Tracy—either because of friendship or because they were intimidated by her manner—or were genuinely torn between different intuitions. But I needn't have worried. They turned up on time, in good spirits, and ready to do battle. I couldn't see any evidence of rancour, and it sounded like the only argument they'd had since our previous gathering was over the choice of food, Astrid having announced quite firmly that she would have no truck with pizza. The group had settled on a mixture of Chinese and Indian (because it had better vegetarian offerings for Antoine) and arrived with a variety of takeout containers, each home to some hellish Western interpretation of an Asian cuisine.

'This menu is a catastrophe,' **I** said. 'How, in this day and age, can any serious establishment claim to be a "Chinese" restaurant? Or an "Indian" one? It's like thinking that labelling something "European food" gave you a serious description of what was to be served.'

'Xandros,' said **Diana,** 'just chill! Try not to turn dinner into a conceptual problem. It's food. And I'm sure that somewhere in China someone once made a honey shrimp.'

'Yes,' said **Temi,** 'and he was caught, tried, found guilty of crimes against cuisine, and deported to Australia.'

DOI: 10.4324/9781003629641-3

'I like honey prawns—or shrimp, as you call them,' said **Kaveh**. 'They're so, so…'

'Nauseatingly cloying?' said **Astrid**.

'Moreish,' said **Kaveh**. 'I think it's because they have a kind of purity that comes from their sheer authenticity.'

'I think you've had one prawn too many,' said **Antoine**, in a grave voice.

'Well, I'm with Xandros,' said **Tracy**. 'As a menu, it's a disaster: we've got Italian and Australian wine, faux Chinese offerings that mix noodles and rice, and an assortment of so-called Indian dishes that all look like they were invented in a pub in 1970s Britain.'

'I also brought some special cheese,' said **Antoine** sheepishly. 'It's from France—a *Mont D'Or*, actually, really delicious.'

'Ah,' said **Tracy** drily, 'the perfect complement to chicken tikka masala.'

'It's all nosh,' said **Kaveh**, 'and we should just enjoy. Remember that the poor would be grateful for any of it.'

'Even the poor can have standards,' said **Tracy**, sounding a little sour.

'What modernity hath wrought,' **I** said, smiling, 'makes being alive bliss and, I'm sure, being young simply heaven.'

'Huh?' said **Temi**.

'It's Wordsworth,' said **Kaveh**. 'Try to keep up.'[1]

'Was he also a Jedi?' said **Astrid**.

'No, more a cloud walker than a sky walker,' said **Kaveh**, with a grin.

'Let's get back to earth,' **I** said. 'We did have an intellectual item on the menu, or should I say agenda. Can we turn to that?'

'Not quickly enough,' said **Temi**.

'Then you're up, Tracy,' **I** said. 'You were going to enlighten us on the state and its significance.'

1 William Wordsworth, *The Prelude, or Growth of a Poet's Mind; An Autobiographical Poem*, includes the famous lines: 'Bliss was it in that dawn to be alive, But to be young was very heaven.' It was originally in his 1804 poem, 'The French Revolution as it Appeared to Enthusiasts at Its Commencement'.

'I don't know that I'm going to give you a fully formed theory of the state,' said **Tracy**, 'since I'm not sure where to start on that topic. But what I have been doing is trying to figure out what we owe to each other if we're really serious about social justice. It seems clear to me that we have obligations to others, but not to everyone, and that we owe more to those we have relationships with than we owe to strangers—even if those strangers are close by, or indeed, in our midst. That means that we owe more to our families, to our friends, to our colleagues, and to our countrymen than to people from other countries. It means working to sustain—sometimes create—the institutions and the policies to take care of our own. It also means making sure that our fellow citizens understand this and are brought up to be responsible for upholding our shared values as well as our common practices and frameworks. I know you guys aren't going to like this, but I think it means educating our compatriots to be, well, patriotic—to be loyal to their country.'

'Why are you bringing up education?' said **Temi**. 'And loyalty? I thought we were going to discuss immigration.'

'Yes,' said **Diana**, 'I'm a bit puzzled too. And patriotism? Seriously?'

'Don't be too quick to judge,' **I** said. 'I think Tracy is on the right track. She's getting to the heart of the issue—though whether you agree with her in the end is another matter altogether.'

'Thank you,' said **Tracy**, 'though you may have an exaggerated opinion of how far I've been able to think things through. I'm just hoping that as I answer your questions my intuitions will be borne out.'

'Go on, then,' said **Antoine**. 'Fill us in on these intuitions.'

'Okay,' said **Tracy**, 'let me start with the most obvious fact. You'll have noticed that the world is divided into states. In fact, there are 195 of them according to *Worldometer*.[2] This is not an accident. The reason we have states is that they perform a vital function. They make it possible for us to act collectively to address

2 https://www.worldometers.info/geography/alphabetical-list-of-countries/.

problems we could not deal with unless we had institutions that enable us to cooperate, particularly in matters where market exchange is not enough. What states do is facilitate the working together of people who have shared interests so that they might be better able to pursue their goals in an orderly way and also take care of one another as members of a shared community.'[3]

'Wikipedia says there are 206 countries,' said **Kaveh** nonchalantly, more engrossed in dissecting yet another honey prawn than in the conversation. 'I looked it up.'

'Maybe that figure is out of date,' said **Tracy**. 'Or is just mistaken? It's Wikipedia.'

'I don't think it's wrong or out of date,' said **Kaveh,** 'but it's really a matter of how you count countries. There are 193 UN member states, and then there are Vatican City and Palestine, and then you have Kosovo and Taiwan, which are recognized by some states but not others. Actually, there are quite a lot of states that are not recognized by everyone—Taiwan obviously, Israel, North and South Korea since they don't recognize one another, and others, I'm sure.'

'Pakistan doesn't recognize Armenia,' said **Astrid** solemnly.

'Turkey doesn't recognize Cyprus,' said **Temi**, 'and Somalia doesn't recognize Somaliland.'

'And then there's Abkhazia,' said **Kaveh**. 'Now that's complicated. Some say it's a country and others say not. I don't think you're off to a good start, Trace.'

'Oh, come on,' said **Tracy**. 'Can't we just use some common sense here? I know there are conflicts and disagreements in politics, and I realize that borders and boundaries change. There are always exceptions and grey areas whenever one tries to categorize anything. Can I just try to make my case?'

'Sorry,' said **Kaveh**.

'Me too,' said **Temi** and **Astrid** in unison.

3 See Christian Reus-Smit, *The Moral Purpose of the State: Social Identity and Institutional Rationality in International Relations* (Princeton: Princeton University Press, 1999).

'We should let Tracy finish her opening move,' **I** said, 'but let's make sure we don't let her off the hook on this matter. It's true that categorization can be difficult, and sometimes even philosophers have to use a little common sense, but we can't appeal to common sense to get us out of philosophical trouble, even if we have to do so for more practical purposes.'

'Er, thank you, I think,' said **Tracy**, looking at me a little uncertainly.

'You're welcome,' **I** said. 'Now carry on.'

'As I was saying before I was interrupted by the encyclopaedia police,' **Tracy** continued, giggling even as she tried to look cross, 'we have states because they bring order and make it possible for us to cooperate. I'm not saying that all states do this equally well, and I know that some states are incompetent or tyrannical or just run by crooks and murderers.'

'When you say, "some" I think you mean "most",' said **Kaveh**. 'Just sayin'.'

Tracy ignored him and continued: 'But that doesn't change the fact that we need states because we need rules and the means of enforcing them—we need institutions. For them to work—and this is why I think some states have no proper institutions—we need both rulers and citizens who accept this story. If either party doesn't, well, Whisky. Tango. And Foxtrot!'

'Hang on a minute,' said **Diana**. 'Are you saying that states are just fictions, only useful ones? I thought you were going to go in a completely different direction once you started talk about family, countrymen, education, patriotism. It sounds like you're now giving a completely utilitarian account for why we have to have states.'

'Yes,' **Antoine** jumped in, 'I thought you were going to start appealing to history and how our forefathers…'

'And foremothers,' **Astrid** added, 'who are always neglected.'

'…and foremothers,' **Antoine** continued, 'how they forged a nation through the sweat of their brows and the blood they sacrificed, and so on, and so on.'

'You're getting a bit overly dramatic, Antoine,' said **Diana**, 'but hey, that's roughly where I thought you were going.'

'That's not a million miles from what I want to say,' said **Tracy**, looking and sounding a little flustered, 'but I thought if I went down that route, all I'd get is the kind of mockery I'm hearing now. But okay, let me try to rescue my case. I think it's both. I think there are good practical reasons of necessity for the state, and I think states have to be established on something real, like history. So yes, we construct it and renew it, but we can't just make it up any way we like.'

'Like writing a chain novel, perhaps,' said **Kaveh**, either helpfully or mischievously.

'Yes, yes,' said **Tracy** eagerly, 'I think that's right.'

'Ronald Dworkin says we should think of the law as a kind of chain novel,' said **Antoine**, 'and each generation adds chapters to keep it going, only they have to do it in a way that's consistent with the story.'

'I don't know,' said **Diana**. 'If the narrative is anything like *Game of Thrones*, where any plot twist is possible, I don't think the past will give us much guidance as to what we must do in the future.'

'I think we have a duty to honour our ancestors,' said **Tracy**, 'and take seriously the fact that they've bequeathed something to us that's made social life possible. Otherwise, their sacrifices will have been in vain.'

'I'm getting a little lost,' said **Astrid**. 'We're a bit all over the place in this discussion. And I don't really see how we're going to get back to talking about immigration.'

'I don't think the discussion is wildly off-track,' **I** said, 'even if it sounds like it. These are the points I think Tracy is trying to make. First, we should accept not only that we live in a world of states but that states serve an important purpose, which is to bring the order and stability necessary to make social life possible. Second, the fact that they have this purpose does not mean that we can just go about creating them as we please since they have evolved along with their populations and are sustained by the attachments their peoples have to them. Third, in order to endure, states need to ensure that these attachments are properly recognized, and also cultivated, through education, for example, though perhaps also through other means that help to foster the loyalty—and, indeed, patriotism—a state needs to survive. From these three claims, I expect, Tracy will want to draw the conclusion we've been waiting for: that immigration control is another vital means of preserving the relationship between state and citizen. If so, she would offer two reasons. The first is that if a state is to endure, it has to look after the interests of its people, and one thing that's in the interest of its population is that the amount of economic, cultural, and political disruption is kept to a minimum—or at least is managed so that people aren't disadvantaged by an influx of outsiders. The second is that a highly mobile population within the state's borders, if it includes large numbers who are sojourners or transients or simply people with other national loyalties, is less likely to evince the kind of loyalty or commitment the state requires to preserve its legitimacy. Some immigration is fine, but too many people immigrating, particularly if they're of the wrong kind, is not.'

'That's just what I was trying to say, thank you,' said **Tracy**.

'Good,' **I** said, 'that means that we can turn to the matter of examining this argument to see if it holds up.'

'Oh?' said **Tracy**. 'I thought we were done.'

'I'm afraid not,' **I** said.

'How cute,' said **Diana**, 'thinking it's all over!'

'It ain't over till it's over,' said **Temi**.

'It's never over,' said **Kaveh**, 'never, ever, ever. Get used to it.'

'Maybe,' said **Astrid**, 'but we're making progress.'

'Towards an answer?' said **Antoine**.

'No,' said **Kaveh**, 'just progress.'

'Towards greater understanding, perhaps,' **I** said, 'which is not something to be disparaged. Right?'

'Okay,' said **Temi**, 'so what are the objections to Tracy's thesis? I don't see any obvious ones, though it leaves me a bit uneasy.'

'I have an objection,' said **Kaveh**. 'Well, maybe it's just a question, but it may also be an objection.'

'Are you being serious, Kaveh?' said **Diana**. 'This isn't just a set up for one of your lame jokes, is it?'

'No, it's serious,' said **Kaveh**, putting on a serious face. 'Seriously serious. Okay, it just seems to me that what you're saying is that we need to control immigration for the sake of the state. Well, isn't that just weird?'

'What do you mean, weird?' said **Temi**. 'Are you objecting to nationalism?'

'Go USA,' said **Antoine**, in an effort to sound ironic.

'Don't be ridiculous, Antoine,' said **Astrid**. 'Leave the bad jokes to Kaveh.'

'No,' said **Kaveh**, 'it's not that. I just don't understand why you want to preserve the state. Or indeed, what it is you want to preserve.'

'I'm not sure what you're getting at, Kaveh,' said **Tracy**. 'I mean, isn't it just obvious? Like Xandros said, states bring order. They bring stability and make social life possible. Without borders there are no nations. Without nations there can be no democracy. No liberalism.'[4]

'No arts, no letters, no society,' added **Astrid**.

'And the life of man, solitary, poor, nasty, brutish,' said **Diana**, with mock solemnity.

'And short!' said **Temi**, thumping his fist on the table with a flourish.

'Funny,' said **Kaveh**, 'very funny. But now I think the point I'm trying to make is too subtle for you.'

'Go ahead and make your point, Kaveh,' **I** said. 'Now I'm intrigued. But I hope this isn't just a long set-up for a joke!'

4 David Frum: 'like so many human institutions, borders are both arbitrary and indispensable. Without them, there are no nations. Without nations, there can be no democracy and no liberalism.' https://www.vox.com/2018/6/22/17488272/open-borders-myth.

'Okay,' said **Kaveh**, 'but prepare to be amazed!'

'Or annoyed,' said **Temi**.

'Or irritated,' added **Diana**.

'Whatever,' said **Kaveh**, 'but here's the thing. I don't think it's so obvious what we want to preserve the state *for*.'

'Of course, it's obvious,' said **Astrid**. 'Xandros just explained it when he summarized Tracy's argument.'

'I don't think so,' said **Kaveh** slowly, 'because there's something odd about this argument. At first, it sounds like we're trying to preserve the state because it serves or protects the interests of the people who live in it or make it up. But if that's the case, surely it doesn't matter who lives in it. People can come and go, move into and out of the state, come to work or study or holiday—or whatever. All the state has to do is maintain peace—law and order—and not worry about immigration.'

'But the state also has to preserve the culture, the history, the very identity, of the population,' said **Tracy**. 'Surely that's obvious. And how can it do that without controlling and limiting immigration?'

'But the culture and the history and the identity of what?' said **Kaveh**.

'Of the state!' said **Tracy**, sounding exasperated.

'But what is the state?' said **Kaveh**.

'It's the people who make it up, obviously,' said **Tracy**, now struggling to conceal her irritation.

'Is that separate from the people,' said **Kaveh**, 'or is it made up of the people?'

'It's made up of the people, I think,' said **Diana** slowly, 'though I'm starting to feel a bit uneasy about this answer.'

'I think you should be,' said **Kaveh**, 'because if the state is just the people who make it up, what does it matter who makes it up as long as the state takes care of them?'

'And who takes care of their culture?' said **Tracy**.

'How is their culture anything other than what is made up by the interaction of the people who are living under the state?' said **Kaveh**. 'And who is the "they" in your question?'

'It's the people who were there first,' said **Tracy**, 'who want to preserve their culture so that it's not transformed by too many immigrants arriving too quickly. And that's why we need the state!'

'I'm not sure you mean "first" literally, Tracy,' **I** said, 'since it would be very difficult to establish who was anywhere "first". I doubt you're referring to native Americans in the case of the United States. But even if you mean the people who settled America from Europe and Africa, they've been followed by wave after wave of immigrants from different parts of Europe, from Central and South America, and from Asia. Who is—or are—the "first" people?'

'The people who share a history,' said **Tracy**. 'That may be a complicated story, but their history gives them continuity—and identity.'

'That's going to complicate things a lot, Trace,' said **Temi**, 'if we go back to the trouble we had with defining civilization when we met for the first time. I mean, histories don't happen within boundaries, history creates boundaries. And uncreates them.'

'That's true,' said **Astrid**. 'Mexico used to include California, Arizona, Nevada, and Oregon. So some of Mexico's history is our history and some of ours in Mexico's—if we can even talk consistently of theirs and ours.'

'I think you're all being a bit obtuse,' said **Tracy**. 'Didn't we all agree that there are 195, or 205, or some number of states in the world? What are they if not 200 histories, even if there are other historical narratives that are possible? We can have a history of Europe, and a history of the EU, and a history of Paris, and a history of New York, and a history of Manhattan—and still have a history of France and the US and Russia and Egypt. Surely we can, can't we? Would that be so hard?'

'Undoubtedly we can,' **I** said, 'but might that not undermine rather than strengthen your point, Tracy? If histories can be overlapping, and if some histories incorporate or subsume some or are internal to others, what does any historical narrative really establish by way of shared identity?'

'We may have many identities, but some identities are more important than others,' **Tracy** replied in a flash.

'And who determines that?' **I** asked. 'And don't say "the state". That would beg the question,[5] since it's the significance and authority of the state we're trying to establish.'

'Maybe I could finish the point I was trying to make,' said **Kaveh** plaintively. 'It's a pretty good point, I promise. No joking, honest.'

'Go ahead,' **I** said.

'Okay,' said **Kaveh**, 'here goes. If the state is made up of people whose interests it serves, there can be no conflict between the interests of the state and the interests of its members, right?'

'Sounds reasonable,' said **Tracy**, sounding a little dubious.

'Right,' said **Kaveh**, 'and that means that if the interests of the people in the state change, as they are bound to as new people are born and ideas percolate and circumstances change, the interests of the state have to change with them.'

'Okay,' said **Tracy**, as the others nodded in agreement.

'So, the state takes it cues entirely from the populace,' **Kaveh** continued, 'and has no business telling people what their interests are or telling them they have to do things for the good of the state.'

'That sounds right,' said **Temi**, 'but I'm a little uneasy about this move. It sounds like a trick.'

'All I'm saying is that there's nothing over and above the people,' **Kaveh** continued, 'and if the people have any duties or obligations, it's to one another. A state or a country is just an abstraction. It doesn't matter in itself; what matters is the lives of the people in it.'

'I think I agree,' said **Antoine**, 'but I don't like it either. Where are you going with this?'

'Neither do I,' said **Tracy**. 'You're talking as though the only thing the state supplies us with is roads and national defence.'

'And welfare,' **Diana** chimed in.

5 The term 'begging the question' is often misused, as though it means 'raising the question'. In fact, to 'beg the question' is to present as evidence in a dispute or debate a claim that itself assumes an answer to question at issue. For example, in a debate over whether the world was created by God, to point to the existence of the world as evidence that it was so created would be to 'beg the question'.

'Yes, yes,' **Tracy** continued, 'but it gives us something more important: an identity. We're Americans, or Italians, or Japanese, or Indians, or Russians. They give us a sense of our place in the world, a sense of fellowship, a sense of belonging. Otherwise, we'd be rootless. Imagine how bad it would be to be a stateless person!'

'Aren't we getting away from the question we're meant to be discussing, people?' said **Astrid** impatiently. 'Which is *immigration*, in case you've forgotten.'

'It's good to be reminded of that, Astrid,' **I** said, 'but I don't think we're off-track. Immigration raises some of the most important and difficult issues in political philosophy—issues that are all too often ignored or obscured by our preoccupation with the economic implications of people moving. It's the conceptual questions that take us to where the real action is.'

'Are you sure you've been on an actual date, Xandros?' said **Diana**. 'I mean one that lasted longer than one drink?'

'I like to be clear,' **I** said. 'Some people find that adorable.'

'You must date in a country we've yet to mention,' said **Temi**.

'Or heard of,' added **Diana**, as the group fell into a fit of giggles.

'Kaveh, back to you,' **I** said, 'before we get caught up in further speculations about my romantic life.'

'Yes, boss, thank you, boss,' **Kaveh** said. 'Now where was I? Oh yes, Tracy. I think you're overstating matters when you say that we need the state to give us an identity. I know some people, maybe even most, believe in the importance of their national identities but surely that's because it's been drummed into them from childhood, by schools and flag-waving and politicians anxious to win their votes. Every election cycle I get letters from Republicans and Democrats addressed to "Dear Patriot" when I'm not even eligible to vote, but it's obvious from the greeting that they're trying to guilt people into sending them money. After a lifetime of this, is it any surprise people think their national identity matters. But even if it does to them, it clearly doesn't to others, and it matters to all of those to varying degrees—ranging from a lot to very little.'

'I think it matters a lot,' said **Tracy** sourly.

'It feels strange to say,' said **Antoine**, 'but I have to admit it doesn't matter much to me.'

'Antoine!' **Astrid** exclaimed. 'You're French. How could it not matter to you?'

'I know, I know,' **Antoine** said slowly, 'but I just don't feel it. Maybe it's because my mother is German and most of my family is. My mother has lots of brothers, sisters, cousins, and my father has only one childless brother he never sees. In the World Cup, I cheer for Germany.'

'Me too,' said **Temi**, 'but mainly because they always win.'

'Whom do you identify with, Xandros?' said **Diana**. 'Do you feel any national loyalty? Where do you belong?'

'I can't say I do,' **I** said, 'and I'm not sure I belong anywhere in any sense that matters to me. I don't feel rejected or unwelcome, but, to be honest, I'm not convinced that a country as such can welcome or reject a person, even if the law or policy can discriminate against some groups. If US immigration law stops people from central America from entering, or ends up deporting them, there are still millions of Americans who want to accept them even though millions of others don't. I feel very welcome among my friends, my colleagues, my neighbours, my profession—and even my students.'

'Which students are these?' said **Kaveh** in a flash.

'Yes,' said **Temi**, 'which? Anyone we might know?'

'No,' **I** said, 'no one any of you would know. Those are really good students—bright, funny, kind, thoughtful, that kind of thing. Not the sort you lot hang out with.'

'Harsh, Xandros!' said **Diana**, 'really harsh!'

'Just fact,' **I** said, 'just fact. But can we get back to the main point?'

'I'm starting to get a lost,' said **Tracy**, sounding a little forlorn, 'even though it's my week, and my theory of the state we're supposed to be discussing.'

'Let me see if I can get us on track again,' **I** said, 'and then hand back to Kaveh. I don't think he's been able to explain fully the point he promised was very important.'

'Ta,' said **Kaveh**, 'that would be brill.'

'What Kaveh was saying,' **I** continued, 'was that even if some people are attached to or identify with their states, we don't need a state to give us an identity. He was saying this because he was trying—struggling, perhaps—to say that while he accepted that states provided certain goods to the people who lived under their authority and conceded that they might give some people a sense of identity, he didn't think everyone needed a state to have an identity that mattered to them. Antoine helpfully supplied an example of someone who didn't need a state-conferred identity. I supplied another when pushed by my prying students, who seem to be all too interested in my thoughts and feelings and indeed my personal life.'

'It's because you're so interesting, Xandros,' said **Diana** in an adoring voice, prompting a mixture of grunts, snorts of derision, and mock agreement.

'Be that as it may,' **I** said, 'or as you young people put it today, *whatever*, Kaveh's point is that if what matters is the good or the well-being of actual people, and if the point of the state is to supply what is needed for the good of the people it serves, what does it matter who comes under its authority? Why can't anybody join this happy band of subjects? And if you say that the state supplies a sense of belonging, the reply is that that's not true for everyone—presumably because some people don't care much about the belonging and just want the other things the state supplies, like law and order or a welfare safety net.'

'But they should care,' **Tracy** said hotly. 'They should.'

'Why?' said **Temi**. 'I mean I'm not certain I disagree with you, but I'm not sure why either.'

'Well, stability for a start,' said **Tracy**. 'Unless people are committed to their country—yes, unless they're patriotic—who will defend it? It could be invaded, and no one would care. Or it could be undermined from within, and there'd be no one who'd be bothered to object.'

'That seems reasonable,' **Temi** replied, 'but is there any evidence that this is true? I mean, are countries with large immigrant populations less stable or more likely to be invaded or overthrown.'

'I think it's just common sense,' said **Tracy** grumpily.

'I think China is not very stable,' said **Astrid** brightly, 'and it has hardly any immigrants. If the Communist Party didn't hold on with an iron grip, I think it would just fall apart.'

'Yes,' said **Antoine**, 'like the former Soviet Union, which also had hardly any immigrants as people were trying to get out rather than get in—and as soon as the state relaxed its control, everybody seceded: all the Baltic states, Ukraine, Kazakhstan, Uzbekistan, and, er, all the other stans, and Belarus, and Moldova and, well, you name it.'

'You've both got a point,' said **Diana**. 'All the high-immigration countries like Australia, Canada, America, France, Germany—all seem very stable.'

'Couldn't it be that people are going there because they're stable and not the other way around?' said **Tracy** hotly.

'Could be,' said **Temi**, 'but their going there doesn't seem to have made those countries less stable. And they've been immigrating to them for decades or even hundreds of years.'

'What about South America, then?' said **Tracy**. 'It has had lots of immigration, but most of the countries there look very unstable.'

'I don't think immigration necessarily leads to stability,' said **Diana**. 'It's just that there's no reason to say it must lead to instability. And there's no reason to think an absence of immigration will bring about stability.'

'Restricting immigration is neither necessary nor sufficient for state stability,' said **Kaveh** with a flourish.

'Any more than immigration itself is a sure way to stability,' added **Diana**. 'How's that for a bit of conceptual clarification?'

'Don't get too carried away,' **I** said. 'It's a nice point, but I'm not handing out cigars.'

'It's not a nice point,' said **Tracy**, 'because we've not established what stability means. I'm not suggesting that immigration will immediately destroy a society, but in the long run there will be a loss of identity if too many people move too quickly. That's a significant kind of loss.'

'Okay, so no cigar,' said **Kaveh**, 'but they're bad for you, Diana, so no harm done. And anyway, the best ones are from Cuba and Cuban cigars aren't allowed to immigrate to the United States.'

'Thank you, Kaveh,' **I** said. 'Now have you finished your point that's led us to this long digression?'

'No, no, absolutely not,' **Kaveh** said. 'That was just a part of the point. There's more!'

'Well, get on with it,' **I** said.

'Okay,' said **Kaveh**, 'the first part of my argument was that, if the point of the state was to supply the populace with certain goods, including the good of a national identity, then it should not matter who is part of any particular state. They pays their taxes and they gets their goods. There's no conflict between the interests of the state and the interests of the people. But I think Tracy's worry is not that people now will lose *their* identities if immigration transforms society. Her worry is that an identity of some kind might *itself* be lost.'

'Huh?' said **Temi**.

'A nicely put question, Temi,' said **Kaveh**, clearly enjoying himself. 'Let me explain. I think what Tracy is worried about is that immigration will, over time, transform a society to the extent that its original distinctiveness will be lost. Maybe she means 'previous distinctiveness', since it's hard to know what 'original' could mean here, but either way the claim is unchanged. What I think is that Tracy has an understanding of the identity of the state that exists over and above the people who make it up and that what she's worried about is the loss of that identity. But I want to ask why we would care about that identity. Isn't it just an abstraction? Surely what matters is the interests and well-being of actual people and not the continued existence of some idea—like Britishness or Frenchness or Chineseness.'

'I don't understand why you think identity is just an abstraction, as you put it,' said **Astrid**, 'unless you're saying all the qualities we possess, like intelligence or colour or tastes, are just abstractions. If so, I'm not sure I'm getting your point. I like some of my abstractions!'

'Okay,' said **Kaveh**, 'I didn't put it very well. I think it's fine that these abstractions—or these qualities—are *your* abstractions or qualities and it makes sense that you care about them. Unless you had your particular qualities, you wouldn't be you. That might include your Britishness or Frenchness if those things happened to be especially important in your life—say, if you were an Olympic medallist who won the gold for France. But that's different from caring about whether certain abstractions or qualities exist, now and into the future. Maybe one day there'll be no such thing as France or Frenchness, Britain or Britishness, China or Chineseness. Why should we care, as long as the state or country or whatever authorities run things in the future allow or enable the people to be happy and free, whatever their identities?'

'I agree that nations probably won't go on forever,' said **Diana** slowly, 'but I'm uncomfortable about making too much of this idea.'

'Our galaxy, the Milky Way, is on a collision course with another, Andromeda,' said **Antoine** solemnly, 'so in about five billion years, boom, no more humanity.'

'Not to mention the second law of thermodynamics,' said **Temi**, 'so if Andromeda doesn't get us, entropy will.'

'Before Kaveh makes another *Star Wars* joke,' **I** said, 'perhaps we could make a distinction or two to clarify matters?'

'Really, Xandros?' said **Diana**. 'More distinctions? I think your epitaph will read: "Here lies Xandros, a man of many distinctions".'

'That would be lovely,' **I** said, 'but I'm still here, so let's press on, shall we?'

'Okay,' **the group** mumbled, in a slightly disorderly way.

'Right, then,' **I** continued, 'I think Kaveh is making quite an important point. We might see it more clearly if we distinguished two conceptions of the group.'

'The group?' said **Astrid**, sounding slightly puzzled. 'What group?'

'Be patient,' **I** said, 'I'm using the term as a placeholder for the moment. Eventually, I want to turn to the entities Kaveh and the rest of you have been talking about: society, community, nation, state. But for now, let's just talk about the group.'

'Go for it, Xandros,' said **Antoine** encouragingly. 'We're ready to be amazed.

'Er, thank you, Antoine,' **I** said, 'so, back to the point. We might distinguish two understandings of the group. On the first, which I'll call the *collective conception*, a group is a gathering of people whose value lies in the fact that the collective provides something to the individuals who make it up.'

'Like what?' asked **Astrid**.

'Goods and services, perhaps,' **I** said, 'like physical premises, if we're talking about a club. Or aid and assistance, if we consider friendly societies—people who band together for mutual support. It might supply the framework of rules that make association possible. Or all of this and more if we think of larger communities in that way.'

'What would be "more"?' asked **Temi**, looking puzzled.

'A collective might provide a sense of community or belonging,' **I** said, 'or even a sense of identity to the extent that community or belonging to this particular collective mattered to those who valued it—or those who did not, for that matter.'

'I see where you're going with this, Xandros,' said **Diana**. 'You're going to say that the state is such a collective. It provides goods and services, it gives everyone a sense of community and belonging, and it gives them an identity—a *national* identity!'

'Let's not jump ahead, Diana,' **I** said, 'though it's possible to see the state in this way. Indeed, many have tried to justify the state in this way, suggesting that its legitimacy rests on its unique ability to supply an identity. At this point, all I'm trying to do is distinguish two different conceptions of the group. The *collective conception* is one.'

'Okay, then,' **Diana** said, 'what's the other?

'It's the *corporate conception*, as I like to call it,' **I** said.

'So how is that different from the *collective conception* of the group,' said **Antoine**, 'because I can't imagine how else one might understand a group? A group is there to give something to its members. Otherwise, why would they be a part of it?'

'Okay,' **I** said, 'the first thing you have to remember is that I'm making a conceptual distinction, not an empirical one. I'm not saying there are two kinds of actual groups and that all groups are of either one type or another. I'm going to explain how groups might be understood in two different ways.'

'Why?' said **Kaveh**.

'You'll see in a minute,' **I** said, 'and, if I may quote you, Kaveh, prepare to be amazed!'

'Very funny,' said **Kaveh**, sounding a little deflated. 'Go on then.'

'The *corporate conception* understands the group a little differently,' **I** continued. 'On this view, a group might have value or purpose regardless of whether it provided some good or benefit to the people who make it up.'

'What would be the point of such a group?' said **Antoine**. 'I don't think it makes sense. Are there any such groups? Anywhere, now or in the past?'

'Yes, Xandros,' said **Tracy**, 'this looks like a totally artificial distinction. Maybe it's possible in theory, but I doubt we'd find such a thing—except in the imaginations of philosophers. You guys—you philosophers—you just make things up. Distinction upon distinction! Here's a distinction: there are two kinds of people, people who make distinctions and those who don't!'

'Very good, Tracy,' **I** said. 'That's a very neat distinction—one with an air of paradox. I like it!'

'Oh, God!' said **Tracy**, sounding exasperated. 'Sometimes you can be so annoying, Xandros.'

'Thank you,' **I** said. 'Then let me press on. There's more. I don't think you should be so quick to dismiss the *corporate conception* of the group. Look at it through the following example. Let's say the government of Australia decided one day to sterilize all of its Aboriginal population so that in a generation or two there were no Aborigines left. Would that matter?'

'Of course,' said **Astrid**. 'It would be a violation of the rights of those Aborigines. It would be monstrous.'

'Suppose it was voluntary,' **I** said, 'say, because the government offered them financial compensation in exchange for their agreement to be sterilized.'

'I don't like this example,' said **Diana**. 'It's creepy.'

'Maybe,' **I** said, 'but it's, sadly, not too far from reality. Governments have tried to "breed out" certain peoples. So, if you think it matters, the question is, why? I agree that forced sterilization violates the rights of those who are made to comply, but what if people agreed to it?'

'I still think it would be monstrous,' said **Astrid** insistently. 'It would be taking advantage of vulnerable people who might not understand the wider implications of what they were doing.'

'What would they be doing?' asked **Temi**,

'They'd be killing off their race,' said **Astrid**, 'or their ethnicity, or their existence as a group.'

'Why would that matter?' **I** asked, 'and I'm not saying it wouldn't, but I want you to give me the reasons it would.'

'I think it's treating the Aborigines very disrespectfully, actually,' said **Antoine**. 'I'm not sure if it's the best reason why it matters, but I think respect is important.'

'I can't disagree,' **I** said, 'but in this case, could we not say that the Aborigines who've decided to take the money have decided that the money, or what it can buy, is more important to them than the respect?'

'We could,' said **Astrid**, 'but I don't know that they should be put in that position—or allowed to make such a choice. After all, their decision affects not just them but all Aboriginal people. If one individual wants to give up the ability to have children, that's his or her choice, but if it's in the context of every member—or enough members—of the race or people doing this and if it means the race dies out, I don't think individuals should have that choice. And it would be wrong for the government to make them such an offer.'

'Even if some or many or all of the Aborigines say they don't care about whether the race dies out?' **I** asked.

'Even then,' said **Astrid** firmly.

'But why does it matter if a race dies out?' **I** said. 'In this case, at least hypothetically, the individual Aborigines think they get more out of the money they're offered than they do out of the continued existence of the race.'

'It would be genocide,' said **Temi** solemnly. 'I don't think it would be okay, even if the people wanted it. They'd be destroying something—a people, a culture, a tradition, or something over and above their individual selves. That can't be justified.'

'I feel the same way,' said **Diana,** 'but I'm not sure why. It just feels wrong.'

'Even if the people who die out aren't going to be there to miss that culture or tradition,' said **Kaveh,** 'or to feel the loss of community, or belonging, or identity?'

'Yes!' said **Diana** and **Astrid,** almost in unison.

'I agree', said **Antoine.** 'The loss may not matter to those who are gone, but it could matter to those who are left, even if they aren't former members of the Aboriginal people. It's their loss too.'

'I wonder if anyone misses the Hittites,' said **Kaveh**. 'I mean, I don't.'

'What are you talking about, Kaveh?' said **Diana**. 'Is this another set-up for one of your lame jokes?'

'No, I mean, does anyone miss the peoples that have disappeared,' **Kaveh** continued, 'since we don't really have any experience of them? I'm sure individual Hittites must have had friends, and when they died out some of those friends would have missed them. But no one misses the Hittites now.'

'Who were the Hittites?' said **Antoine**.

'The people of a kingdom in Anatolia, but they were killed off by the Assyrians, around 1100 BCE, I think,' said **Temi**.

'Yes,' said **Kaveh,** 'some of their descendants were probably incorporated into the Assyrian empire. I've always wondered whether some of my ancestors were Hittites.'

'So, what does your family tree have to do with anything we're talking about?' said **Astrid**. 'How is any of this relevant?'

'Very relevant,' **Kaveh** shot back. 'The question is why should we care about peoples that have disappeared, and I'm saying maybe we shouldn't—or, in fact, don't, since there are many peoples that have disappeared without our lamenting the loss, either of the individuals or of the culture.'

'But there is a loss,' said **Astrid**, 'even if we don't notice it. The world is poorer, even if no one knows it.'

'I believe you've all hit on the point that makes the distinction between the *collective* and the *corporate* conceptions of the group relevant,' **I** said, 'since we're now asking whether it could matter that a group exists or continues to exist regardless of the wishes or the interests of its members. On the *collective* conception, it would make no sense, since the whole point of the group is to serve the members—there's no conflict between the interests of the members and the interests of the group. On the *corporate* conception, however, there could be a conflict because the group as an entity may be valuable or have interests even if it does not benefit the members, who might not even care whether it continues to exist.'

'How is this relevant to anything we've been discussing?' asked **Temi**.

'Let's go back to the point Kaveh raised,' **I** said. 'He suggested that Tracy was wrong to think we should care about the possibility that immigration might transform the state to the extent that it lost its identity and became something different. His reason was that what Tracy was concerned about preserving was an abstraction, as he put it. What I'm suggesting is that Kaveh is invoking a *collective* conception of the group by saying that a group has value only if it serves the interests of its members. Tracy is invoking a *corporate* conception of the group by suggesting that it matters that the group—in this case, the state—continues to exist even if its current members don't care about it.'

'They should care about it!' said **Tracy**. 'It would be unpatriotic not to!'

'But why should they?' said **Antoine**. 'I mean, 1500 years ago there was no France—until Clovis was named king of the Franks, and even then, he was king of lands that include what are now Belgium and The Netherlands and parts of Germany. Maybe in 1500 years from now, there will be no France, just the Republic of Europe. Why should I care, as long as the people in this future are governed justly and are free and happy?'

'There was no Germany 150 years ago,' said **Astrid**, 'so I guess it's possible there won't be one in 150 years from now, though it feels weird to say that.'

'Hang on, Antoine,' said **Diana**. 'Didn't you say a few minutes ago that you thought the disappearance of the Aborigines would be a loss, even though there'd be no Aborigines to lament it?'

'I did,' said **Antoine**. 'I guess I've not been consistent, and I don't know how to reconcile these two intuitions. I feel it would be sad to see the end of a people, but I don't feel the same way about the end of a political association.'

'Aren't the French and the Chinese and the Americans and the Germans and the Egyptians and other members of states all peoples too?' said **Tracy**. 'It seems to me that they are. And you can kill off national peoples just as you can kill of racial ones. In this case, it would be through too much immigration that could mean that, in 200 years, America is nothing like it is today. It wouldn't even be America, except in name.'

'This sounds like a variant of the Ship of Theseus paradox,' **I** said.

'Remind me what that is, Xandros,' said **Antoine**. 'I remember it only vaguely.'

'I can explain,' said **Diana**. 'Theseus, according to Greek legend, saved the children of Athens by slaying the Minotaur and then escaped on his ship to the island of Delos. After his death, the Athenians would commemorate Theseus by sailing his ship to Delos every year, but after several hundred years, philosophers began to ask whether this could be the same ship, since it had been repaired so many times that no plank of the original remained. Was this now the ship of Theseus or had that ceased to exist, to be replaced by another vessel altogether.'

'So, the question is whether immigrants would turn a country into a different one,' said **Tracy**, 'and I say yes. They will replace us.'

'But by that logic, today's America is not the same America of 1776,' said **Astrid**.

'Or even 1922, if you consider that there are no Americans alive today who were also alive then,' said **Diana**.

'There's Maria Morera,' said **Temi**. 'She's alive and was born in 1907.'

'Yes, but she was an immigrant,' said **Kaveh** with a grin and looking very pleased with himself.

'Okay, 1907,' said **Diana**. 'There are no Americans alive today who were alive before Maria Morera was born. By Tracy's logic, either that wasn't America then or we aren't living in America now, because they're two different places.'

'Yes,' said **Antoine**, 'and the United States has also changed a lot culturally since then and not just because of immigration. I mean, there was the Civil Rights Act in 1965, there have been huge changes in sexual morality, and there's been an end to the oppression of women.'

'Really, Antoine?' said **Astrid**. 'An end to women's oppression?'

'Does that include an end to the era of mansplaining?' said **Diana**. 'Because I'm thinking not so much.'

'Okay, okay,' said **Antoine**, 'poor phrasing, very poor phrasing, but I was trying to agree with you, Diana.'

'He was trying to show solidarity with the sisters,' said **Kaveh**, 'or at least, some of them. Never a good idea.'

'It's not the same,' said **Tracy**. 'It's different when the source of change is internal. Immigrants will change us from the outside.'

'I don't see what difference that makes,' said **Temi**, 'and besides, you could say that all kinds of things that change us come from the outside, especially ideas, which we could learn about from tourists, or from our citizens returning from abroad, or just from the internet.'

'Immigration would change us more quickly,' said **Tracy**.

'Maybe,' said **Temi**, 'but that means you accept that we're going to change anyway and that a lot of it is going to be because of outside influences we can't do much to prevent.'

'It seems to me that we have two different, though related, questions,' **I** said, 'whether social transformation that leads to the disappearance of a state matters and whether what really matters is the rate or speed of transformation.'

'Yes,' said **Antoine**, 'I agree.'

'One could argue that the only thing to worry about is the speed of transformation,' **I** continued, 'but those who care about the transformation itself would think it's wrong at any speed. Where do you guys stand? If you think it's wrong at any speed, you're with Kaveh, and you're going to have to invoke a *corporate* rather than a *collective* understanding of the group—in this case, of the state.'

'I have to confess I'm a bit unhappy with this very stark presentation of the alternatives,' said **Tracy**, 'since it might be too much to expect any society never to be transformed, even after a thousand years, into something quite different. Can't there be a middle way?'

'Those who stand in the middle of the road get run over,' said **Kaveh** gleefully, to groans from the others, who chose nonetheless to ignore him.

'What I'm trying to get at is that we have to take seriously the question of what it is that we value,' **I** said. 'Is it what Kaveh has called an "abstraction" that matters most? Does it matter at all? Clearly, many have devoted themselves to trying to ensure that something is preserved, and in principle want it to survive indefinitely. That might include a religion, or a race, or a tradition, or a nation. We seem to agree that indefinite survival is unrealistic. But perhaps even trying to preserve some things for a very long time is almost as unrealistic and, maybe more importantly, incompatible with attending to the interests or the well-being of actual people, whether now or in the future.'

'What matters more, America or Americans?' said **Kaveh**. 'I say Americans.'

'But if there's no America, there'd be no Americans,' said **Tracy**.

'There would,' said **Temi**. 'They just wouldn't be called that. As individuals, they'd still exist, but not as Americans. The question is, what is more important when we think about what we want for future people, that they be free and happy or that they have a particular identity? I guess I'm with Kaveh on this.'

'Me too,' said **Antoine**.

'I'm not ready to concede,' said **Tracy**. 'I think identity is more important than you're allowing. Imagine if you were Jewish and belong to a tradition that's thousands of years old and has endured a history of persecution and even attempted extermination. I think you'd put a pretty high price on the ideal of identity preservation. Maybe you'd even sacrifice your life for it.'

'I get that,' said **Diana**. 'If there are things that people are prepared to die for, they've got to be important, and surely dying for your country is one of those things. I don't disagree with Antoine and Temi, but I can't help feeling that Tracy has a point.'

'I don't,' said **Kaveh**. 'I can imagine sacrificing my life to protect my friends and family, and even for my fellow citizens if the country were under attack, but not for an abstraction. If I were Russian, I might fight to defend my fellow Russians from violent enemies, but I would not lift a finger to support the idea that Russia includes Ukraine. And if California wanted to secede from the United States, I would not, if I were an American, support efforts to force it to remain in the Union. Same for Quebec and Canada. If America or Canada ceased to exist, I don't think it would matter as long as the people in these places were free and happy. I think the disappearance of the Soviet Union was a good thing because a lot of people became freer. All they lost was a symbol.'

'I just don't see how you can say that Kaveh,' said **Tracy**. 'It's so… so…'

'Obvious?' said **Kaveh**.

'…unpatriotic,' said **Tracy**, at last. 'More than that, anti-patriotic. If you don't have patriots, you won't have a country.'

'Really?' said **Kaveh**. 'I'm not so sure. I mean, how many patriots do you need?'

'I think most of the people living in a country have to be patriots to at least some degree,' said **Tracy**. 'Otherwise, there'd be no social solidarity, no political community. People need to feel they belong, or you couldn't sustain a defence force, or welfare institutions, or even basic taxation. People just wouldn't go along willingly with policies that distribute goods and responsibilities unless they feel they are part of a community. They have to love their country more than they love their souls.'

'And you're saying if there are too many immigrants, people wouldn't feel that sense of solidarity?' asked **Astrid**.

'Yes,' said **Tracy**. 'You need to see some commitment from others you can regard as your fellow nationals.'

'I hate to do this, Tracy,' **I** said, 'but what do you mean by a "national" or, for that matter, an "immigrant".'[6]

'What do you mean by "what do you mean", Xandros,' said **Diana**, brightly with an exaggerated smile.

'Diana, what do you mean by what do you mean by what do you mean,' said **Temi**, in a deep voice and mock-serious tone.'

'This is important, guys,' **I** said. 'So Tracy, I'd like to hear what you mean by a national or an immigrant.'

'An immigrant is someone who is out of his or her country of nationality for twelve months or longer,' said **Kaveh**, 'at least according to the UN.'

'Very good, Kaveh,' **I** said.

'Does that include students?' asked **Astrid**. 'I mean, a lot of them are out of their countries for two or three years. Are they immigrants?'

'Yes, obviously,' said **Tracy**, 'though I'm not sure how to consider them when trying to control immigration numbers.'

'Students! Who needs them?' said **Kaveh**, with a grin.

'Why twelve months?' asked **Antoine**. 'I mean, it seems a bit arbitrary. Why not two years? Or six months?'

'There's no *natural* definition, if I can use the word *natural* loosely,' **I** said. 'The definitions we find have been settled upon by government agencies or immigration researchers so they can identify and count people who belong in this category. Otherwise, every tourist could be an immigrant, or no one would be an immigrant.'

'I'm shocked!' said **Diana**.

'Why?' **I** said. 'Do you think there has to be a natural definition?'

6 For an extended discussion of the definitions of immigrant and native or national, see Kukathas, *Immigration and Freedom*, Chapter 2.

'No,' **Diana** replied. 'I'm shocked that you'd admit to using a word loosely. I thought you prided yourself on using words carefully and precisely.'

'Our world must be collapsing around us if Xandros has started to speak loosely,' said **Temi**, to general laughter.

'I blame capitalism,' said **Kaveh**.

'I blame liberalism,' said **Antoine**.

'It could be due to climate change,' said **Diana**.

'Okay, okay,' **I** said, 'have your fun. But I hope you get the point, even if liberalism and climate change have addled your brains. I know I make a big deal of clarity in our use of language, but the reality is that the world around us is not easy to describe precisely because things come in variations or gradations, whether we're talking about trees or trousers or tourists. Sometimes, it may not matter much, but sometimes it does.'

'And you think that's the case with immigration or immigrant,' said **Astrid**.

'Yes,' **I** said, 'these are concepts that need to be understood in their contexts.'

'And what are those contexts?' asked **Diana**.

'Well,' **I** said, 'the first thing we need to appreciate is how relatively new these words are. Or perhaps I should say this word, "immigrate", since the others are variants. The word "migrate" is much older but was generally used as part of other words, like "remigrate" or "commigrate" or "transmigrate". It signified movement, usually between places, but had no particular political connotation. It was Noah Webster, it has been argued, who in 1828 introduced the modern conception of "immigrant" by defining "immigrate" to mean "to remove into a country for the purpose of permanent residence".[7] Of course, this didn't say anything about how to establish intention or purpose, what was to be understood by permanent, and who was to do the removing. Were slaves immigrants on this definition? What counts as moving if, as happened

7 See Neil Larry Shumsky, 'Noah Webster and the Invention of Immigration', *The New England Quarterly*, March 2008, 81 (1), 126–135.

to residents of Mexico who became Americans when the boundary shifted in 1848 and territories like Arizona, California, and Oregon became part of the United States?'

'That's all very interesting,' said **Tracy**, 'but I'm not sure how it's relevant. How do we define immigrant now.'

'My purpose in drawing attention to this,' **I** said, 'is to point out that the meanings of words change, are often contested, and can be shaped by a variety factors, including political ones. They can also have political consequences.'

'Did you know that St Paul's Cathedral, when it was first built, was described as awful, mediocre, and pathetic?' said **Kaveh** brightly.

'Nice example,' **I** said. 'Back then, awful meant awesome, mediocre meant balanced, and pathetic meant having the power to evoke a feeling of compassion—pathos. In the case of immigration, the important thing is not so much any change of meaning but the fact that the word immigrant came to be associated with foreigner or outsider—someone from another country coming to settle. It suggests a contrast with native or national.'

'That sounds like an inevitable development given that the modern state was emerging at this time,' said **Tracy**, 'perhaps even a desirable one, since we need terms to separate categories: insiders and outsiders, natives and foreigners. The point of immigration control is, after all, to protect the interests of natives from harm resulting from too many outsiders or foreigners moving.'

'And that's the function of the state, Tracy?' said **Antoine**.

'Precisely!' said **Tracy**, 'precisely!'

'So, on your view,' **I** said, 'the state is like the agent of the natives, looking out for their interests and making sure that too many outsiders don't enter—and that those who do aren't a danger to the natives. Correct?'

'Correct,' said **Tracy**. 'If you want open neighbourhoods, you need to close national borders.'[8]

8 See Michael Walzer, *Spheres of Justice*, 38.

'But who decides who are the natives and who are the foreigners?'[9] I asked.

'Shouldn't that just be obvious?' asked **Diana**.

'I'm not so sure,' said **Temi**. 'I think Xandros is laying a trap.'

'Lay a trap?' **I** said, making clear I felt a little hurt. 'Moi?'

'Yes, it's a trap,' said **Astrid**. 'He wants you to say the state decides, and then he'll say that the state might not be neutral or might be corrupted and sell out to those who want to move if they're able to pay or offer the state some advantage.'

'That's not quite what I had in mind,' **I** said, 'though that's not a bad point. The state, or parts of it, might not be entirely disinterested and could well play favourites. Indeed, it does. If you're wealthy enough, you could obtain permanent residence in the UK, for example, by buying two million pounds of government bonds. Since these bonds pay interest, you could say that if you're wealthy enough, the government will pay you to immigrate.'[10]

'Sweet!' said **Kaveh**. 'That sounds like a nice little earner. Cool Brittania!'

'I think that's not a bad idea,' said **Tracy**, though she sounded a little hesitant. 'I mean, it's to the benefit of the citizens. It's raising revenue and not taking work away from people in the country.'

'All interesting observations, but I had something a little different in mind,' **I** said. 'Consider the fact that before Britain lost its

9 For an interesting historical account, see Kunal M. Parker, *Making Foreigners: Immigration and Citizenship Law in America 1600-2000* (Cambridge, UK: Cambridge University Press, 2015).

10 This UK Tier 1 (investment) visa programme has been discontinued. However, it remains possible to purchase residence or even citizenship through investment or donation in many countries. For example, it is possible to obtain a permanent residence visa in Italy, Spain, Greece, Portugal, Latvia, Cyprus, and Malta by investment (in real estate, property, or government bonds). Citizenship can be purchased in Vanuatu, Cambodia, North Macedonia, El Salvador, Egypt, Jordan, Turkey, and Malta. Donation or investment amounts range from US $115,000 to $1.5 million. Other countries charge more: Singapore (S$2.5 million), Australia (A$5 million), and France (€10 million) are some examples. The United States EB-5 visa has since 1990 enabled investors to secure permanent residence if they invest at least US$ 1,050,000 in businesses that created ten or more full-time jobs.

empire after the Second World War, it ruled over something like 800 million people, all of whom had British nationality and the right of abode in the UK. Over a period of about 35 years, all of those people except those who lived in the British Isles or were direct and immediate descendants of Britons living in Britain could claim British nationality.'

'Who decided that?' asked **Antoine**.

'The British government,' **I** said.

'Wasn't there a vote?' asked **Astrid**. 'I mean, didn't those British subjects across the empire have a say in it, as taxpayers?'

'Not so much, I'm guessing,' said **Kaveh**.

'I'm afraid you're right, Kaveh,' **I** said. 'These were cabinet decisions taken to amend the British Nationality Act—sometimes over the objections of some Members of Parliament of both major parties.'

'Why?' said **Diana**. 'Why not allow people to keep their British nationality?'

'Probably because those who took the decisions wanted to make sure the wrong people didn't exercise the right to move to Britain,' **I** said, 'and the best way to achieve this was to reclassify some people as not British nationals and as not, therefore, possessing the right to move there.'

'That doesn't seem right to me,' said **Antoine**. 'I find that very disturbing. Do other countries do this sort of thing?'

'They have, and they do,' **I** said. 'The definition of nationality is an ongoing affair and not just for philosophers.'

'I think you're exaggerating, Xandros,' said **Tracy**, a little grumpily. 'I'd like to hear some examples.'

'Okay,' **I** said, 'consider that in the United States African Americans were not recognized as citizens until the passing of the 14th Amendment to the Constitution in 1868—and even then, they were not recognized as equals in practice in many places, especially in the American South. Native Americans were not granted citizenship until 1924. American women who married foreigners were, until 1922, stripped of their citizenship. Before 1948, British women who married foreigners lost their nationality, and as late as 1983, British women were not able to pass on their nationality. And, of course, even today, there are those who call for the repeal of the citizenship clause of the 14th Amendment that provides that anyone born on American soil is automatically an American citizen.[11] The British Nationality Act of 1983 did just that for British citizenship, incidentally—it removed *jus soli* as a principle by which citizenship is acquired.'[12]

'That's a lot of examples, Xandros,' said **Diana**, 'for a philosopher, I mean.'

'I know stuff,' **I** said, 'and there's lots more where that came from.'

'Well, someone's got to make a decision about who counts as a national,' **Tracy** said hotly, 'and it can't just be left to chance. Maybe there have been some injustices in the past, but I say we move on from that. Anyway, there'll always be injustices, and people who get caught on the wrong side of definitions. We can't have perfection.'

'I don't know, Tracy,' said **Antoine**. 'Depriving a few hundred million people of their nationality doesn't seem quite right to me. Weren't all these people subject to British laws, obliged to pay British taxes, and asked to fight in the British army? How are they not British. And all those people who moved to the UK from the

11 See H.R.—140 Birthright Citizenship Act of 2021, introduced by Representative Brian Babin (Republican, Texas) 'This bill limits birthright citizenship by redefining what it means to be *subject to the jurisdiction* of the United States. Currently, a person born in the United States and subject to U.S. jurisdiction is entitled to citizenship. Under the bill, a person is subject to U.S. jurisdiction if he or she is born to a parent who is (1) a U.S. citizen or national, (2) a lawful permanent resident residing in the United States, or (3) an alien performing active service in the Armed Forces.' At the time of writing, this bill has been referred to the Subcommittee on Immigration and Citizenship but has yet to be presented to or passed in the House or Senate.

12 The principle of *jus soli* holds that rights of nationality are acquired by birth on the territory of the state. *Jus sanguinis* holds that such rights are acquired by birth to one or more parents who is a national or citizen. Joachim Stern coined the term *jus pecuniae* to distinguish citizenship acquired through monetary purchase. On the ethics of birthright citizenship, see Ayelet Shachar, *The Birthright Lottery: Citizenship and Global Inequality* (Cambridge, MA: Harvard University Press, 2009).

Caribbean—they came because they were encouraged, and they were British nationals. I don't think they should have been turned into foreigners. They should at least have had a say in the question.'

'Yes,' said **Astrid**, 'a democratic vote was needed.'

'And who would have been eligible to cast a vote on the question of who is British?' **I** asked.

'The British, of course!' said **Kaveh** triumphantly. 'The British!'

'Thank you for your enthusiasm, Kaveh,' **I** said. 'I see you get my point.'

'Obviously, a democratic vote won't do,' said **Tracy**, 'but I think it goes to show that the basis of national membership is not to be settled by giving all affected[13] people a say. We have to go back to history, to a society's origins. That's how we settle the question of who belongs—and who doesn't.'

'I don't think that's going to be so straightforward,' said **Temi**. 'We've already struggled to find a way of deciding which bits of history to choose, just as we struggled at the beginning to figure out where to draw the boundaries of a civilization. It sounds we'd just be creating a myth. A lie, really.'

'Maybe it is partly myth,' said **Tracy**, 'but without stories, you can't hold a society together. I don't think we can make up just any old story, but we need to tell people something about who they are and why they belong. Otherwise, society just won't work, and no state would be legitimate. Maybe it's a bit of a lie, but not wholly, and in a good cause.'

'A white lie,' said **Kaveh**, putting his hands together as if in prayer and gazing innocently up to the heavens. 'A noble lie.'

'But who gets to tell this lie,' **I** asked, 'or to enforce it?'

'The majority,' said **Tracy**. 'Who else?'

13 The 'all affected principle' holds that all those impacted by a collective decision should be included in the decision. The idea goes back at least as far as the Justinian Code (V,59,5,2) in Roman private law: 'what touches all must be approved by all'. It is now part of discussions of democratic theory. See on this Robert E. Goodin, 'Enfranchising All Affected Interests, and Its Alternatives', *Philosophy and Public Affairs*, 35 (1), 2007, 40–68; Robert E. Goodin, 'Enfranchising All Subjected, Worldwide', *International Theory*, 8 (3), 2016, 365–389.

'But the majority of whom?' asked **Diana**. 'We've agreed we need to know who the people are before we can ask what counts as the majority.'

'It's the majority of those who are in power, then,' said **Tracy** impatiently. 'Who else could it be?'

'That doesn't seem fair,' said **Astrid**, 'or just.'

'It's perfectly just,' said **Tracy**. 'That's what justice is, it's about what's right in the right context. And the context is the community of people who are the actual people. Those who decide are those who represent those people and serve their interests. And they are responsible for interpreting to the people the identity of the people.'

'I'm getting lost,' said **Antoine**. 'We seem to be going around in circles.'

There was a sudden silence as everyone looked at one another as though stumped by a particularly infuriating riddle.

'I think we're getting lost because we're trying to find a philosophical answer to a political question,' said **Tracy** abruptly. 'The reality is that we have states and rulers who are in power and those rulers exercise power to settle questions like this. It's not that we can't address some ethical questions internally, but we can't settle foundational questions. The state has the power to govern us, and it should do so in our interests. The way it will succeed is by making sure we obey the law, and the way they get us to comply is by making good laws and ensuring that there's a story that we can believe that unites us all.'

'And justice?' **I** asked.

'Ooh, that's one of the best stories,' said **Kaveh**.

'Well, I think there's got to be more to it than that,' said **Astrid** firmly. 'Tracy makes it all sound so, so…'

'Communitarian?' said **Kaveh**.

'So parochial,' said **Astrid**. 'It's just a defence of established power. And I don't think saying the problem can't be solved philosophically is much of an argument. It's no less a philosophical statement than anything else. We have to be able to do better than this.'

'I'd like to think we can,' **I** said, 'but I think you'll all agree we've got our work cut out for ourselves.'

'You said it, boss,' said **Diana** wearily. 'I don't think there was enough bad food to give us the energy we need to solve this problem.'

'Let's call it quits, then,' **I said**, 'and try again next week or whenever it is we're scheduled to meet again.'

'I think I'm up next,' said **Astrid,** 'though I'm not so sure what I'm going to say now. Things have gotten mighty confusing.'

'Welcome to my world, everyone,' **I** said. 'Welcome to my world.'

4 Rights and Refugees

Astrid arrived early for our next meeting, carrying several plastic bags that looked like they were about to burst. They turned out to be filled with food for the evening's conversation, but on this occasion, it was not the smorgasbord to which we'd been subjected at the last gathering. This was a carefully curated repast and Astrid was the sole author.

'I'm sorry I'm a little early, Xandros,' **Astrid** said, as she shuffled through the door and down the corridor into the kitchen, 'but I've a little prepping to do for dinner. I hope you don't mind.'

'No problem,' **I** said. 'Can I help?'

'Sure,' **Astrid** replied, 'but 'it's mostly assembly, since everything's pre-cooked. Well, almost everything. The avocados need to be mashed—didn't want them turning brown, so I brought them over whole. And we need to juice a couple of lemons.'

'What is it you have in store for us?' **I** said. 'It sounds like quite a feast.'

'It is!' said **Astrid**, clapping her hands and smiling happily, 'and I have some really good tequila in the car. I'll go get it now. I hope you have some nice glasses.'

With that, Astrid turned and strode out almost hurriedly, making me think that she wanted to make sure everything was ready before the rest of the group arrived. She was still beaming when she returned with two bottles of Patrón Reposado.

DOI: 10.4324/9781003629641-4

'This will go perfectly with everything,' **Astrid** said. 'It'll even shut Kaveh up!'

'What's on the menu,' **I** asked, 'and yes it will go perfectly, though for the sake of a favourite cocktail of mine, an El Diablo, put a little aside for me.'

'Mexican and Central American, basically,' **Astrid** said, 'including tortillas, tamales, and lots of lovely chicken and pork fillings, all nice and spicy.'

'What about Antoine?' **I** said. 'Vegetarian?'

'Absolutely!' said **Astrid**. 'It's a totally inclusive menu.'

A knock on the door told us the others had arrived and soon they were inside, shuffling off coats and slumping into chairs to assume their usual positions. They were clearly as comfortable in my home as they were in each other's company. Even Tracy, who I feared might be a bit standoffish after our last little symposium, seemed very chirpy. Only Diana looked a little downcast, though she brightened up when Antoine and Temi started teasing her about looking too serious.

'Okay, Astrid,' said **Kaveh**, 'what sort of nosh have you got for us?'

'Yes,' said **Diana**, 'we're dying to know, though by the look of the tequila I think we can guess.'

'Why is Astrid providing dinner?' **I** asked.

'She wanted to,' said **Temi**. 'In fact, she insisted. Told us she didn't want another hodgepodge, and when we said maybe she should cater, she said yes.'

'Yes,' said **Antoine**, 'and then we couldn't talk her out of it. She wouldn't let us even bring some wine.'

'She wouldn't even let us bring wine,' **Kaveh** repeated.

'But that part we took no notice of,' said **Temi**, with a broad smile, pulling out a bottle of red wine from behind him as the others did the same.

'Hey, you promised,' said **Astrid**, trying to look cross.

'It's okay, Astrid,' said **Diana**. 'It's for Xandros.'

'Yes,' said **Antoine**, 'we decided we needed to bring him something to replenish his stocks since we've been enjoying his hospitality.'

'Yeah,' said **Kaveh**, 'totally appreciated, dude.'

'That's very kind, everyone,' **I** said. 'I do appreciate the gesture, though I'd appreciate it even more if none of you ever again calls me "dude". That would be wonderful.'

'Done,' said **Kaveh** firmly. 'It's time these guys started to show a little class. So, Astrid, explain the menu.'

'Yes,' said **Tracy**, 'I'm intrigued. And starving!'

'Well, it's something in keeping with the theme of tonight's discussion,' said **Astrid**, 'and I'm thinking of calling it "the people's repast".'

'All very nice,' said **Kaveh**, 'but what and when do the people eat? The people are hungry.'

'Quite hungry, actually,' said **Antoine**.

'Massively,' said **Temi**.

'Give us your poor, your hungry masses, yearning to feed free,' said **Kaveh**, 'give us this day our…'

'Okay, okay,' said **Astrid**, laughing. 'It's a mix of Mexican and Central American. Probably nothing new to you, but all very good. There's a collective that runs a refugee relief program, and they have a kitchen that cooks for fundraising drives. And they also feed poor people, mostly immigrants. I made the pork and the chicken, but I got the tortillas and tamales from friends who work there.'

'And me?' said **Antoine** plaintively.

'Don't worry,' said **Astrid**. 'There are plenty of vegetarian things—the tamales are all beans or cheese.'

'Excellent, really excellent,' said **Antoine**, smiling happily.

'You're welcome, Antoine,' said **Astrid**. 'You're all welcome. And just to show you how welcome you are, here are some flyers about the refugee relief collective with a link to their website, which also has a donation button you can click when you're feeling rich.'

'It might be a while before I'm feeling rich,' said **Kaveh**. 'My car needed new tires this week, so I had to choose between meals and wheels. Lucky there's free food tonight.'

'Didn't I see you going to the movies a few days ago?' said **Diana**. 'I mean, the expensive one with the golden lounge?'

'Yes,' said **Temi**, 'and you went to dinner at Bismillah Biryani! That's a pricey establishment and not in most people's budget.'

'Yeah, Kaveh,' said **Diana**, 'you dress like a bohemian, but you have expensive tastes.'

'I'm just a poor boy, from a poor family,' said **Kaveh**, grinning.

'Open your eyes, man,' said **Antoine**. 'For you, it's easy come, easy go.'

'I'm hurt,' said **Kaveh**, trying to suppress the huge smile that still lit up his face.

'Didn't mean to make you cry,' said **Temi**. 'Poor Kaveh.'

'Yes, poor Kaveh,' said **Antoine**.

'Poor, poor Kaveh,' said **Diana**, pretending to wipe away a tear.

'You guys!' said **Kaveh**. 'You send shivers down my spine.'

'Enough already,' **I** said. 'Maybe it's time to bring this fandango to an end—if you're actually interested in getting to the conversation we're here for.'

'Okay, no escape from reality,' said **Temi**. 'Just as we were starting to enjoy giving Kaveh some of his own back after putting up with his lame jokes for so long.'

'Thanks, Xandros,' said **Kaveh**. 'I was caught in a landslide of abuse. As anyone can see.'

'You get no sympathy,' **I** said, 'but Astrid might soon. You're up, kiddo.'

'Okay,' said **Astrid**, 'I guess my time has come. So, I thought I'd start with the refugee question.'

'I thought we were going to discuss the rights question,' said **Diana**. 'In fact, wasn't Antoine going to do that?'

'Yes, he was,' said **Astrid**, 'but we talked about it and decided that our topics—and our views—overlapped somewhat, and it might be better to begin with the more practical question. Antoine will come in with his bit later, if that's okay with Xandros. Will you let me go first?'

'Carry on, carry on,' **I** said. 'I don't think it really matters what order you go in. Besides, you brought enough food and tequila for an army. Anyone can see you've earned a little indulgence.'

'Okay, great,' said **Astrid**, who was suddenly surprisingly nervous. 'So, I'm going to start by going back to something Kaveh said a while ago, maybe in our first conversation.'

'Seriously?' said **Tracy**, who'd been silent for some time. 'Something Kaveh said?'

'Yes,' said **Temi**. 'I mean, why don't you just put a gun against my head and shoot me?'

'You're all just jealous,' said **Kaveh**, clearly enjoying himself enormously.

'Kaveh said something like "open borders for refugees", if I remember correctly,' said **Astrid**.

'Correct,' said **Kaveh**. 'Open borders for refugees, the rest pay cash.'

'Oh dear,' said **Tracy**, 'was that serious? Sometimes I wish I'd never been born at all.'

'Goodbye, I've got to go,' said **Antoine**, laughing.

'Come on you guys,' said **Astrid**. 'I should never have brought the tequila.'

'She did,' said **Diana**, 'she did. I think we're obligated to play along with this fantasy.'

'Thank you,' said **Astrid**, 'but please give me a chance.'

'Carry on, Astrid, carry on,' **I** said.

'I think there's something to what Kaveh said,' **Astrid** continued, 'even if he was just trying to be funny. Most people writing about immigration, even those who are wary of admitting too many, think refugees are special. They recognize that refugees fall into a separate category and aren't like ordinary immigrants. People who are fleeing persecution or war or natural disaster aren't moving voluntarily, their lives are at stake. They have a claim to our help in a way that immigrants don't. I'm not an advocate of open borders, but I can't see how we can justify turning away people who are in danger or who might not survive without us. Simple humanity demands that we not turn our backs on them. That means that we can't pick and choose among refugees in a way that we might wish to with immigrants.[1] And that means open borders for refugees. Though I don't agree with the part about others paying cash.'

'Do you know what you're saying, Astrid?' said **Tracy**. 'I mean, there must be tens of millions, maybe hundreds of millions, of refugees in the world today. Do you really think they should be able to go anywhere they want? And to be clear, they're not going to India and China, they're going to go to the United States and Europe.'

'And Canada,' said **Kaveh** helpfully.

'And New Zealand,' said **Antoine**. 'I hear it's really nice there.'

'It won't be once it's flooded with refugees,' said **Tracy**.

'There aren't hundreds of millions,' said **Antoine**. 'Closer to 30 million, though once you include another 50 million internally displaced people and 5 million asylum-seekers we're getting up around 90 million.'

'That's not trivial,' said **Tracy**. 'I mean, how many immigrants are there in the world in total?'

'In 2021, about 272 million,' said **Antoine**.

'Antoine, go you,' said **Diana**. 'All these stats at your fingertips!'

'I prepped for this, remember,' said **Antoine**, 'so I also know a lot of stuff.'

'Does that figure include refugees?' asked **Temi**.

'Yes,' said **Antoine**, 'but not internally displaced people.'

1 Though the idea that refugees have stronger claims to admission than (other) migrants is widely held, the extent of such claims is a subject of considerable debate and disagreement. For an introduction to the topic, see David Owen, *What Do We Owe to Refugees?* (Oxford: Polity, 2020). See also Chandran Kukathas, 'Are Refugees Special?', in Sarah Fine and Lea Ypi (eds.), *Migration in Political Theory: The Ethics of Movement and Membership* (Oxford: Oxford University Press, 2016), 249–268.

'Then the number of potential refugees looking for someone to let them in is definitely over 50 million, I'd say,' said **Tracy**, 'and it could go up to a hundred million quite easily, in my opinion—especially if it became easier for self-proclaimed refugees to be admitted.'

'What exactly is a refugee?' **Diana** asked suddenly. 'Xandros, all this time and you've never asked for some conceptual clarification, but this surely is a question we need to ask, right?'[2]

'Maybe Xandros is unwell,' said **Kaveh**. 'I saw him licking his lips over the tequila.'

'I'm very well,' **I** said. 'Thank you for asking. But you're quite right that this is an important question. Once again, the matter of definition is not a straightforward one. There is, of course, a legal definition insofar as international law includes a refugee convention.'

'Yes,' said **Astrid**, 'it says a refugee is someone who, because of a well-founded fear of persecution on the grounds of race or religion or nationality or opinion or membership of a particular group, is outside of his or her country of nationality and too afraid to return to that country—and doesn't have a second nationality.'

'Very good,' **I** said, 'though obviously there's more in the convention, which goes on to specify the rights and duties of refugees and of those claiming refugee status.'

'What do you mean, "claiming"?' said **Temi**.

'Since being a refugee in international law means having a particular legal status, a determination has to be made by a court that any particular individual who claims to be a refugee is in fact a refugee,' **I** said.

'Which courts?' asked **Diana**.

'The domestic courts in the country in which protection under the convention is being sought,' **I** said. 'If you seek asylum in Australia, your case will be heard by an Australian court; if you seek it in the United States, it will be heard by an American court.'

2 Andrew E. Shacknove, 'Who is a Refugee?', *Ethics*, 95 (2), 1985, 274–284. See also William Maley, *What is a Refugee?* (London: Hurst, 2016).

'What if you're not fleeing persecution?' asked **Temi**. 'Suppose you're trying to escape being bombed—in Libya or Syria or Ukraine?'

'Then you're out of luck,' said **Kaveh**. 'No ticket, no start.'

'Is that true?' asked **Diana**. 'That hardly seems fair. Say it isn't so, Xandros.'

'I'm afraid it is,' **I** said, 'so let's look at an important distinction. The picture that dominates the popular imagination, as well as the academic literature to some extent, is one of refugees as people who've been forcibly displaced and crossed a border. The *humanitarian* understanding of refugees imagines them to be people fleeing war, famine, or failed states like Venezuela. But international law arising out of World War II and the Holocaust has emphasised the distinctively *political* nature of refugees as people who are trying to escape persecution in or by states that refuse to offer them protection as members but discriminate against them on grounds of religion, race, or nationality—or group membership or opinion, as Astrid noted.'

'So, Ukrainians or Syrians trying to get out of the way of Russian bombs aren't refugees under international law?' asked **Diana**. 'That doesn't seem right.'

'No, it doesn't,' **I** said, 'and so it has seemed to many people, so other, more capacious, definitions have been offered. But in international law, what countries have signed up to is the 1951 Convention, which supplies the architecture for the international regime that governs the treatment of refugees.'[3]

'Then why have the Ukrainians been admitted into Poland and Germany and even into the UK?' asked **Temi**. 'And why didn't the UK take in more than a handful of Syrians?'

'There's nothing to stop a country taking anybody in,' **I** said. 'The US took in an enormous number of refugees long before it ever signed on to the Refugee Convention. And there are countries

3 For the 1951 Refugee Convention and the 1967 Protocol, see the United Nations Commissioner for Refugees website: https://www.unhcr.org/about-unhcr/overview/1951-refugee-convention.

that have signed the Convention but have limited their intake of people seeking asylum.'

'Like Australia,' said **Kaveh**. 'It's been pretty creative.'

'How so?' asked **Diana**.

'If you're a signatory to the Convention, you're obliged to hear the case of anyone who arrives in the country seeking asylum, to determine if he or she is genuinely a refugee,' said **Antoine**, 'so Australia just stopped anyone trying to land on its shores. You can't make a claim and you have no right to unless you're in the country.'

'Yes, it was brilliant,' said **Kaveh**.

'Why?' said **Diana**. 'That's awful!'

'So it's awful,' said **Kaveh**, 'but credit where credit's due! So creative! Stop poor people from landing, ship them off to another country, pay other governments to lock them up, don't allow anyone to visit, and get the word out that it's too risky to try to come to Australia. All while staying within the Convention. It's genius.'[4]

'You're a strange, strange, man, Kaveh,' said **Temi**.

'Thank you,' said **Kaveh**.

'It costs the Australian government over two million dollars a refugee,' said **Antoine**. 'American dollars too, not the Aussie peso.'[5]

'Good ideas are expensive,' said **Kaveh**, grinning. 'You get what you pay for.'

'Kaveh, are you serious?' said **Diana**. 'I can never tell. Does anything matter to you.'

'I'm mysterious,' said **Kaveh**, 'get used to it. And nothing really matters. Really. Nothing.'

4 In 2001, the Australian government, in a move to limit the number of asylum claims, declared through legislation that some parts of its territorial waters were not part of its territory for the purpose of making asylum claims. According to Catherine Dauvergne, while this was a move 'within Australia's legislative competence, it [was] nonsensical from the perspective of international law.' See Dauvergne, *Making People Illegal: What Globalization Means for Migration and Law* (Cambridge, UK: Cambridge University Press, 2009), 58.

5 https://www.kaldorcentre.unsw.edu.au/publication/cost-australias-asylum-policy.

'But surely we owe refugees something,' said **Diana**. 'They're not like other immigrants. And I mean both kinds of refugees, the humanitarian cases and the fleeing persecution cases.'

'That's my point,' said **Astrid**. 'That's why I quoted Kaveh the Indifferent. "Open borders for refugees".'

'I prefer "Kaveh the Insouciant",' said **Kaveh**. 'I think that would make a cool title.'

'Kaveh the Impossible,' said **Diana**.

'Kaveh the Insufferable,' said **Temi**.

'The Inexcusable,' said **Antoine**.

'You guys,' said **Kaveh**, hand over his heart and fluttering his eyes, 'you're so sweet. You like me, you really like me.'

'Thank you, Sally,' **I** said, 'but maybe someone could advance a thesis for us to consider. I hear a lot of emoting but not much in the way of argument or analysis.'

'I thought I did have a thesis,' said **Astrid**, 'which is that there should be no restrictions on the movement of refugees. People fleeing war, persecution, famine, state collapse, should all be welcomed. I'll go further and say we have no right to exclude them. If you see a drowning child, you have a duty to save it if you can without danger to yourself, and you definitely have no right to stop someone else trying to save the child. If others are trying to save refugees, it would be wrong to stop them. It would be immoral. I think we should be more hospitable, especially to the vulnerable.'

'I agree,' said **Kaveh**, 'completely.'

'What?' said **Temi**. 'I thought you favoured the Australian policy.'

'No,' said **Kaveh**, 'I just said full credit to the government for creativity. Doesn't mean I have to agree with it. Like admiring a really nicely tied hangman's noose, even if you're against the death penalty.'

'Well, I have some serious objections,' said **Tracy**, 'even if the rest of you don't. I don't think open borders for refugees is remotely viable as an option—or justified.'

'I thought you'd been a little quiet, Tracy,' **I** said. 'Still waters run deep.'

'I wish I could say I was thinking deep thoughts,' said **Tracy**, 'but to be honest, I've just been getting more and more annoyed.'

'Liberalism is to blame,' said **Kaveh**, 'and climate change.'

'No, seriously, you people,' said **Tracy**, 'you're all just so unrealistic. I mean, it's not that I don't feel sorry for the victims of war and wicked states, but the idea of just opening our borders to anyone in a particular category is just ridiculous. It would be a disaster.'

'Why?' said **Temi**. 'And by the way, Trace, I haven't said I buy the open-borders-for-refugees argument, I've just asked a few questions. I don't know what I think yet, except I too think Kaveh is pretty insufferable.'

'I believe the word you're looking for is "insouciant",' said **Kaveh**.

'Okay, sorry, Temi,' said **Tracy**. 'I shouldn't have lumped you together with the others. But I do think they're being unrealistic. Why? Because they're not acknowledging that while refugees are a particular category of immigrants, they're immigrants all the same. They have the same effects on a host society as any other immigrant. They affect the size of the labour pool and therefore the labour market, they reshape the society if they're culturally different, they use public services just as much as other immigrants do, if not more, and they add to the pool of residents who have no loyalty to the country, making the state less stable.'

'But they're people in distress,' said **Astrid**, 'and they're vulnerable.'

'So are a lot of our fellow citizens,' said **Tracy**, 'and for that matter, so are a lot of other migrants. That's probably why it's so hard to sustain the distinction between different kinds of refugees. It's not obvious that someone fleeing persecution is so much more vulnerable than someone fleeing a war zone or someone trying to escape poverty. The people from Central America riding the "beast" to try to get to the United States are at least as vulnerable as people like the Hazara[6] fleeing persecution in Afghanistan.'

6 The Hazara are an ethnic minority found predominantly in Afghanistan. Shi'a Muslims, they have been among the most persecuted of the minorities in the region.

'The Hazara have it pretty tough,' said **Kaveh**, sounding uncharacteristically serious, as though a nerve had been touched.

'And what about the Rohingya?' said **Astrid**. 'They're probably the most persecuted minority in the world right now. Surely, they're different from economic migrants.'

'I think you're missing my point,' said **Tracy**. 'I'm not trying to play the game of "Who's suffering most?". I'm just saying that you can't draw a clear distinction between refugees and other immigrants either on the basis of vulnerability or on the basis of impact on the host society. Refugees are not special, even if we should be sympathetic to them.'

'So, you don't think the Holocaust survivors would be a special case then,' said **Temi**. 'They were just immigrants like everybody else when they were trying to escape Nazi Germany. Is that right?'

'I don't know why you would say that, Temi,' said **Tracy**, sounding quite hurt. 'Of course, I recognize that the Holocaust was a great evil. I'm not trying to say that persecution, let alone genocide, is okay or that refugees don't suffer or that they don't have any claim on our sympathy and help. But I think the distinction between the claims of refugees and the claims of other kinds of immigrants is not as clear-cut as you're all suggesting—or at least some of you are suggesting.'

'Freddie was a kind of refugee,' said **Kaveh**.

'Who?' said **Astrid**.

'Freddie,' said **Kaveh**, 'Mercury. Freddie Mercury. You know, the lead singer of *Queen*, the band.'

'How was he a refugee?' said **Antoine**. 'I thought he was British.'

'He was,' said **Temi**, 'but he moved to the UK as a child. His parents were Indian Muslims, as I recall. I don't' see how he was a refugee, though.'

'Because his parents moved to the UK to escape from Zanzibar before the revolution,' said **Kaveh**, 'knowing that Indians would not be welcome. And they were right. Lots of Indians were killed. They got out in the nick of time.'

'That doesn't make him a refugee,' said **Astrid**.

'It does,' said **Kaveh**. 'His parents were in danger, so he was.'

'But they left before anything happened,' said **Antoine**. 'Does that count?'

'Some think it does,' **I** said, 'because you can be an anticipatory refugee. Though, in a way, all refugees who've not been directly threatened are "anticipatory" refugees since they're trying to get away before the danger arrives.'[7]

'How far ahead are you allowed to look to claim you're an anticipatory refugee?' said **Diana**. 'I mean, could minorities in any tyrannical regime claim refugee status to immigrate on the grounds that there's a possibility that they'll be targeted in the future?'

'That's an interesting problem,' **I** said, 'though I have a different question for Kaveh about Freddie's status. His parents could move to the UK because, as subjects of the British Empire, they had the right to move to Britain. They didn't need visas or permission because they were British nationals. Could they be classified as refugees, anticipatory or otherwise?'

'Huh!' said **Kaveh**, looking a little dumbfounded. 'I dunno.'

'Nicely put, Kaveh,' said **Tracy**. 'Very pithy. You'll make a philosopher yet.'

Kaveh scowled for a moment before his face brightened into a smile and he said, cheerfully, 'Well, Gromit, that went about as well as could have been expected,' causing the rest of the group to break into laughter.

'Making distinctions and clarifying concepts is tough,' said **Antoine**, 'really confusing sometimes. How do you keep doing this, Xandros?'

'It's my job,' **I** said.

'Do you like it?' said **Astrid**.

'It's a living,' **I** answered, 'but not a career for the faint of heart.'

'Yeah,' said **Temi**, 'you philosophers are the bad boys of the academic world.'

7 See E.F. Kunz, 'The Refugee in Flight: Kinetic Models and Forms of Displacement', *International Migration Review*, 7 (2) 1973, 125–46, for the origin of the term 'anticipatory refugee'.

'Well,' said **Astrid**, 'I'm not sure how useful it's turning out to be. I mean, if we can't make precise distinctions, what do we do about the problems we're trying to address? Even if it's difficult to distinguish refugees from immigrants in certain respects, there's still a difference between someone running from Russian bombs in Syria or Ukraine and someone applying for a work visa to leave Slovakia for a tech job in the Bay Area. We should treat the first case as urgent and cut those being bombed a break, while those trying to get into Silicon Valley can be processed in the normal way, taking into account labour market conditions, qualifications, and whatever else might be relevant for admission. Would that be so hard? After all, there are hundreds of thousands of people who've been stuck in refugee camps for years, with little prospect of finding a proper home and leading a proper life, and others who are in limbo because they've found their way to our societies but have insufficient rights to be able to do more than just survive.'

'I'm all for common sense,' said **Tracy**, 'but you'll recall that you started with a more extreme position, which was "open borders for refugees", not this more moderate view you seem to be espousing now. Are you ready to acknowledge that we have to strike a balance between admitting people for humanitarian reasons and making sure we don't open the door so wide that we encourage more people to come than we can handle—or than is good for refugees themselves?'

'I'm not sure I know what you mean, Tracy,' said **Temi**. 'How can opening the door wider be bad for refugees?'

'In lots of ways,' said **Tracy**. 'For a start by encouraging more people to begin presenting themselves as refugees, thereby crowding out the real refugees. If you want to make refugeehood the fast-track to entry, you can't make it an open track, or everyone will consider using it and soon it will become as slow as the alternatives.'

'That's probably true,' said **Antoine**. 'The more people claim to be refugees, the longer it will take to process their cases to see who is genuinely a refugee.'

'Then there is the problem of people traffickers and smugglers,' said **Tracy**, 'who will encourage those who are desperate to take the illegal migration route in the hope they'll be able to secure asylum. It puts genuine refugees in danger while encouraging criminals.'

'I don't think it's the smugglers who are creating the demand,' said **Astrid**. 'I mean, it's not as if those being smuggled have a lot of better options.'

'They could go to refugee camps and wait for their claims to be heard,' said **Tracy**. 'There's an option.'

'I don't think so,' said **Diana**. 'The camps are pretty bad, and people can get stuck there for years. And besides, it's not as if there's a camp in every neighbourhood or even every country. How are people going to get there?'

'With the help of people smugglers, of course,' said **Kaveh**. 'Cos' there's a hole in the bucket, dear Liza, dear Liza...'[8]

'Yes,' said **Diana**, 'though I have no idea who Liza is. But if you're going to have to use your life's savings and borrow money to pay a people smuggler, you may as well do it to get to your final destination. It makes no sense to go somewhere else that will cost you the same, bring you the same risk, be just as uncertain, and definitely take longer.'

'People should wait their turn and not jump the queue,' said **Tracy**, a little sourly. 'Just because you're desperate doesn't entitle you to take the place of someone else whose plight is no less desperate than yours.'

'But there's no queue,' said **Astrid**. 'It's not like you arrive at a camp and take a ticket.'

'And go shopping while you wait for your number to come up on the board,' said **Diana**, 'or take the kids to the merry-go-round until B17 comes up.'

8 See the song 'There's a hole in my bucket', recorded in 1960 by Harry Belafonte and Odette.

'I can hear the kids crying,' said **Kaveh**, '"Please Mister, please, please call B17".'

'It's more like a lottery than a queue,' said **Astrid** solemnly.

'At least they're not dying at sea,' said **Tracy**, 'or being sold into slavery by traffickers in human misery.'

'I don't think that's quite fair,' said **Antoine**. 'From what we know, a lot of smugglers are just former refugees themselves who help people to cross borders, sometimes for very little or nothing. And a lot of those who charge a lot are the ones who take the most risk. They know that if they're caught, they could go to prison or have their boats impounded or destroyed. And most of the people they help turn out to have a legitimate case for refugee status.'[9]

'Yes,' said **Astrid**, 'and we should also make a distinction between people traffickers and people smugglers. Traffickers take people against their will and sell them into servitude, while smugglers help people who want to escape to escape.'

'I'm sure smugglers are paragons of virtue,' said **Tracy**, making no attempt to suppress the contempt in her voice.

'Well, I'm sure that we'll find a lot of people movers have mixed motives,' said **Astrid**, 'and maybe some smugglers will morph into traffickers, but surely it's because helping people move is illegal. If it were legal, it wouldn't attract so many criminal types.'[10]

'British Airways moves people legally for money,' said **Kaveh**, 'though I have to admit their level of service is criminal.'

'Guys, I think we're starting to go around in circles,' said **Temi**. 'We're trying to make sharp distinctions but maybe it's impossible. All categories shade into one another. And when you classify people, it's not as if they just quietly comply and sort themselves into one group or another—they redefine themselves to fit the classification that's most useful. We're trying to make rules to govern

9 See Peter Tinti and Tuesday Reitano, *Migrant, Refugee, Smuggler, Saviour* (Oxford: Oxford University Press, 2017).

10 See Chandran Kukathas, 'In praise of the strange virtue of people smuggling', *Quadrant*, 47 (9), 2003, 40–41. See also Javier Hidalgo, 'The Ethics of People Smuggling', *Journal of Global Ethics*, 12 (3), 2016, 311–326.

people with different identities, but the rules also create identities. Xandros, what do we do?'

'Xandros to the rescue!' said **Kaveh**.

'The world is more complicated than it appears,' **I** said.

'Great,' said **Diana**, 'that's very helpful.'

'Yeah, thanks a bunch, Xandros,' said **Tracy**. 'That's clarified things.'

'I think we can go home now,' said **Antoine**. 'Xandros has tied things up very neatly.'

'Do I detect a hint of sarcasm?' **I** said.

'No,' said **Diana**.

'Whatever gave you that idea?' said **Tracy**.

'Perish the thought,' said **Antoine**.

'Why did I ever agree to this?' **I** said, laughing, 'I feel like I'm in the hands of smugglers, only being smuggled into the bizzarro world of students. Is there no way out?'

'You'll have to wait your turn,' said **Diana**, 'take a ticket and join the queue.'

'Actually, I think there is a way out,' said **Antoine** quietly.

'For Xandros?' said **Kaveh**, 'I don't think so. He's doomed. He's trapped in a world of endless distinctions.'

'Yes,' said **Diana**, 'he's facing the Hydra, and every time he makes a distinction, two more puzzles pop up and he has to make more distinctions.'

'Even his distinctions have distinctions,' said **Tracy**, 'poor guy.'

'No,' said **Antoine**, 'I think there's a way out of the problem. I mean, we can't make a clear case for giving refugees special treatment, because the more special we make them, the more they become like other immigrants—or other immigrants become like them. But what if we said immigrants had more rights or just rights? Then they'd be less likely to self-classify as refugees.'

'What do you mean, immigrants have rights?' said **Temi**. 'Are you saying that we should accord them rights or that they just do have rights?

'I'm not sure,' said **Antoine**. 'I was going to do my part today by saying that people have a right to migrate—that is, they have the right to emigrate because they have the right to leave their country, and the right to immigrate because they have the right to enter another country if they wish to. But the discussion of refugees has made me less clear about whether we just have rights or whether states should recognize certain rights. Like the right to move.'[11]

'Are you saying that it would be unjust to prevent people from moving or to deny them the freedom to enter a country?'[12] asked **Temi**.

'I'm not sure,' said **Antoine**. 'I don't think I know how justice and rights are related.'

'Are you arguing for open borders?' asked **Astrid**.

'It sounds like you are,' said **Diana**.

'I don't know,' said **Antoine** a little forlornly. 'Maybe I am. Help! I'm a bit lost.'

'Very, very frightening,' said **Kaveh**, 'very, very frightening. Still, you have to admire Antoine's gumption, going out on a limb like that with nothing to break his fall if he slips. All I can say is, magnifico!'

'We can leave Kaveh to wax rhapsodic,' said **Tracy**, 'but I don't see how saying there is a right to immigrate can be serious, though I accept that there's a right to emigrate, if only because no one has the right to stop you from leaving.'

'Surely, it's symmetrical,' said **Temi**. 'The right to exit is meaningless unless you have a right to enter somewhere else.'

'Not necessarily,' said **Diana**. 'You might have the right to go to Disneyland in the sense that no one has the right to stop you taking vacation, leaving your house, driving to Anaheim, and going to the gates, but no one at Disneyland is obliged to let you in if it's

11 Kieran Oberman, 'Immigration as a Human Right', in Sarah Fine and Lea Ypi (eds.), *Migration in Political Theory: The Ethics of Movement and Membership*, 32–56. For a contrary view, see David Miller, 'Is there a human right to immigrate?', in Sarah Fine and Lea Ypi (eds.), *Migration in Political Theory: The Ethics of Movement and Membership*, 11–31.

12 For a general theory of the right both to immigrate and emigrate, see Lea Ypi, 'Justice in Migration: A closed borders utopia', *Journal of Political Philosophy*, 16 (4), 2008, 391–418.

after hours or they're closed for repairs or you don't have a ticket. No one has the right to stop you leaving your country, but that doesn't mean every country from Andorra to Zimbabwe is obliged to admit you.'

'Hmm,' said **Temi**, 'that's all very well, but it's not much of a right if you can't exercise it. All you can really do is sail the seas.'

'I think there are a few things we need to clear up before we go much further,' **I** said, 'since none of you has specified what it means to have a right to immigrate.'

'I thought we made clear it means the right to enter a country,' said **Diana**, 'just as the right to emigrate means the right to leave your own.'

'Some countries won't let you even leave,' said **Kaveh**, 'like North Korea.'

'That's a rare exception,' said **Astrid**, 'not even worth talking about.'

'Singapore won't let you leave without permission if you've not done your national service,' said **Kaveh**, 'and the Philippines won't let you leave to take a job abroad without permission, though I don't think you need permission to go away on holiday.'

'All good observations that help me bring you people to see the point I want to make,' **I** said, 'which is that it's not clear what you mean by the right to leave a country or the right to enter one.'

'My point exactly,' said **Kaveh**, to groans from everyone.

'So,' **I** said, 'by a right to enter a country, do you mean just the right to set foot on its soil—which you might do as a transit passenger or a tourist or a flight attendant or truck driver passing through—or do you mean a right to do more than just visit briefly?'

'Lots of Africans can't even get a tourist visa to visit the UK or US,' said **Temi**, 'so a right just to visit would be a good start.'

'It's not enough, though, seriously,' said **Astrid**. 'I mean, a right to be a tourist? That's ridiculous. You wouldn't list that in a declaration of human rights.'

'Okay,' **I** said, 'what other rights would you say people do or should have? The right to stay for as long as they like? The right to work? The right to buy land? The right to open a business or to trade? The right to vote? The right to stand for public office? The right to use the public health services or to receive a welfare check? None, some, or all of the above?'

'None,' said **Tracy**.

'Some,' said **Diana**.

'Yes, some,' said **Antoine**.

'Some,' said **Temi**.

'All,' said **Astrid**, 'all or nothing.'

'I'm leaning towards all,' said **Kaveh**, 'though not at once. Eventually, though.'

'Astrid,' **I** said, 'does that mean you're in favour of open borders?'[13]

'I think I must be,' **Astrid** replied, 'because I don't see how, once you commit to saying we should admit refugees, and take that idea seriously, you can avoid opening up to other immigrants as well. The more you restrict immigration, the harder it will be to be humanitarian. It's not that it's impossible to draw a line, but that line's going to be arbitrary and unfair and maybe even cruel.'

'I get it,' said **Kaveh**, 'being a weekend humanitarian does sound a bit lame. Better than nothing, though.'

'Most of our rights are qualified, aren't they?' said **Antoine**, 'so I think immigrants must have a qualified or limited right to move, not an absolute one. And I see Xandros's point, we need to specify what they have to do if they immigrate. I would say that they have a pretty extensive right to enter a country, subject to reasonable checks to make sure they aren't criminals or spies for other governments or infected with dangerous diseases. And they should

13 For an analysis of the concept of an 'open border,' see Kukathas, *Immigration and Freedom*, Chapter 2. For defences of open borders, see Chandran Kukathas, 'Why Open Borders?', *Ethical Perspectives*, 19 (4), 2012, 650–675; Bryan Caplan, *Open Borders: The Science and Ethics of Immigration* (New York: First Second, 2019); Michael Huemer, 'Is there a right to immigrate?', *Social Theory and Practice*, 36 (3), 2010, 429–461; Joseph Carens, 'Aliens and Citizens: The Case for Open Borders', *Review of Politics*, 49 (2), 1987, 251–273.

be free to work and stay as long as they like. But I don't think they should have the right to welfare or the right to vote or the right to stand for public office. Those rights should be reserved for citizens.'

'Britain allows non-citizens to vote,' said **Kaveh**.

'Really?' said **Diana**.

'Yes,' **I** said, 'citizens of Commonwealth countries like Australia and Canada who are legal residents of the UK—including students—can vote in local and national elections and even stand for office, though I'm not sure about the students standing for election as opposed to just voting. And, of course, some countries allow even non-resident foreigners to vote— like Italy, which allows people of Italian descent who've never even been to Italy to vote in Italian elections. There's a lot of variation in voting rights. And welfare rights, come to that.'

'I suppose Commonwealth citizens having the right to vote is a holdover from the colonial era,' said **Tracy**, 'but presumably this will go the way of the other rights they had when their own countries became independent.'

'You're right to anticipate this, Tracy,' **I** said, 'but as we discussed last time, I don't think it's clear that they somehow were not British nationals before that or that some British nationals stripping other British nationals of their nationality is ethically defensible.'

'They paid their taxes,' said **Kaveh**, 'just like everybody living in Britain—except for the very poor and some of the wicked.'

'But this would be irrelevant if everybody is deemed to have the right to move anywhere,' **I** said. 'History would be irrelevant.'

'History can't be irrelevant,' said **Tracy**. 'If history is irrelevant, well, we just won't have a country. Anyway, I simply don't see what basis there is for saying that everyone has the right to immigrate, even if it's just a right to enter a country, let alone to reside and work or be given welfare benefits and citizenship. Where does such a right come from?'

'Maybe people from former colonies should have the right to move to the motherland,' said **Kaveh**, 'or the former motherland, anyway. Special immigration rights for victims of past injustice. That's what history shows, surely.'[14]

'Oh, be serious, Kaveh!', said **Tracy**.

'I was being,' said **Kaveh**, sounding a little forlorn.

'I know,' **I** said, 'and it's a nice point.'

'Where do any rights come from?' said **Antoine**. 'That's a really difficult question and maybe one that just can't be answered, since there are so many theories, and none seems to be totally acceptable. But we still have recognition of human rights even if we don't know where they come from. There are all the UN declarations, for example, on universal human rights, on the rights of children, of the rights of women. It must be possible for us to have rights.'

'You can't just make up more rights on the grounds that there are other rights that are recognized,' said **Tracy**. 'That's not a good reason.'

'That's fair,' said **Astrid**, 'but what are some good reasons?'

'Maybe it's time for a distinction,' **I** said. 'I know you're all ready for one.'

'You're like a distinction junkie, aren't you, Xandros,' said **Diana**, 'and you just need a fix. So, okay, go ahead, before you start experiencing withdrawal symptoms.'

'Thank you, Diana,' **I** said, 'but I think you'll like this one. We need to distinguish between what are called *liberty rights* and *claim rights*. To have a liberty right is to have an entitlement to act without hindrance or interference, whereas to have a claim right is to have an entitlement that imposes on others stronger duties not just to refrain from hindering you but also to ensure that your entitlements are respected.'

'That's a bit too abstract for my taste,' said **Astrid**. 'I'm not sure I get it.'

'Okay,' **I** said, 'let's consider some examples. Suppose that Kaveh is going to his favourite restaurant, Bismillah's, and there's free

14 On this, see Lea Ypi, 'Irregular Migration, Historical Injustice, and the Right to Exclude', *Royal Institute of Philosophy Supplements, Volume 91: A Philosophers' Manifesto: Ideas to Change the World*, May 2022, 169–183.

parking in the area. Kaveh has a liberty right to park in any available space. If he parks there, no one has the right to prevent him. But he doesn't have a right to any particular space, and if all the spaces are occupied, it's tough luck on Kaveh, but he does not have a right that's been violated.'

'It's like he has a right to hunt but not a right to succeed,' said **Diana**.

'Yes,' **I** said, 'but now suppose that Kaveh owns the land on which he intends to park, then what he has is not a *liberty* right but a *claim* right, because he can justifiably demand that no one else park there and that anyone who does must vacate that space so he can park—or, knowing Kaveh, so he can enjoy watching them drive around in frustration, looking for a free space and praying for someone to leave the parking lot.'[15]

'One of the underappreciated things about rights is that they can give you the power to make others suffer, to bend them to your will,' said **Kaveh**, flashing his eyes in a pitiful attempt to look forbidding.

'So, it looks like we agree that everyone should have a liberty right to migrate,' said **Temi**, 'since we think there's a right to emigrate, but what's at issue is whether people have a claim right to immigrate because countries have a duty to let them in.'

'Very good, Temi,' **I** said, 'but then it gets a bit complicated, as rights-talk often does.'

'No, no,' said **Diana**, 'no, no, no! Why must you always complicate things?'

'Sorry,' **I** said, 'but someone might assert that he has a right to emigrate that's so strong that his country not only ought to let him leave but also should make it possible. If he's too poor to buy an airline ticket, maybe he has a claim right to assistance—what good's a right if you're too poor to exercise it.'

15 For a fuller account of the concept of a right and its usage, see Leif Wenar, 'Rights', *Stanford Encyclopedia of Philosophy* (Spring 2023 edition), Edward N. Zalta and Uri Nodelman (eds.), https://plato.stanford.edu/archives/spr2023/entry/rights.

'Yeah,' **Tracy** snorted, 'that's where all rights-talk ends, with people demanding a right to everything. Ridiculous.'

'Equally, if there were no borders, or no one's permission was required to cross one, you wouldn't be asserting a claim right in looking to do so, only a liberty right,' **I** said.

'But we do have borders, and we do need permission to cross them because that's the way the world is set up,' said **Temi**.

'Yes,' **I** said, 'so the question is whether those responsible for granting permission have a duty to give it or, to put it differently, whether refusing to grant permission violates the rights of people who are entitled to be let in.'

'Is the world really set up in this way?' said **Kaveh**. 'Maybe it's not really, and we're just going through a phase, so all it takes is for someone to challenge it and it will just fall apart. Someone like Galileo.'

'Galileo?' said **Astrid**.

'Galileo,' said **Kaveh**.

'Galileo?' said **Antoine**.

'Galileo!' said **Kaveh**.

'What is Kaveh talking about? Seriously!' said **Diana**.

'Go figure,' said **Tracy**.

'Galileo challenged the heliocentric worldview of the Catholic Church,' **I** said, 'so I assume Kaveh is referring to that, maybe to question our own national-geography-centric perspective.'

'Magnifico!' said **Kaveh**, 'down with this methodological nationalism.[16] This monstrosity!'

'Methodological nationalism, as you call it, is unavoidable,' said **Tracy**, 'so the question is precisely whether there is a right to immigrate that imposes duties on the citizens of countries to admit would-be immigrants and to allow them not only to enter but also to stay, to work, and to become full members. If you have states,

16 See Alex Sager, 'Methodological Nationalism, Immigration and Political Theory', *Political Studies*, 64 (1), 2016, 42–59; Alex Sager, 'Political Philosophy Beyond Methodological Nationalism', *Philosophy Compass*, 16 (2), 2021, e 12726.

you have methodological nationalism, and there's no use pretending or theorising otherwise.'

'That's a pretty firmly stated opinion,' I said, 'so what say those of you who think countries are duty-bound to let people enter, settle, or even join? What arguments do you have.'

'The critical argument has to be the argument from poverty,' said **Astrid**. 'We owe duties to the poor, and especially because the reason they are poor is that the basic structure of society—global society—causes some people to prosper and others to struggle. There's nothing fair about it. Indeed, it's quite unjust. Immigration will go a long way towards eliminating poverty and is justified on those grounds. People's right to immigrate derives from their right to try to lift themselves out of poverty, and we have at the very least a duty not to prevent them from helping themselves. I think we also have a duty not to make it difficult, let alone illegal, for those among our fellow citizens who help immigrants by offering them jobs or trading with them or giving them charitable assistance. So, both immigrants and our fellow citizens have certain claim rights as well as liberty rights.'[17]

'Go Astrid!', said **Kaveh**, to which Astrid responded with a bow and curtsey and broad smile.

'Bah! Humbug!' said **Tracy**, also with a smile but one that left it unclear whether she was being serious or funny.

'I'm not sure about the poverty argument,' said **Diana**, 'though not because I disagree that immigration would do an enormous amount to reduce poverty throughout the world. But what about those who aren't poor? Don't they have a right to immigrate? It seems to me that they do. Maybe they want to be with their families? Maybe they find they like a place they visited? Maybe they fall in love with someone in another country. Do they also have to be poor to have the right to immigrate?'

17 For a subtle analysis, see Kieran Oberman, 'Poverty and Immigration Policy', *American Political Science Review*, 109 (2), 2015, 239–251, which argues that while immigration is a powerful tool for reducing poverty, the justification for freedom to immigrate cannot rest on this empirical claim but is grounded rather in the normative claim that everyone has the right to migrate.

'Imagine if you needed a visa to fall in love,' said **Kaveh**. 'Hey, wouldn't that be a great title for a song?'

'The rich have no trouble immigrating,' said **Temi**, pretending to ignore Kaveh. 'The purpose of immigration controls is to keep out the poor.'

'Maybe it depends on who you count as rich,' said **Diana**. 'I'm sure Nicole Kidman can move anywhere she wants to, but what about a middle-class woman from London or Chicago, who'd count as rich by global standards—and definitely by historical standards—but wouldn't have the kind of wealth you need to be welcome anywhere?'

'That's true,' said **Astrid**. 'There was a case of someone in Britain who went to Brazil and married a doctor but couldn't sponsor him to immigrate because she'd stopped working after having a baby and so didn't meet the income requirement. His income didn't count.'[18]

'Yes,' said **Antoine**, 'there are also all those people who just want to move to be with their families, you know, like retired parents whose children have emigrated. They can't just move, even though they're not poor. Surely, they have a right to be with their children, and maybe their children have the right to bring their parents to live close to them?'

'Maybe poverty is a sufficient but not necessary justification for the right to immigrate,' said **Astrid**.

'But what's the basis for such a right for the non-poor?' said **Antoine**.

'They want to break free,' said **Kaveh**, 'that's all.'

18 As of April 2024, British citizens or residents have had to show that they had an income of at least £38,700 to be eligible to sponsor a spouse for a visa to enter or remain in Britain as a legal resident. This amount was raised from the previous minimum of £18,600. Only 27% of Britons earn the requisite amount. The purpose of the increase was to reduce the net migration rate. Family visas counted for a net migration total of 39,000 in the 12 months up to June 2023. See https://www.euronews.com/2023/12/11/anguish-grows-over-effective-ban-on-most-uk-citizens-marrying-foreign-nationals.

'What are you talking about, Kaveh?' said **Diana**, 'and what do you mean, "that's all"?'

'I mean, maybe it's enough simply to say that everyone has a basic right to freedom,' said **Kaveh**, 'and we'd need to have a pretty good reason to stop them from exercising it. But the default is that everyone is free, and that means free to move about, including across boundaries.'

'What would count as a good reason?' said **Temi**.

'Easy,' said **Kaveh**, 'harm to others.'

'And what counts as harm to others,' said **Temi**.

'Not so easy,' said **Kaveh**. 'Over to you, Xandros.'

'Thank you for this can of worms, Kaveh,' **I** said. 'This is going to be interesting.'

'But what about the rights of states and their citizens to exclude others from immigrating?' said **Tracy**. 'Surely, they have rights, too! Maybe people have the right to be free to move around, but that can't be an absolute right. I mean, I have the right to move around in my country, but I can't just walk into your house uninvited, or enter the University President's office whenever I like, or wander into the Pentagon. Nor can I join any club or organization I want without the members' agreement. I think rights to exclude trump rights to move.'[19]

'Tracy's got a point,' said **Temi**.

'Indeed, she does,' **I** said. 'I told you this was going to get interesting.'

'Then it's up to you, Xandros,' said **Diana**. 'You have to sort all this out.'

'And if I can't?' **I** asked.

'Then we will, we will mock you,' said **Kaveh** firmly.

'We will,' said **Diana**, 'absolutely.'

19 On the right to exclude, see Christopher Heath Wellman, 'Immigration and Freedom of Association', *Ethics*, 119 (1), 2008, 109–141. For a contrary view, see Sarah Fine, 'Freedom of Association is not the Answer', *Ethics*, 120 (2), 2010, 338–56. See also Christopher Heath Wellman and Phillip Cole, *Debating the Ethics of Immigration: Is there a right to exclude?* (New York, Oxford University Press, 2011).

'Totally,' said **Antoine**.

'I don't think I can take it,' **I** said, laughing. 'You can't do this to me.'

'Yes, we can,' said **Kaveh**. 'We will not let you go.'

'Be a man,' said **Diana**, 'not just a philosopher.'

'Yes,' said **Kaveh**, 'are you a man or just a silhouette of a man?'

'Okay, okay,' **I** said, 'I can see my time has come. So, let me open your eyes. But allow me to do this in an orderly way. First, we should address the harm question. Then we can turn to the matter of whether there's a right to exclude that trumps the right to move.'

'Okay, Xandros,' said **Diana**, clapping her hands, 'make some distinctions, clarify some concepts, we can't wait!'

'Right,' **I** said, 'let's start by outlining Kaveh's contention. As I understand it, he proposes that we take the default rule to be that everyone has a right to move across international boundaries, so any restriction on movement has to be justified—and justified to those wishing to move.'

'And maybe also to those who want them to move,' said **Kaveh**, 'like potential employers, or families wanting to be reunited, or charitable organizations who want to help others but can't if they aren't allowed to exercise their right to be a good Samaritan.'

'Let's leave those cases aside for the time being,' **I** said, 'and focus on those who want to move, though we will return to the examples you raise.'

'Sure,' said **Kaveh**.

'It's not an unreasonable starting point,' **I** said. 'Most of us would probably want a good reason for preventing us from acting—including moving about. But it's not the only possible starting point.'

'What else could there possibly be?' asked **Temi**. 'I'm no libertarian, but even most socialists would probably agree that you have to have a reason to interfere with someone's freedom.'

'Not a libertarian, perhaps, but clearly someone for whom the claims of the individual come first,' **I** said, 'or at least someone who thinks the interests of the individual are the measure of all things.'

'What else could be?' said **Temi**.

'Well, we did have a long discussion, last time we met, about whether value had to be understood in term of individual well-being or could inhere in other things, like the community or the state,' **I** said. 'For some, the starting point might be, let's say, national sovereignty, or the common good, or even "total utility". For anyone starting from one of these perspectives, it is the failure to limit liberty that might have to be justified.'

'Seriously?' said **Antoine**.

'Yes,' **I** said, 'but let's leave aside discussion of these alternative starting points for another occasion. I'll have something to say about them at our next meeting. In the meantime, let's take a closer look at the argument that that people should be free to move unless moving causes harm to others.'

'That's fine,' said **Diana**, 'but promise you won't forget about this. I'm especially puzzled by the national sovereignty and common good arguments.'

'What about the total utility argument? said **Astrid**. 'Doesn't it get a place on stage?'

'No,' said **Kaveh**, unable to suppress his giggling, 'no utility billing.'

'Thank you, Kaveh,' **I** said, 'but I will say a bit about it when the time comes. For now, though, let's focus on harm. As you are all no doubt aware, there are several difficulties that have to be overcome when invoking the harm principle—that is, when arguing that liberty can be limited only in order to avoid harm to others. These include, in no particular order, the questions of what counts as harm, both quantitatively and qualitatively, who should count as the actual or potential victims of harm, and whether some kinds of harm may be justified, or even warranted. There is also the question of whether harm to others is a test only for interference with certain *basic liberties*, but not for interference with liberty as such. If so, what needs to be settled is whether the freedom to move is one of the basic liberties such as freedom of religion or freedom of conscience.'

'I think I'd go along with Kaveh a bit of the way,' said **Tracy**. 'I agree that limiting liberty has to be justified, but I don't think the freedom to move is a basic liberty, at least not internationally, even though I agree everyone ought to be free to leave their country if they wish—provided someone else will have them. And if no one will, well, that's just too bad. You're not being coerced because you're not welcome.[20] It's like being free to marry—you can have that freedom all you want, but if no one wants to marry you, well, you can't say your rights have been violated. Oh, and I think immigration does harm others, so we should limit it.'

'Then let's take a look at the arguments,' **I** said, 'beginning with the matter of whether harm to others can ever be justified. It seems to me it can. Thoughts.'

'Absolutely,' said **Diana**. 'Kaveh is definitely crying out to suffer some serious harm, and it would be totally justified.'

'I agree,' said **Temi**, 'but in this case it would be a case of deserved punishment, and I don't think that's the kind of harm we're talking about.'

'I think so too,' said **Antoine**. 'We're really talking about third-party effects, not punishment that's just. I would say that harm to third parties can be justified sometimes because having an effect on others is unavoidable. If I take the parking space Xandros mentioned before, I might harm Kaveh if I take the last spot, but I don't think that would be unjustified. It has to be deliberately inflicted harm or harm resulting from negligence.'

'Does that mean competition in the marketplace is harmful?' said **Diana**. 'After all, one business might try to drive out another by lowering its prices, but even if it's deliberate I can't see that there's anything wrong with that.'

'What about predatory pricing?' said **Antoine**. 'That's got to be wrong.'

20 On this topic, see the exchange between Abizadeh and Miller: Arash Abizadeh, 'Democratic Theory and Border Coercion: No Right to Unilaterally Control Your Own Borders', *Political Theory* 36 (1), 2008, 37–65; David Miller, 'Why Immigration Controls Are Not Coercive', *Political Theory* 38 (1), 2009, 111–120; Arash Abizadeh, 'Democratic Legitimacy and State Coercion: A reply to David Miller', *Political Theory*, 38 (1), 2010, 121–30.

'I'm all for predatory pricing,' said **Kaveh**. 'It's good for consumers, and we get to watch capitalists trying to destroy each other.'

'I think we're starting to wander into a stream of topics,' **I** said, 'and while they're undoubtedly related to our concerns, it's not helping us focus—though it does suggest how difficult it is to develop rules or principles that apply straightforwardly. Let me see if I can summarise before we go any further.'

'Please do, Socrates,' said **Diana**, fluttering her eyelashes. 'I mean Xandros.'

'Try to get your ancient Greek philosophers right, Diana,' **I** said. 'We have work to do. First, we're agreed that we start with the assumption that harms to others have to be justified. Let's also agree that punishment can be excluded from consideration, if only on the assumption—not always warranted—that those being punished have been given a justification through the legal process for the harm to be inflicted on them. We should also accept that harms that we inflict through the exercise of our liberty rights (for example, through competition in the marketplace), that do not violate anyone else's claim rights, are also justified.'

'Oh, wow, Socrates, so clear,' said **Temi**.

Ignoring the provocation, **I** continued: 'That brings us to the question of whether immigrants or immigration imposes unjustifiable harms on others.'

'Clearly, they do, or it does,' **Tracy** blurted out. 'Isn't it obvious? Immigrants take jobs away from our fellow citizens, they lower wages by adding to the pool of labour, they absorb welfare benefits paid for by citizens, they compete for scarce social services and public goods, and they dilute or weaken the culture. How much more harm do you want? I say we aren't violating anyone's rights when we limit immigration, because here interference with liberty is warranted to prevent harm to others—namely to our fellow countrymen.'

'And women,' said **Kaveh**.

'Yeah, thanks,' **Tracy** snorted.

'That sounds reasonable,' said **Diana**, 'but I'm not entirely convinced. When I was researching the economics of immigration, it became pretty clear that the effects of immigrants on wages and employment were pretty minimal. And I don't think you can say that they both take jobs and go on welfare, at least not collectively. I mean, which is it: are they taking jobs or taking unemployment benefits? It surely can't be both.'

'I think you're making it more complicated than necessary,' said **Tracy**. 'The simple fact is that if an immigrant takes a job, a citizen doesn't get it.'

'Even if employers can't find citizens to do some of those jobs?' said **Diana**.

'That just means they aren't paying enough,' said **Tracy** flatly.

'Sure, though that may be because if they paid what citizens expect, they'd go out of business,' said **Diana**.

'If they can't pay fair wages, they don't deserve to be in business,' said **Tracy**. 'End of story.'

'Harm to employers is okay, because they're horrible capitalists,' said **Kaveh** solemnly.

'That does seem a bit harsh, Trace,' said **Temi**. 'I mean it might be easy—or at least easier—for big corporations to pay the wages needed to attract employees, but a lot of small and medium-sized businesses would struggle. And there are some jobs that almost no one in America wants to do that immigrants will. I tried fruit picking as a summer job one year, and I have to admit I quit after two weeks. I thought it would be a bit of an adventure, but an internship was way easier and much more attractive even at below minimum wage.'

'Quite substantial businesses would struggle, too,' said **Diana**. 'Their margins are sometimes quite fine, but even if they're not, at some threshold it stops making sense to hire workers if the price of labour is too high. They have to compete with other businesses.'

'Okay,' said **Tracy**, 'maybe if employers *really* can't find workers, it would be permissible for them to hire foreign labour, but I think that would be the minority of cases.'

'And who decides whether or not the right workers are available domestically?' **I** said. 'After all, an employer could claim there's no one suitable, and who's to say there is, since no one knows better than the employer herself what kind of person is needed? I have to confess that when I got my job here, I displaced a citizen who might otherwise have been employed.'

'That's awful, Xandros,' said **Diana**. 'How could you live with yourself after that? What happened to the poor guy? Or woman?'

'He took to drink,' **I** said, 'ended up trying to make a living selling Amway. Very sad, very, very sad.'

'Still, his loss is our gain,' said **Kaveh**. 'No one would beat Xandros in open competition. Don't you agree, Trace?'

'That's an irrefutable argument,' said **Tracy**. 'There's no doubt that some immigrants bring more value than we can imagine. Xandros is a man of distinction. Distinctions! Still, just because there are exceptional cases, that doesn't mean the exceptions should become the norm.'

'Nice move, Tracy,' **I** said. 'Very nice.'

'Huh?' said **Kaveh**.

'I'm not arguing for zero immigration,' said **Tracy**, 'nor am I suggesting that every harm resulting from immigration must be prevented or rectified. I'm just saying that immigration harms some people in immigrant-receiving societies and that this should be taken into consideration before we decide that outsiders have the right to immigrate. I think we have the collective right to control immigration, and a duty to protect those who might be harmed—indeed, to protect the *rights* of those who might be harmed by immigration.'

'That sounds very reasonable in theory,' said **Diana**, 'but what about those who are harmed by the absence of immigration of insufficient immigration. Without immigration, some jobs would not exist, some industries would not be possible, some services would not be delivered. And in the longer run, if able people are stuck in societies that aren't going to make the best use of their talents, we'll all be a little poorer collectively and the poorest will feel it the most.'

'That seems right to me,' said **Temi**, 'so the best way to decide what rights there should be is to figure out what would lead to the best outcome overall.'

'Are you saying that we should try to maximize utility?' asked **Antoine**. 'Is that the standard?'

'I guess so,' said **Temi**. 'I think I should go where the argument leads.'

'Whose utility are we maximizing?' said **Astrid**. 'I'm getting confused. Do we maximize global utility? Or national utility? Or something in between?'

'Er, global, I think,' said **Temi**. 'I mean, it would be weird to say we're obligated to maximize national utility.'

'It has to be national,' said **Tracy**. 'It's impossible to figure out the effect on total utility at the global level. If everyone had the right to move anywhere, and ten million decided to move to Sweden, I'm sure the immigrants would see their utility improve for the most part—unless the Swedish people got really mad at them and made life difficult—but surely the utility of a lot of Swedes would go down. How do we measure the utilities and compare them?'

'GDP per capita?' said **Temi**, though without much confidence. 'PPP, of course.'

'I don't think it's reducible to income,' said **Tracy**, 'or anything, really.'

'Well, then how are you going to know if you're maximizing national utility?' said **Diana**. 'Surely, that's going to be difficult for the same reasons.'

'I don't know,' said **Tracy**. 'Maybe the whole idea of maximizing anything is just silly—or at least unrealistic. I mean, what's utility? It's not a real thing you can see or count. And if you say let's maximize happiness, it sounds very vague.'

'We could maximize preference satisfaction,' said **Antoine**. 'Maybe that would work.'

'Maybe in principle,' said **Tracy**, 'but we aren't going to be able to count preferences, and we will have to figure out how to weigh trivial preferences against substantial ones, and we'll just end up guessing—or making claims about why one outcome is better than another without being able to justify any of them to anyone's satisfaction but our own. Whether we say preference satisfaction or utility or happiness, it all comes down to the same thing: better outcomes in some way we can't identify with any precision.'

'Tracy!' **I** said. 'You sound just like a philosopher!'

'Oh, no!' said **Tracy**. 'I had no idea it was contagious. Is there a vaccine?'

'There is,' said **Kaveh**. 'It's called tequila. Have some.'

'Surely, there's a commonsensical way of dealing with the question,' said **Temi**. 'After all, consequences are morally relevant. If ten million unvaccinated libertarians infected with Covid wanted to move from America to Sweden, it would be pretty bad for a lot of Swedish people.'

'True,' said **Antoine**, 'even if none of Sweden's citizens got infected, their health-care system could come under pressure if a lot of Americans arrived and started getting sick or dying.'

'Yes,' said **Astrid**, 'and they travel with so much luggage. Sorry, a bit of an over-generalization, I know, but seriously.'

'I have to confess, I don't really much care for examples that begin with statements like "What if so many million people did this or that?",' **I** said. 'What if a billion people walked into McDonald's and all ordered Whoppers—wouldn't that show that capitalism fails because it can't meet demand? What if a billion people decided they want to move to Singapore—doesn't that show we need more immigration controls? It's not a helpful way of reasoning.'

'McDonald's don't make Whoppers,' said **Kaveh**, 'though they do tell some.'

'Whoppers,' said **Astrid**, 'Burger King. Try to keep up, Xandros, if you want to maintain some credibility.'

'Thank you,' **I** said, 'and please pardon my lack of familiarity with the varieties of hot dog. But I hope you see my concern.'

'Burger, Xandros,' said **Astrid**, 'but never mind.'

'All that said,' **I** continued, 'I think the point Temi is trying to make is reasonable. Even if we can't calculate utilities precisely, we should be able to make some judgments about the consequences of actions or regulations or policies and make some moral assessments accordingly. Making immigration to Sweden freer would undoubtedly bring the country many advantages and also benefit many immigrants, but there would clearly be some risks, for Swedish citizens in particular. Some sort of cost-benefit analysis is possible, even if we have to do it by prescinding from a whole range of other considerations about the long term because we just can't do the math.'

'Does that mean ignoring the interests of people wanting to immigrate?' said **Astrid**. 'All because it's too hard to do the math when more people or more issues are taken into consideration?'

'That does sound a bit unfair,' said **Antoine**, 'especially if we're considering refugees. It would be harsh to qualify the right to immigrate to save your life by invoking the harm principle backed up by a cost-benefit analysis.'

'"Sorry, you have to drown because it's just too expensive to allow you crawl ashore",' said **Kaveh**. '"We've done the math and, sadly, it didn't work out".'

'I know this is going to sound awful,' said **Tracy**, 'but Kaveh is right. I know he was being flippant and ironic—and moronic—but it is the truth, isn't it? We can't take everybody, we can't give everyone rights to move, and this means that some people will suffer. Bluntly, they will suffer even more than the people whom we're protecting would have had we let more immigrants in. It's a trade-off, and it's one we make all the time. Get used to it. The world is not just.'

'Power rules,' said **Kaveh**, 'okay?'

'Actually, yes,' said **Tracy**, 'and that's the way it's always going to be.'

'What is it exactly you're saying now, Tracy?' **I** said, 'because it looks like you've switched from saying immigrant rights have to be qualified because of our moral concerns about the harm others will suffer if we accord them those rights to saying that we keep immigrants out because we have the power to do so. Are you now saying that ethical considerations are irrelevant because the powerful simply do as they wish? Or are you saying that keeping immigrants out is ethical—or even just—because we are strong and they are weak?'

'I'm not sure,' said **Tracy**, sounding a little flustered. 'This is getting awkward.'

'Maybe justice is defined by power,' said **Kaveh**, 'since only the powerful can enforce their definitions of justice.'

'Kaveh, can you go back into your cave for just a little while?' said **Diana**. 'Xandros, help! I think we're getting lost.'

'I think we've made splendid progress,' **I** said, 'and sometimes getting a little lost isn't a bad thing, provided we know how we've come to be lost and also know where we've been. We are at least aware of some directions we can't take.'

'Okay,' said **Antoine**, sounding a little dubious.

'We have one more meeting scheduled,' **I** said. 'So that might be the opportunity we need to figure out where we'll go from here.'

'Where will that be, Xandros?' said **Diana**. 'Where will we be going?'

'Any way the wind blows,' said **Kaveh**, 'any way it blows.'

5 Immigration and the Open Society

Since this was to be our last gathering, I felt that I should go to a little extra trouble with dinner and told the group not to worry about food. I would cater. No one objected, though I sensed a few eyebrows being raised when I said I would cook. Eastern Mediterranean would be best, I thought, with a wide array of dishes to lend a festive air to proceedings. Yes, that seemed satisfactory, especially with some fine wine: a little Assyrtiko from Santorini to begin with, and for those wanting to move on to red, an exceptionally tasty Brunello. Of course, the important thing is the company. A little bread with cheese among friends can be as good as a feast. But I can't resist preparing a feast.

Everyone arrived at once, or at least were all on my doorstep when I answered the knock, and they blundered in noisily, shedding coats and hats along the way.

'Something smells good,' said **Astrid**. 'Have you really been cooking, Xandros?'

'Since the moment I could walk,' **I** said, 'and all day today.'

'Fancy-schmancy,' said **Kaveh**, looking at the table I'd set, with the silver cutlery and Riedel stemware in place of the everyday dinner service I normally pulled out.

'I'd like to say you're all worth it,' **I** said, 'but perhaps we should wait till the end of the evening to decide that question. Though I have to admit, I think even the least deserving merit a little hospitality.'

'Amazing, Xandros,' said **Antoine**. 'What's on the menu?'

DOI: 10.4324/9781003629641-5

'Welcome to Club Med,' **I** said. 'I hope you're all hungry.'

'We are,' said **Temi**, 'or at least I am.'

'And thirsty,' said **Tracy**. 'Is that wine chilled? And what are we eating? Is there a starter?'

'You can all help me put everything on the table,' **I** said, 'and then we can just help ourselves to anything in any order we want.'

'And from time to time you'll step in to clarify what we're consuming,' said **Diana**, 'right?'

'Or make sure we understand the distinction between one kind of falafel and another,' said **Antoine**. 'I can see them.'

'Well spotted, Antoine,' **I** said. 'I made one traditional falafel and another one baked with herbs.'

'What else is on the menu?' said **Kaveh**. 'All this talk is making me even hungrier.'

'Falafels aside, we have mostly vegetarian dishes, but some meat,' **I** said. 'Of course, there's a tabbouleh salad, a tomato-olive-cucumber-parsley salad dressed in olive oil and lemon juice, some green beans in oil and tomato sauce, a little hummus, some baba ganouj, bell peppers filled with savoury couscous, roast chicken stuffed with basmati rice, and lamb koftas, in a cloyless sauce, naturally.'

'Wow!' said **Temi**.

'And for dessert?' said **Kaveh**.

'For dessert we'll have to go on a diet,' said **Astrid**.

'I picked up a few sweets,' **I** said. 'I didn't make these, I'm afraid.'

'Shame on you, Xandros,' said **Diana**. 'What did you get?'

'The usual,' **I** said, 'Turkish delight, some baklava, honey cakes, halva, rolled dates, and a little lemon sorbet—which is not quite in keeping with everything else, I know, but in case anyone needs something lighter yet sweet, well, it's there. Actually, I made the baklava—it's my specialty. But the other sweets are from *Just Sweets*, my favourite store.'

'Okay, you're forgiven,' said **Diana**, 'but you do realize this doesn't mean we're going to go easy on you tonight. You can't buy us off with a few falafels and some cheap liquor.'

'Hey!' **I** said. 'What do you mean "cheap"? The quality of the wine is better than any argument any of you have ever offered!'

'Harsh, Xandros!' said **Astrid**. 'Harsh!'

'Let's sit,' **I** said, 'and don't be shy about helping yourselves, as I won't be serving anything but insights.'

'Here we go,' said **Diana** with a groan, 'but I guess we asked for it when we accosted you.'

'This is your night, Xandros,' said **Temi**, 'so I hope you're going to have something substantial to say instead of just lurking about ready to pounce with a question or a bit of conceptual clarification.'

'Yes,' said **Antoine**, 'it's time to deliver.'

'I can't wait,' said **Tracy**. 'Let's see how you hold up when everyone is trying to tear you down.'

'You want a positive thesis,' **I** said, 'about immigration. Right?'

'Yes,' said **Astrid**, 'absolutely.'

'Well,' **I** said, 'I'll give you that, but not till we've walked through a few preliminaries to make sure we're clear about what we're looking for.'

'Oh, for Locke's sake,' said **Diana**, 'how much clearing up do you have to do before you actually start to build something?'

'Just a little,' **I** said. 'I'm trying to set the mood. And also, I want to make sure we know what we are and are not doing.'

'Sounds great,' said **Kaveh**. 'We don't want to go too fast, or we'll be done before we've finished all the grub. Thinking fast by thinking slow.'

'Thank you, Kaveh,' **I** said. 'So, down to work. I'd like to start by saying what it is I think we're doing. On the surface, we've been exploring various aspects of the immigration question. We've asked whether immigration is a danger to Western civilization and whether it poses an existential threat, we've asked whether the economics of immigration means immigration does or does not make sense for countries, we've considered whether immigration threatens to undermine the state, and we've examined the refugee issue and asked whether or not immigrants have rights. In all these efforts, we've begun with immigration and ended up exploring larger questions about culture, about well-being, about value—among other things.'

'True,' said **Astrid**, 'we did tend to get distracted.'

'It was more than a tendency,' **I** said, 'it was an inevitability. We can't look at immigration without having to engage with some more general questions about how we should relate to one another. Indeed, we can't avoid asking who we mean when we talk about one another.'

'Our fellow countrymen,' said **Tracy** with a grin, pretending to bang her fist on the table. 'No one else!'

'And who are those countrymen, and what holds them together?' **I** asked.

'People inside our borders, held together by justice,' **Tracy** said, without missing a beat. 'It's all about justice. Without justice, you can't have a country. Without a country, you can't have justice. The two go together like, like, like hummus and pita bread, or lemon juice and olive oil.'

'Excellent,' **I** said. 'Very well put. Bravo!'

'So, you agree with me, Xandros,' said **Tracy**, 'that justice is what is important and above all? And that we need the state to secure it?'

'Not at all,' **I** said. 'I disagree with you completely, I just appreciate how plainly you've put the view I plan to question.'

'Hang on,' said **Diana**, 'you can't be serious. You aren't against justice.'

'Yes,' said **Antoine**, 'I'm confused. What about poverty? What about George Floyd? What about the evils of colonialism?'

'What about these falafels?' said **Kaveh**, 'I mean, good work Xandros. They're just, just, just, just delicious.'

'We get it, Kaveh,' said **Temi**, 'we get it. Just eat more, just talk less.'

'Just sayin',' said **Kaveh**, 'just sayin'.'

'I'm not against justice,' **I** said. 'I don't think justice is bad or injustice is good. Nor am I indifferent in matters of right and wrong. But I'm not persuaded that justice is the right concept to use—or ideal to invoke—when considering the question of immigration.'

'Why not?' said **Diana**. 'Justice for migrants—it sounds like a good idea, and a good slogan too. It goes straight to the heart of the matter.'

'Justice for people on the move,' said **Kaveh**.[1]

'All we have to do is figure out what justice is,' said **Diana**.

'Oh, is that all?' said **Temi**, rolling his eyes. 'Yeah, that'll be a piece of cake.'

'Mmmm, cake,' said **Kaveh**, 'but no piece without justice—no pieces of cake, that is.'

'Are you against justice for immigrants?' asked **Antoine**, looking puzzled. 'Or are you saying we owe them something different, like charity?'

'Or hospitality?' said **Astrid**.

'Let them eat cake!' said **Kaveh**, pretending to pound his fist on the table. 'That's it!'

'Give it a rest, Kaveh,' said **Diana**, 'this is serious. And we're seriously confused by Xandros.'

'Sorry,' said **Kaveh**, picking up a kofta and chomping into it enthusiastically with evident enjoyment.

'I don't think immigrants, or would-be immigrants, have claims of justice against us,' **I** said, 'or against anyone, for that matter.'

'What about refugees?' said **Diana**. 'Not even refugees?'

'Not even refugees,' **I** said.

'Harsh!' said **Diana**, 'very harsh. That's not very kind. Or hospitable.'

'Not at all,' **I** said. 'I think we should be very generous with refugees and should welcome immigrants from everywhere. Indeed, I think all countries should, some to a greater extent than others. I just don't think it's a matter of justice.'

'What else could it be,' said **Astrid**, 'or are you just saying it would be good to be nice? Surely, you're saying more than that?'

'Yes, what is justice?' said **Kaveh**.

'What a good question,' **I** said, 'a very good question.'

1 Gillian Brock, *Justice for People on the Move: Migration in Challenging Times* (Cambridge, UK: Cambridge University Press, 2020).

'Funny, that,' said **Temi**. 'You've totally set us up to ask this, haven't you, Xandros.'

'We were going to get to this eventually,' **I** said, 'so I thought I'd speed things up a bit. But since we're now on the topic, here's my concern. Well, actually, I have several concerns, but let's begin with one.'

'One's good,' said **Antoine**, 'one step at a time.'

'Thank you,' **I** said. 'My first worry is that making immigration a matter of justice raises the stakes unnecessarily high. To say that something is a matter justice is to say one is committing a serious wrong if one doesn't comply with the demand in question. Justice doesn't easily admit compromises. If something is required or must be done as a matter of justice, a failure to comply may mean punishment or some kind of sanction is warranted. Justice is a very demanding virtue.'

'Let justice be done though the earth perishes,' said **Kaveh**. 'That's cool.'

'Yes,' **I** said, '*fit justitia pereat mundus* is one view, though I doubt too many people would go that far. Still, my point is that justice is too strong a standard even if we don't go to extremes, because it imposes a very demanding set of requirements on everyone—on us all.'

'But isn't that a good thing?' said **Astrid**. 'I mean, we should abide by the requirements of justice, surely?'

'We should,' **I** said, 'which is precisely why we should be careful about making too many things requirements of justice.'

'I'm not getting it,' said **Diana**. 'You'd better explain.'

'I'll try,' **I** said, 'I'll try.'

'Didn't John Rawls say that justice is the first virtue of social institutions, or something like that?' said **Temi**.

'As truth is of systems of thought,' said **Kaveh** helpfully. 'I know my Rawls.'[2]

2 'Justice is the first virtue of social institutions, as truth is of systems of thought. A theory however elegant or economical must be rejected or revised if it is untrue; likewise laws and institutions no matter how efficient and well-arranged must be reformed or abolished if they are unjust.' John Rawls, *A Theory of Justice*, 3.

'So it would seem, Kaveh,' **I** said. 'I'm impressed.'

'It's not that impressive,' said **Diana**. 'Everyone knows that line—especially after you drummed it into us in class.'

'There was a class?' said **Kaveh**, feigning shock.

'But you don't think justice is the first virtue, do you, Xandros?' said **Temi** quietly.

'No, I don't,' **I** said. 'It's one virtue, but only one—among several.'

'But one of the biggies, yeah?' said **Kaveh**. 'I mean more important than efficiency or being dressed in cheerful colours.'

'It's a biggie, yes,' **I** said, 'but not big enough to defeat all other considerations.'

'I'm not following this,' said **Temi**. 'I mean, if justice is so important—a biggie as you call it—then it will defeat all other considerations. If it's not, it won't. I don't think you can have it both ways, saying that justice is more important than other virtues but can be put aside when we don't like what justice demands.'

'I think he's got you there, Xandros,' said **Antoine**. 'You can't have it both ways.'

'Nice try, gentlemen,' **I** said, 'but I think you're both in error.'

'This had better be good,' said **Diana**, with a big smile.

'What's at issue here,' **I** continued, 'is not whether justice is a very important virtue—whether of individuals or of social institutions—but whether it is of such importance that it must always—always!—trump other considerations. I say it is very important, but not so important as to be deemed the *first* virtue. I don't think there is a "first virtue". Sometimes, we have to trade off one virtue or good against another. For example, I'd promised you all dinner—with a touch of enlightenment—tonight, and ordinarily promises should not be broken. But if I'd come across a lost child on my way to the supermarket, I'd have prioritised her welfare over your promised dinner to make sure she was returned to safety.'

'That's too trivial an example,' said **Astrid**. 'A promise like that is conditional—we all understand that. We'd have been upset if you told us you saw a lost child but ignored her because you felt obliged to cook for us.'

'Even though we're hungry, and there's six of us to just one child?' said **Kaveh** mischievously.

'That's true,' said **Temi**, playing along. 'It's six to one, or seven if we count you, Xandros.'

'Very funny,' **I** said, 'but to answer Astrid's more serious point, I don't think the reasoning would change if we adjusted the example. Let's imagine there's a presidential election and you're certain you've won but have been denied by an incorrect determination by some public official or court. Justice is on your side, but it's not clear that you should pursue justice if that will mean a delayed settlement of the issue and possibly deepening social division brought about by continued political bickering. Might it not be nobler to concede defeat in the interests of peace and stability?'

'But Trump didn't win,' **Diana** blurted out, 'so I don't think this is a great analogy.'

'Actually, I was thinking of the US presidential election of 2000,' **I** said, 'when Democrat candidate Al Gore conceded even though he lost as a result of an unfavourable Supreme Court ruling and despite securing a majority of the popular vote.'

'Still not convinced,' said **Temi**. 'I don't think that case is clear enough, and it pits an individual's interests against the interests of society as a whole.'

'Okay,' **I** said, 'let me try another example, though I think you've been too quick to dismiss the one I've just presented. Let's say you're Germany in 2015 and you've suddenly been confronted with the prospect of a million Syrian refugees coming into the country. Other European countries wring their hands but close their borders to all bar a relatively small number of immigrants, and many people within Germany express serious misgivings about accepting so many people seeking asylum. They worry that this will tear at the social fabric of a nation founded on Christian values, and also point to the impact this will have on the poorest people among their fellow citizens, who will have to share the financial burden of caring for all these outsiders and also compete with them for jobs, social services, school places, and public space. They think it's unjust. But couldn't we also say that, even if it's unjust, humanitarian considerations outweigh any commitment to justice?'

'I don't think Angela Merkel had any right to let in so many people like that,' said **Tracy** hotly. 'It was democratically irresponsible as well as unjust.'

'I think it would have been unjust not to let in the Syrians fleeing war and catastrophic social breakdown,' said **Astrid**, 'and all those European nations that wouldn't let them in acted unjustly.'

'Catastrophic moral horror,' said **Kaveh**.

'Oh, be serious, Kaveh,' said **Tracy**, looking exasperated.

'I was being serious,' said **Kaveh**, sounding a little hurt. 'That's what Robert Nozick says, isn't' it, that maybe sometimes we can justify rights violations if they would avert catastrophic moral horror?'

'Quite correct, Kaveh,' **I** said, 'but we now have two problems. The first is to figure out whether justice trumps all other considerations and the second is to decide what to do when claims of justice are contested or straightforwardly in conflict.'

'What do you mean?' asked **Antoine**.

'Well,' **I** said, 'Tracy thinks letting in the Syrians was unjust and Astrid thinks refusing to let them in would have been unjust. Two quite different views about justice, indeed two views that look directly opposed to one another.'

'Obviously, we need to work out which view of justice is correct,' said **Temi**. 'I'm not saying it's easy. Clearly, it's not. But what else can we do? People with the responsibility for making decisions have to make them, and they have to give reasons. If they reject claims to the contrary, well, then they have to say why.'

'Politics as a seminar!' said **Kaveh** brightly.

'I'm not that naïve, Kaveh,' said **Temi** quietly. 'I know that policy is not always, if ever, the result of rational deliberation and a careful weighing of ethical alternatives. It's politics. It's a dirty business full of people with egos and interests.'

'Try coming to a faculty meeting,' **I** muttered, not wanting and yet wanting to be heard.

'But,' **Temi** continued, 'since we are trying to figure out the principles that should guide our thinking, and what institutions we need, I don't see that we have any choice but to ask which view of justice is right.'

'I'm with Temi,' said **Antoine**. 'Anything else would be a counsel of despair.'

'I have to admit I feel the same way,' said **Astrid**.

'Me too,' said **Diana**.

'I guess I agree,' said **Tracy** grumpily, 'though I can see you're all going to have a different view of justice. So, yes, me too.'

'What about the last one of you?' **I** said. 'The one busy eating. *Et tu*, Kaveh?'

'Et too? Yes. Delicious grub, boss!' said **Kaveh**, grinning. 'Me too? Not so much. I want to see what Xandros has to say.'

'Seriously, Kaveh?' said **Diana**. 'Do you have a view or are you just trying to be clever?'

'Both,' said **Kaveh**. 'Don't be jealous.'

'Well, Xandros,' said **Temi**, 'do you have something to say? Are we at an impasse?'

'Yes and no,' **I** said, 'yes and no.'

'Xandros!' **the group** exclaimed, almost in unison.

'No, I'm not trying to be evasive,' **I** continued, 'but I think we need to approach this problem carefully. After all, no one said that questions of justice must be straightforward.'

'Fair enough,' said **Diana**, her shoulders slumped in feigned resignation. 'Tell us more, sensei.'

'It's the Xandros swerve,' said **Temi**. 'It gets us every single time!'

The others raised their arms high and began bowing to me in mock adulation.

'Oh, mighty Xandros!' said **Kaveh**, unable to contain his giggles.

'Thank you,' **I** said, 'so pay attention. There are two issues before us. The first is whether considerations of justice can be overridden by other ethical concerns, or we must regard justice as uncompromising—like truth. The second is whether we should approach conflicts over what justice demands by trying to settle what justice truly requires or seek some other form of resolution. My view is that, sometimes, justice must take a back seat or give way to other, more pressing, concerns. And I also think sometimes disagreements about justice cannot be settled, for different conceptions of justice will turn out to be irreconcilable, and the disputing parties will not find the common ground needed to reach agreement on what justice commends. Sometimes, the same conception of justice could yield conflicting conclusions and we have to decide who will receive justice and who will not. Justice cannot bring order into a world which is incapable of sustaining it for more than a moment, if at all.'

'Wow, Xandros!' said **Diana**. 'Look at you, advancing an actual position! No "either or", no "on the one hand but on the other hand", no conceptual mumbo-jumbo. A proper thesis!'

'I speak when I have something to say,' **I** said, to a murmur of groans.

'Me too!' said **Kaveh**, to louder groans.

'Well, as much as I'm pleased to hear you take a position, Xandros, I'm going to ask for a bit more convincing,' said **Temi**. 'You'll need to give us something by way of explanation. For a start, I don't understand how justice can issue conflicting recommendations. If two recommendations conflict, one of them is not a recommendation of justice.'

'An entirely reasonable request,' **I** said, 'so let me try to answer. Imagine the following case. There are two brothers whose father bequeaths to each of them one of his two identical flutes, family heirlooms that have been passed down from father to son for several generations. In a fit of jealousy, their sister steals them and by the time she is persuaded to return the valuables, one of them has been destroyed. Who should get the remaining heirloom? Both brothers have just claims. If one is given the heirloom, the other's just claim must remain unsatisfied.'[3]

'They could share the heirloom,' said **Diana**, 'maybe taking turns.'

3 This is a variant of Amartya Sen's flute example. In *The Idea of Justice* (Cambridge, MA: Harvard University Press, 2009), 12–13, Sen raises the question of which of three claimants to a flute should have it: Anne, who knows how to play the flute; Bob, who is poor and has no toys of his own; or Carla, who made the flute.

'Maybe one will be generous and tell his brother to keep it,' said **Antoine**.

'I'd just toss a coin,' said **Astrid**.

'Give it to the poorer brother,' said **Diana**.

'Have a flute-playing contest and give it to the one who sounds better,' said **Kaveh**.

'All possible solutions,' **I** said, 'but my point is not that such problems can't be resolved. We resolve them all the time, whether personally or institutionally. But sometimes we find solutions that have nothing to do with justice because justice simply cannot be done without also causing injustice. And not because we disagree about what justice requires but because we cannot do what it requires without also violating justice.'

'I agree that there are cases like this,' said **Temi**, 'but I'm not persuaded that unresolvable cases excuse us from thinking harder about the problem and trying to create just outcomes or just institutions wherever we can. Can one flute put an end to justice?'

'The answer, my friend, is blowing in the wind,' said **Kaveh**, 'or should I say, woodwind?'

'It's alright, Kaveh,' said **Diana**, 'don't think twice, and maybe don't speak once.'

'It ain't me, babe,' said **Kaveh**, with a wide smile, 'it's Xandros and all his crazy examples. Times are changin'.'

'Babe?' said **Diana**, 'babe?!'

'Sorry,' said **Kaveh**, 'I couldn't help it.'

'You could have, Kaveh,' **I** said, 'but I'm sure Diana will forgive you. Playing with words and playing with fire are equally dangerous, and it's easy you find yourselves doing both at the same time.'

'Be careful, Kaveh,' said **Diana**.

'And, no, one flute does not put an end to justice, Temi,' **I** said, 'and I wasn't trying to suggest that a single example was enough to settle everything. But there is a problem. A part of it is that demands of justice can conflict.'

'Sometimes,' said **Temi**, a little sourly.

'I can see you're not persuaded,' **I** said, 'so let's consider the problem not of conflicting demands of justice but of disagreements over what justice requires. Astrid's and Tracy's differing views on how to respond to the Syrian refugee crisis is a case in point.'

'Well, one of them is wrong,' said **Temi**. 'We need to figure out who. And why, obviously.'

'Okay,' **I** said, 'let's try. Whom would you side with, and for what reasons?'

'I thought you were going to be doing the theorising, Xandros,' said **Antoine**, 'not us. Aren't you being a bit sneaky, turning things around and asking questions instead of providing answers?'

'Swervability,' said **Kaveh**, 'that's Xandros's superpower!'

'I promise I won't just ask questions and try to trip you all up,' **I** said, 'but this is a dialogue after all, and I've been challenged by Temi, who says we should figure out what justice is. I'm not asking him for a full theory, just whose side he's on and why.'

'That's okay,' said **Temi**, 'that's fair. I'm with Astrid.'

'I knew it!' said **Tracy**, with a scowl.

'I think it would be wrong to turn away someone in distress if you can help at relatively little cost to yourself,' **Temi** continued, 'and the greater their distress, the greater the wrong. Justice entitles us to keep what is ours, but the definition of what is ours is dependent on circumstances. You can't refuse shelter to someone stranded by a hurricane and in danger, even if you're justified in refusing to let in a stranger who just wants to take a nap because he's tired. Rights, including property rights, are conditional. And you definitely don't have the right to stop other people helping those in distress. If you don't want to house a Syrian refugee, fine, but it would be unjust to prevent your neighbour from doing so.'

'That would be fine if letting someone into your house didn't mean letting them into the country,' said **Tracy**, 'but it does. It means letting them use roads and public parks. It means letting them access public transport and public health care. It means letting them take jobs or welfare benefits, and either way it means citizens losing jobs or wages or paying higher taxes. That's not just.'

'We could let refugees work and make them pay higher taxes,' said **Kaveh** helpfully. 'Win-win.'

'And our jobs?' said **Tracy**, looking incredulous.

'They're not our jobs,' said **Kaveh**, with a grin. 'What are you? Some kind of socialist? Jobs are created by people who want to hire other people. They're not obliged to hire anyone. Why would you force them to hire someone they don't prefer? Surely, that's unjust.'

'Justice means putting your own people first,' **Tracy** retorted. 'Not strangers!'

'We'll make friends with them,' said **Kaveh**. 'They won't be strangers for long. And some of "our" people, well, they're a little strange to say the least.'

'Yeah, Kaveh' said **Diana**, 'like you.'

'You're very kind,' said **Kaveh**, 'thank you. That's probably the nicest thing you've ever said to me.'

'What's your ideal of justice then, Kaveh,' said **Antoine**. 'I mean, I'm actually a bit sympathetic to what you said, but what's the general theory behind it?'

'I don't have a general theory,' said **Kaveh**, 'but I like Amartya Sen's view that we shouldn't be looking for an ideal to guide us. He's against transcendental theories and I am too. We don't need to imagine a perfect world in order to ask what a better one would look like, and we don't need an ideal of justice to figure out what justice requires.'

'Is this some sort of joke?' said **Diana**, smiling. 'I can't believe you said something serious.'

'Who is this impostor,' said **Astrid**, 'and what have you done with Kaveh?'

'And whatever you've done with him, thank you!' said **Temi**, laughing.

'Yes, but I still don't know what Kaveh means,' said **Antoine**. 'Can you explain, whoever you are, just what this Sen view is all about?'

'Er, gosh,' said **Kaveh**, 'I don't really have Sen at my fingertips. Maybe some dessert would help, but I can't promise. Xandros? Help?'

'Have some dessert, everyone,' **I** said. 'It's good. And I'll try to fill you in on Sen's view.'

'Is that your view?' asked **Temi**.

'No,' **I** said, 'but it's an important view, and engaging with Sen is always a good idea, since there are few people around who are smarter.'

'And an immigrant,' said **Kaveh** helpfully.

'They seem to be everywhere,' said **Diana**.

'Immigrants. They get the job done,' said **Kaveh**.

'Thank you, Mr Miranda,' **I** said, 'but let's turn to Sen's ideas rather than his origins. He has a theory of justice, like everyone seems to have these days, but he thinks that we don't need to come up with transcendental theories the way people like John Rawls and Ronald Dworkin have in order to make judgments about justice.'

'Oh, tell us more, Socrates, I mean, Xandros,' said **Diana**, fluttering her eyelashes.

'Very funny,' **I** said, 'but before I go further, can any of you summarize some of the prominent theories Sen wants to reject?'

'Well, Rawls's theory, of course,' said **Temi**, 'which tries to identify the principles of a just society. In his view, those principles are ones that would be settled upon by people in an Original Position, thinking behind a Veil of Ignorance about their own identities. He concludes that they would choose "justice as fairness", which prescribes a principle of the priority of some basic liberties that cannot be violated no matter what, and a subordinate principle that says institutions should be arranged so that the least advantaged are better off than they would be under any other arrangement.'[4]

4 Rawls's two principles of justice as set out in *A Theory of Justice*, 266: 'First: each person to have an equal right to the most extensive scheme of equal basic liberties compatible with a similar scheme of liberties for others. Second: social and economic inequalities are to be arranged so that they are both (a) to the greatest benefit to the least advantaged, consistent with the just savings principle, and (b) attached to positions and offices open to all under conditions of fair equality of opportunity.'.

'Good,' **I** said, 'though there's more to the second principle, which comes in two parts. Still, we needn't go into that for today's purposes. Who else?'

'Well, Nozick's view, obviously,' said **Kaveh**, 'which says really nice things about Rawls's theory and then totally trashes it.'

'A bit of an exaggeration,' **I** said, 'but go on.'

'Well, Nozick thinks people have rights,' **Kaveh** continued, 'though he never says exactly what they are or where they come from. Anyway, he thinks it's wrong to violate their rights, which generally means not interfering with them physically—violating their freedom—and not taking their stuff—their property. Doing anything that violates their rights is unjust, so you can only take from them with their consent. Any distribution of property is just if it's the outcome of voluntary exchanges, and it would be unjust to try to change the pattern of distribution by taking from some to give to others. It's okay if some people are rich and others poor if there was no injustice committed in the process, though he agrees that in reality there was lots of injustice, so we also need a principle of rectification of injustice.'[5]

'Very succinct, Kaveh,' **I** said. 'Nice job.'

'It's what I do,' said **Kaveh**.

'Sure it is,' **I** replied, 'sure it is. Anybody else we should consider?'

'What about Ronald Dworkin?' said **Antoine**. 'I think he has a theory of justice too.'[6]

'Go for it,' **I** said.

'Well, he believes that everybody is entitled to equal concern and respect,' said **Antoine**, 'and that means that everything should be distributed so we have equality of resources, so that if we are the victims of brute bad luck—like being disabled, whether by birth or accident—society will make sure you have what you need to live a good life. Though if you suffer because of your own bad choices, that's on you.'

5 Robert Nozick, *Anarchy, State, and Utopia* (Oxford: Blackwell, 1974).

6 Ronald Dworkin, *Sovereign Virtue: The Theory and Practice of Equality* (Cambridge, MA: Harvard University Press, 2002).

'It's a luck-egalitarian theory,' said **Astrid** helpfully.

'Yes,' said **Antoine**, 'yes, and Professor G.A. Cohen also advocates something like this, only I think he thinks everybody should get the same income after we tax everybody at 100%.'[7]

'Yeah, that'll work,' said **Kaveh** dryly, 'because everyone's going to work even harder when they know all their earnings are taken away and that they'll get back however much the government decides to give them.'

'I think it could work,' said **Antoine**. 'There's a book by a guy called Carens that works it all out, and Cohen cites it.'[8]

'Rich people will still work,' said **Temi**, 'because they like the thrill of success. After a while, money stops being a motivator.'

'Yes,' said **Kaveh**, 'but everyone with a boring job will quit and start businesses selling their poems or making stuff no one wants but is fun to make.'[9]

'So?' said **Antoine**. 'Why not?'

'Because we're already drowning in bad poetry,' said **Kaveh**, 'and we'll probably also get a lot more articles by Xandros on the meaning of meaning or the concept of a concept or analyzing analyzing, and we'll all die of starvation.'

'More of my baclava, Kaveh?' **I** said.

'Sorry, boss,' **Kaveh** said, 'got a bit carried away.'

'Not for the first time,' **I** said, 'and probably not the last. But no matter. Let's return to the issue at hand. So, we have all these theories of justice. What shall we do to address the immigration question?'

'Aren't we forgetting Michael Walzer,' said **Astrid**. 'I mean, he actually addresses the immigration issue in his book, doesn't he?

7 G.A. Cohen, *Rescuing Justice and Equality* (Cambridge, MA: Harvard University Press, 2008). See also Cohen, *If You're an Egalitarian How Come You're So Rich* (Cambridge, UK: Cambridge University Press, 2000).

8 Joseph Carens, *Equality, Moral Incentives, and the Market: An Essay in Utopian Politico-Economic Theory* (Chicago: Chicago University Press, 1981).

9 See Chandran Kukathas, 'The Labour Theory of Justice', in Alexander Kaufmann (ed.), *Distributive Justice and Access to Advantage: G.A. Cohen's Egalitarianism* (Cambridge, UK: Cambridge University Press, 2014), 235–248.

I don't think Cohen and Dworkin even mention the word. I'm not even sure Sen does, does he? Does Rawls? Nozick?'

'The more theories, the merrier,' **I** said, 'and yes, Rawls does talk about immigration briefly, and we should consider his view. Walzer's too.'

'You're sneaky, Xandros,' said **Diana**. 'You're back to your old tricks, turning everything back on us with your questions. What's your theory of justice?'

'I don't have one,' **I** said.

'Are you working on one?' said **Antoine**. 'When do we get to hear it?'

'I'm not,' **I** said, 'so the soonest you can hear it is "never". Is "never" good for you? Because it works for me.'

'We're going to get you, Xandros,' said **Diana**, trying to sound menacing. 'You're going to tell us what you think if it's the last thing you do.'

'Of course,' **I** said, 'but let's get back to Sen's view first, since you asked for my views on that.'

'Fine,' said **Diana**, folding her arms and straining to look cross, 'fine.'

'As has already been noted,' **I** continued, 'Sen has it in for what he calls transcendental theories of justice, which he thinks are unnecessary and unhelpful. He says they don't give us the guidance they're meant to, largely because we don't need to know what justice is ideally in order to work out what justice requires in any specific context. It's as if these theorists believe that if we're trying to decide if one mountain is higher than another the way to the answer is to ask first how high the highest mountain is anywhere. I think he's right.'

'So, you're a Senian,' said **Kaveh**, 'and now we know.'

'Well, no, I'm not,' **I** said, 'not really.'[10]

'You're as slippery as an eel,' said **Diana**. 'It would be easier to pin down a raindrop. Do you wrestle?'

10 See Chandran Kukathas, 'On Sen on Comparative Justice', *Critical Review of International Social and Political Philosophy*, 16 (2), 2013, 196–204.

'Only with philosophical puzzles,' **I** said, 'and sometimes my conscience. But I can tell you why I'm not a Senian. In the end, he too wants a theory of justice, only he calls it a comparative theory. Some think it's not that different in nature from the transcendental theories he criticizes. I don't think a comparative theory is really possible—at least, if one wants something that's genuinely different from a transcendental theory.'

'So, you agree with Sen that we shouldn't be looking for transcendental theories,' said **Antoine**.

'Yes,' **I** said.

'But you don't think he has supplied an alternative.' said **Temi**. 'Right?'

'Not in the form of a theory of comparative justice,' **I** said, 'though I like a lot of what he's said.'

'What do you like, then?' asked **Diana**.

'Okay,' **I** said, 'I like the view that we should focus less on an imaginary just world and more on the concerns that engage people, questions about social conditions that need remedying—poverty, hunger, arbitrary incarceration, torture—though I'm not sure we always need to use the language of justice. I also like the idea that we make comparative judgments, say by concluding that a world without slavery is better than a world with slavery. We can "rank order" alternatives, to use Sen's terminology. But he's also insistent that we cannot rank order everything, so while we can say that a society without slavery is better than a society with it, and that a society without hunger or poverty is better than one with these conditions, we can't readily say that a society without slavery is better than a society without hunger or poverty.'

'Couldn't we do this by using a common measure?' said **Astrid**. 'Don't utilitarians do just that? Whatever produces the most utility is just.'

'We could,' **I** said, 'but I'm not sure how convincing it is, even if utilitarians thought they had a theory of justice.'

'What do you mean?' asked **Temi**. 'Doesn't Rawls include utilitarianism as one of the theories of justice for us to consider, even if he rejects it?'

'I'm not sure that I'd consider utilitarianism a theory of justice,' **I** said, 'though I agree that's it's a variety of ethical theory. The utilitarian philosopher J.J.C. Smart once began a seminar presentation in a series on theories of justice by saying "utilitarians don't really have a theory of justice, so I'm just going to tell jokes". And he did.'[11]

'Is that true?' said **Antoine**.

'Yes, it is,' **I** answered. 'He did say that, and it's true that utilitarians have no theory of justice. Their theory is that you should do whatever maximizes utility, so if injustice achieves that, that's what you should do, though you should also take into account whether committing injustice ends up reducing utility overall if it leads people to behave badly by undermining morality.'

'Surely, that's a kind of theory of justice,' said **Tracy**, who'd been rather silent for a while. 'It sounds very practical.'

'It is,' **I** said, 'though I'm not sure why you need to invoke the concept of justice here, except for, well, utilitarian reasons. In any case, Sen doesn't think we can find a metric or measure to reduce all judgments of value to some common denominator, so all our comparative judgments are basically one-on-one comparisons—pairwise comparisons, if you like.'

'Can we say a society with immigration control is better than one without?' said **Kaveh**, smirking.

'Yes, Xandros,' said **Diana** excitedly, 'can we? Straight answer, please. And nice move, Kaveh!'

'Well, it all depends on what you mean by society,' **I** said, causing a mild uproar.

'Xandros! Come on!' said **Diana**, genuinely exasperated.

'We're caught in an endless loop,' said **Temi**.

'Loops don't have ends,' **I** said.

'There you go again,' said **Astrid**. 'Now we're going to go round and round discussing the concept of a loop.'

11 Personal recollection of a talk given by Professor Smart at the Australian National University circa 1980 in a seminar series on justice, hosted by Eugene Kamenka.

'Until we die,' said **Diana**.

'Like a morbidius loop,' said **Kaveh**.

'We want to break free,' said **Antoine**, 'we want to break free.'

'Don't worry,' **I** said, 'life goes on. As I said earlier, we will come full circle and return to the beginning and then know it for the first time.'

'Aaaargh!' said **Diana**.

'Ditto,' said **Antoine**.

'You've beaten us,' said **Astrid**.

'That's his tactic,' said **Tracy**. 'He looks like he's going to answer, then he asks a question that's so exasperating that it makes you want to leave in a huff.'

'For once, we agree, Trace,' said **Temi**. 'You feel our pain.'

'Actually, no,' said **Tracy**, laughing. 'I'm rather enjoying it, seeing you guys squirm instead of me.'

'Oh, don't be such snowflakes,' **I** said. 'Philosophy is a blood sport, so just toughen up. We're on a journey. Just try to keep up. We will reach our destination.'

'Can a journey be a blood sport, Xandros,' said **Kaveh**, 'or are you mixing your metaphors? I don't think a blood sport is usually a journey, conceptually speaking.'

'Go Kaveh!' said **Antoine**, and the rest of the group fell into a fit of giggles.

'Okay,' **I** said, 'you got me. Shall we get back to the question at hand?'

'Why not?' said **Astrid**. 'We've come this far. And you did cook.'

'Right,' **I** said. 'You've asked if a society without immigration control is better than one with, and I've said it all depends on what you mean by society. I say this because immigration controls exist in all sorts of contexts and take a variety of forms. For example, South Africa under apartheid practised a form of immigration control when it restricted the movement of black people into white areas. The government wanted and couldn't do without black African labour but didn't want racial mixing or competition with the white workforce. It thought this was better for South Africa. But that surely depends on what you mean by South Africa. It's one thing if you mean South African whites, quite another if you mean all South Africans.'

'It has to mean all South Africans,' said **Diana**. 'Anything else would be wrong. Unjust!'

'My sentiments precisely,' **I** said, 'but not those of a good many South Africans at the time and indeed many people around the world. Still, let me give you another example. Take the European Union. If we ask if a society without immigration controls is better than one with, what is the relevant society here? Is it the whole of the EU? Or Europe as a whole? Or each country? What are we comparing? Or what should we be comparing? And what is the basis for comparison?'

'A country, or a union of countries, or a world, without immigration controls is better than any of these things with immigration controls,' said **Diana** firmly, 'and it's better because it would be more just.'

'Let's leave justice to one side for the moment,' **I** said, 'since we're trying to settle a different question right now, the question of whether we can make comparative judgments. I think we can, but I don't think it's always straightforward. Few would disagree that a world without hunger is better than a world with. We have a single measure: hunger. And less is better than more. That a world without slavery is better than one with slaves is also fairly easy to defend today, though slavery persists. There is a single measure: freedom, understood in a particular way. I'm simplifying, of course, since there have been many kinds of slavery, but I think you get the point. But if we ask whether a society is better without immigration controls, I don't think we have a single measure we're using to make a comparative judgment. The obvious bad that comes with immigration control is the loss of freedom of those who are stopped from moving or working or hiring others, but the trade-off for many is the preservation of social solidarity or national identity. And which identity we're talking about depends on whether we're talking about a nation, or an interstate federation like the EU or a region like Europe, or another kind of grouping altogether.'

'But what's your view, Xandros,' said **Temi**, 'since you don't seem to think much of anyone's solutions? And don't give us the famous Xandros swerve.'

'Yes,' said **Astrid**, 'no swerving!'

'Yes,' said **Antoine**, 'do you prefer freedom or national solidarity?'

'I prefer freedom,' **I** said.

'What?' said **Diana**. 'I mean, seriously, you just gave us a straight answer.'

'You did,' said **Antoine**. 'You said you prefer freedom. You didn't say, "it depends on what you mean by freedom," or ask, "what do you mean by national solidarity," or anything!'

'Are you feeling okay, boss?' said **Temi**. 'You look like you might be running a fever. Should we call a doctor?'

'I am a doctor,' **I** said, 'but thank you all for your concern. I'm just fine. And you're right, we do need to ask what we mean by freedom, and what we mean by national solidarity for that matter, but I'm fairly clear about what I think on this issue. So, you're welcome.'

'So, let me see if we have this right,' said **Diana**. 'You like freedom, you're a bit indifferent to justice, and you don't like national solidarity. Is that right? Are you some kind of anarchist?'

'How can you not value national solidarity?' said **Tracy**, sounding a little troubled. 'I mean, aren't you a patriot or just a little bit of a patriot? You can't have justice, or freedom, without order. That's what the state gives us, but it works only if people are loyal citizens.'

'I think I agree with Tracy,' said **Temi**, 'at least I do a little bit. I'm not saying that other people don't matter, but we have to privilege our own at least to some degree, surely? I guess that's why I'm a Rawlsian, isn't it? I think we have to figure out what's just for our own society, and part of justice is freedom. And equality.'

'I'm in agreement too,' said **Antoine**, 'though I'm more with Michael Walzer than Rawls. I mean, we should care about the poor, but the first question is the question of membership. Solidarity before philosophy! Democracy before philosophy!!'

'I guess I think the same way,' said **Astrid**, 'though saying it out loud is a little scary.'

'It definitely is,' said **Diana**, 'definitely.'

'I can't believe what I'm hearing,' said **Tracy**. 'You guys sound like me!'

'That's why it's scary,' said **Temi**, laughing.

'I mean, you were all ready to defend letting in a million refugees, and now you say you think national solidarity matters most,' said **Tracy**, 'which makes me think you're all hopelessly confused. Seriously confused!'

'Xandros to the rescue!' said **Kaveh**, brandishing a rolled date like a sword and scattering flecks of pistachio around the room.

'I fear that you're all beyond rescue,' **I** said, 'but let me at least offer you a few insights. I doubt that they'll provide you with much comfort, but at least you'll be less ignorant.'

'Xandros!' exclaimed **Diana**. 'Very harsh! Even for you.'

'Sorry,' **I** said. 'Just trying to toughen you all up a little, philosophically speaking.'

'Well, that's all right then,' said **Temi**, rolling his eyes. 'Enlighten us, boss.'

'Let's turn out attention to Messrs Rawls and Walzer, shall we?' **I** said. 'They're both what we might call liberal nationalists, though they theorize in quite different ways. Both are somewhat wary of immigration, and both see national solidarity as important. Both think justice is very important, though they think about justice in rather different ways. Perhaps we should treat them in turn.'

'In turn's good,' said **Kaveh**. 'Go for it.'

'Thank you,' **I** said. 'Let's start with Professor Rawls, who takes the view that in a world of just and decent societies there would be no need for immigration, since no one would have any reason to move.'[12]

'Really?' said **Astrid**. 'Did he really think that? How odd!'

12 John Rawls, *The Law of Peoples with 'The Idea of Public Reason Revisited'* (Cambridge, MA: Harvard University Press, 2002), 39ff.

'Perhaps it depends on what you mean by immigration,' said **Diana**, with a grin, before she broke into a fit of giggles.

'It does,' **I** said, 'though Rawls doesn't explain what he means by it.'

'Bad Professor Rawls,' said **Kaveh**.

'Indeed,' **I** said, 'but we're here to learn, not judge.' This was greeted by guffaws of laughter, but **I** continued undeterred. 'Rawls thinks that a people has at least a qualified right to restrict immigration to protect its constitutional principles and political culture. But once we have a world of liberal and decent peoples, in what he calls a realistic utopia, there would be no need for such restrictions as there would be no need for people to move, since factors such as poverty and persecution that push them to do so will have been eliminated.'

'That sounds a little optimistic,' said **Tracy**. 'I mean, I agree about people having the right to protect their cultures and principles, but I rather doubt that there will come a time when we've eliminated all the push factors, or the pull factors for that matter. People will want to move from worse places to better ones.'

'It does seem like rather an unrealistic utopia,' said **Antoine**, 'though utopias aren't meant to be realistic, are they?'

'In that case, we might be waiting rather a long time for utopia to arrive,' **I** said, 'but till it does, Rawls says, the territory of a people is their asset, and they have the right and responsibility to manage it well, so it has the capacity to support them in perpetuity.'

'In perpetuity is a long time,' said **Astrid**, 'isn't it?

'It is,' **I** said.

'Like the amount of time it takes you to grade our term papers?' said **Diana**.

'Not as long as that, surely!' said **Temi**, with a grin.

'Given how difficult they are to understand, even when they're submitted on time, you're lucky to get them back at all,' **I** said, 'but we're not here to discuss your deficiencies.'

'You're on fire today, Xandros,' **Diana** said with a laugh.

'Back to Rawls,' **I** said. 'He does say "in perpetuity". He thinks the people itself as politically organized is the agent responsible for the husbandry of the territory and government is the agent of the people that must manage the territory, the size of the population, and the environmental integrity of the land.[13] We should think of countries as closed societies and that the role of its institutions is to maintain stability in long-run equilibrium.'

'What?' said **Kaveh**. 'Is there a translation?'

'Yes,' **I** said. 'It means that since the long run means generations into the future, what must be kept stable and constant are the institutions that make up the political society, whose resources and population need to be managed to ensure that perpetuity.'

'That seems reasonable enough,' said **Tracy**, 'though I never thought I'd say that about Rawls. I think I agree with him.'

'He sounds like a nationalist,' said **Astrid**, 'though I never really pictured him as one.'

'He's not really,' said **Temi**, 'not really, surely?'

'Just a little bit, maybe?' said **Antoine**.

'Just a little bit pregnant?' said **Diana**.

'He's a methodological nationalist!' said **Kaveh** triumphantly. 'That's it!'

'That's not a real thing,' said **Diana**. 'Can you be serious for a minute, Kaveh?'

'Actually, that's not a bad description,' **I** said. 'In building his theory of justice, Rawls does say that we need to assume a closed society. What he says about immigration is consistent with this, even though now he's presenting not a theoretical abstraction in the form of a conception of justice but a general account of how we should view a society. We should see the world as made up of separate nations, each responsible for its own affairs.'

'I like it,' said **Tracy**.

'I have a sneaking suspicion you don't, Xandros,' said **Temi**, 'do you?'

13 *Law of Peoples*, 8.

'It depends on what you mean by "like",' **I** said.

'Oh, for the love of Hobbes!' said **Diana**. 'I don't believe it! Do you not know what "like" means? Like it means, like, like!'

'Just kidding,' **I** said, 'just kidding! But you have to admit I got you!'

'Nice one, Xandros,' said **Kaveh**. 'Epic!'

'Okay, okay,' **I** said, 'I'll stop tormenting you. You're right, I don't like Rawls's view here. And I'm going to tell you why.'

'This had better be good,' said **Tracy**, 'and not just a bunch of distinctions to distract us. We live in a world of states. We belong to countries. We form groups. We're not isolated, atomistic, individuals. People see peoples, but I think maybe you see only atoms.'

'People who see peoples are the luckiest people in the world,' said **Kaveh**, with a grin.

'You're right, of course, Tracy,' **I** said, ignoring Kaveh altogether. 'We do live in groups, and in states, though I do also think that we're made up of atoms—purposeless bits of stuff that have come together at random to create that unfathomable thing that is human consciousness. But we don't see atoms, we see people and things, so we had better play the game by engaging with each other as individuals who are shaped by others, by groups, and by all our histories. They're real, even if only in the sense that they're real enough.'

'You sound like Rawls,' said **Temi**, 'political not metaphysical, but with a little metaphysics all the same.'[14]

'Maybe,' **I** said, 'but let me explain why I'm not with Rawls, least of all on the immigration question.'

'At last!' said **Diana**.

'Rawls wants us to think about the world as made up of more or less closed, territorially based, societies that are self-sufficient,' **I** said, 'and to regard them as occupied by peoples who collectively possess and are responsible for managing their lands and populations "in

14 John Rawls insisted that his political philosophy did not depend on any controversial metaphysical theses. See Rawls, 'Justice as Fairness: Political Not Metaphysical', *Philosophy and Public Affairs*, 14 (3), 1985, 223–251.

perpetuity". He thinks this is the starting point for reflecting on the principles of justice that should govern them, but he also thinks that this is what we should try to perpetuate in the real world, in his ideal real world. I think all the assumptions he's made ought to be rejected.'[15]

'That's a bit bold, Xandros,' said **Temi**. 'Do you really mean to reject all these assumptions? They sound pretty commonsensical to me.'

'Yes,' said **Antoine**, 'at least mostly. I think. Probably. Though I'm not sure.'

'Nicely put, Antoine,' said **Kaveh**. 'Very pithy.'

'Shut up,' said **Antoine**, giggling, and shaking his fist at Kaveh in mock aggression.

'Have some halva, Kaveh,' **I** said, smiling, 'and listen. To begin with, societies are never closed, though some are open or closed to varying degrees. They're open to people everywhere to some extent, whether to traders, or itinerants, or immigrants, or, more abstractly, to ideas, which might be communicated without anyone crossing a boundary or sending a physical product, especially nowadays when electronic traffic dwarfs every other form of engagement between people.'

'Tell us about the old days when you were young, Xandros,' said **Diana** mischievously. 'You know, when you corresponded by snail and told stories by the fireside for entertainment.'

'Have some halva,' **I** said. 'I think there's some in the garage. Meanwhile, I'll explain for those who care why it's important not to start by assuming closed societies. I'm going to start by saying something about Aristotle.'

'I'm definitely going in search of halva,' said **Diana**. 'Not Aristotle, please!'

'I'll help,' said **Temi**. 'We all will. But you keep going, Xandros.'

15 Chandran Kukathas, 'Immigration and Liberal Freedom', in Duncan Ivison (ed.), *Research Handbook on Liberalism* (Cheltenham: Edward Elgar, 2024), 210–224.

'Very funny,' **I** said, 'but you're in for a treat. And it's not the halva.'

'Epic!' said **Kaveh**.

'Quite,' **I** said. 'So listen. Aristotle says that the polis, or what some misleadingly call the state, is a kind of association. All associations, he says, aim at some good.[16] He goes on to suggest that "the association which is the most sovereign of all and embraces all the others aims highest, that is, at the most sovereign of all good."[17] This is what the polis amounts to: an association that embraces all other associations in order to achieve the highest good. The first associations are the natural associations between male and female and between master and slave.[18] Out of these two arises the association that is the household, whose purpose is to serve the everyday needs of these original associations.'[19]

'Okay,' said **Diana**, 'so where are we going with this?'

'Ah,' **I** said, 'but the polis, Aristotle tells us, is a special form of association. It is the complete association, made up of several villages, and one that reaches the limit of total self-sufficiency. Total self-sufficiency! For Aristotle, the polis is the end to which all other associations tend, and its purpose or point is the achievement of what is best, which is self-sufficiency.'

'Still not seeing it, Xandros,' said **Diana**.

'Let me explain,' **I** said. 'The polis, on this view, is the end to which all other associations tend. Now the polis, Aristotle says, is "a plurality of some sort",[20] consisting of persons who differ in type. Like Rawls, he thinks political society is not an alliance of people who are alike but an association of people who are different. It is not something that exhibits the unity of a household, but it is a kind of unity that arises out of the combination of diverse persons and diverse households. The question is, how much unity

16 Aristotle, *Politics* (translated by T.A. Sinclair, revised and edited by Trevor J. Saunders, London: Penguin, 1981), I i, 1252a1–7.

17 *Politics* I i, 1252a1–7.

18 *Politics* I ii, 1252a24–39.

19 *Politics* I ii, 1252b9–15.

20 Politics II ii, 1261a10–22.

should political society possess? Aristotle's answer is that it should possess as much unity as is necessary for self-sufficiency—no more and no less.[21] For example, it needs to be united inasmuch as all the citizens share a common territory but not so united that they all share each other's wives, children, and possessions.'[22]

'Seriously?' said **Astrid**.

'Sorry,' I said. 'People in the past were not as gender-sensitive or as nice as we are today. But his point is this: the self-sufficiency in question, here, is the self-sufficiency of the association called the polis. It is the level of association that is most capable of being self-sustaining or self-perpetuating—more so than is an individual on his own, more so than a household, which has a greater capacity for self-sufficiency than an individual. The polis, on this understanding, is the highest form of human association, for it is the only form that is capable of standing on its own. Neither individuals nor households—nor even villages—can sustain themselves without the cooperation of others. The polis, however, can sustain itself without the cooperation of other associations and has no need of being subsumed by other forms of organization in the way that it subsumes the associations that comprise it.'

'And we should care about Aristotle's view why?' said **Diana**.

'Because Rawls's view is just like this,' **I** said. 'Well, almost. Without wishing to overstate the similarities between Rawls and Aristotle, not least because ancient Greece was a slave society and Aristotle defended it as one that was rightly divided into citizens and other subordinate categories of person in a way Rawls could never contemplate, they hold in common an understanding of political society as bounded by territory and membership and self-sufficient because capable of standing on its own. By this they mean not simply that it is self-sufficient in material goods. Indeed, a society might not be so to the extent that it cannot produce on

21 *Politics* II ii, 1261a6–15.

22 *Politics* II i, 1260b36–1261a9. (The target of this observation is Plato's understanding of unity and his argument for the elimination of the family among rulers in the *Republic*.).

its own all the things its members might want. The point is rather that it is capable of sustaining a kind of identity now and into the future. Both Rawls and Aristotle think that political society is needed not just for life but for the good life. Households and civil society will not suffice for this—persons need to be part of something greater to make the good life or a complete life possible!'

'You seem to be getting a little excited, Xandros,' said **Kaveh**, 'and you're scaring us.'

'Don't you see?' **I** said. 'For Rawls, as it was for Aristotle, a political society is not something that comes into existence because individuals choose to remain in or to form it, in order better to pursue their own ends, but rather an association that makes possible meaningful lives for persons who, only within it, can relate to one another as individuals.'

'Sounds good to me,' said **Tracy**. 'We have to be part of something bigger than ourselves.'

'Chain yourself to a building,' said **Kaveh**. 'That'd work.'

'Thank you, Kaveh,' **I** said. 'But moving on, what makes things difficult is the persistence of differences in the ways in which people understand the ethical ideas that underpin social relations—ideas such as freedom and equality, for example. In the United States, Rawls says, these differences have been quite stark: the pro-slavery South understood freedom as something to be accorded only to the white population, and equality as something that could not be extended to inferior races. Finding a way of reconciling such differences was, for him, crucial to preserving that which was most needed to enable people to live complete or meaningful lives: political society.'

'What could be wrong with that?' said **Tracy**.

'Well, if that is the way one looks at the world, it is difficult to see how the figure of the immigrant can be incorporated,' **I** said. 'And Rawls can't, in my view.'

'Again, what's wrong with that?' said **Tracy**.

'Wasn't Aristotle an immigrant?' said **Astrid**. 'I'm sure he was.'

'Interestingly enough, he was,' **I** said. 'He was a metic, not a full citizen of Athens, so there's a certain irony in his account of the importance of membership of the polis, since he did not possess all the rights the Athenians did.'

'You mean, the top Athenian men,' said **Diana**, 'not the women or the slaves.'

'Yes,' **I** said, 'Aristotle was someone who lived most of his life as a resident alien, in places in which he was not a citizen, and from time to time in Athens, which he had to leave in periods of strife between the city and his native Macedon. He was not a slave, but he could not take part in political life, or indeed, own property, as could well-born Athenians.'

'Cool,' said **Antoine**, 'but I'm not sure about where all this is leading.'

'You distracted me,' **I** said, 'though without taking me too far astray. I think Rawls and Aristotle go wrong in trying to present political society as a self-sufficient and united whole. It's not that they don't recognize differences within society. Aristotle famously criticizes Plato for not appreciating that in order to work any society must be composed of different kinds of people. And Rawls thinks people need to come to a deep shared understanding that allows them to reconcile themselves to one another despite their differences. But societies are not and cannot be self-sufficient—not once they are big enough to depend on a division of labour and start to engage in trade. Once that happens, they'll be filled with all sorts of people, including immigrants, or people who are regarded as outsiders. Rawls's ideal society is filled only with members.'

'Like Aristotle's,' said **Astrid**.

'Funnily enough, no,' **I** said, 'because Aristotle actually thinks that metics, along with other foreigners and slaves, are economically indispensable to a city.[23] Self-sufficiency depends on the existence of non-citizens—to do the things citizens can't or don't want to do. But they're not members and generally don't have a path to membership. A resident foreigner might be needed but has no status and is not someone who has any right to honours.'[24]

23 *Politics* 1326a18–20.
24 *Politics*, 1278a37–39.

'And Rawls?' said **Astrid**.

'His ideal world has no immigrants or foreigners,' **I** said, 'since no one would have reason to move. Very different from Aristotle, who accepted that the ideal polis would still contain foreigners. He thought they were economically needed. And he seems to have had no trouble accepting that they would be politically excluded.'

'I think I prefer Rawls's view,' said **Antoine**. 'I don't like the idea of a country with a lot of second-class citizens.'

'I agree,' said **Temi**. 'It's one thing for the ancient Greeks to have done it, excluding women and slaves too, but this sort of thing has no place in modern society.'

'Are you so sure about that,' **I** said. 'After all, how many of you here as students have full political rights? Or a pathway to citizenship. All I have is a Green Card.'

'I'd kill for a Green Card,' said **Kaveh**. 'Though only someone who was really bad.'

'Still not sure I'm getting your point, Xandros,' said **Diana**. 'Are you trying to defend Aristotle? It doesn't sound like you're defending Rawls.'

'Neither,' **I** said. 'I'm trying to criticize them both for a view they hold in common, though each also holds views to which I'm sympathetic.'

'What do you like about Rawls's view?' said **Astrid**.

'The rejection of slavery,' **I** said. 'I start from the assumption of human equality and, like Rawls, interpret that in a way that makes slavery indefensible.'

'Big call, Xandros,' said **Tracy**, 'going out on a limb like that.'

'Yeah,' said **Diana**, 'you radical, you!'

'Mock me all you wish,' **I** said, 'but you wanted to know where I disagreed with Aristotle and agreed with Rawls. And I don't think this is a trivial matter just because we're all so confident of our virtue. It's not that long ago that slavery was formally abolished, and I'm not so sure there aren't some people who'd welcome it back.'

'Actually, I went to one of the old slave plantations in Louisiana as a tourist last year,' said **Diana**, 'and the guide told me not to believe all those liberals up north because the slaves were happy.'

'Seriously?' said **Antoine**.

'Seriously,' said **Diana**. 'My husband and I felt very awkward.'

'Thanks for sharing that,' **I** said. 'Rawls takes this matter seriously, and I'm with him on this commitment, even though there are serious critiques questioning whether his theory is able to escape the racial assumptions he rejects.[25] I am not so happy, however, with his assumption that political society must be understood as self-sufficient. Especially since his understanding of self-sufficiency seems to require economic self-sufficiency.'

'Does he really think a country can be self-sufficient, economically speaking?' said **Astrid**.

'Well, to the extent that he thinks that the context of justice is the basic structure of society,' **I** continued, 'and society is to be viewed as "a fair system of cooperation over time, from one generation to the next,"[26] yes, he does. In such a society, he says, the people are jointly responsible for its economic productivity and should arrange their institutions to ensure basic freedom and a fair distribution of their joint product. That means making sure that the rules ensure that the least advantaged are taken care of but also that the most productive have an incentive to produce enough so the living standards of all are lifted.'

'Sounds like trickle-down economics to me,' said **Antoine**, 'and I'm not sure that's okay.'

'That's a nice criticism,' **I** said, 'but Nozick has a better one. If the social product is really joint, how do we know who was the greater contributor? We could give the better off a larger share to incentivise them, but how do we know which contributors make the difference that gives us greater productivity?'

'Nice,' said **Antoine**, 'nice.'

'Ah, but I have an even deeper criticism,' **I** said.

'Gosh, is that the time?' said **Temi**. 'Shouldn't we be leaving?'

'Listen,' **I** said, 'and prepare to be amazed.'

'Really?' said **Diana**. 'Amazed?'

'Yes, '**I** said, 'and this will get us to what I'm trying to tell you all. You see, Rawls and others who buy into his intuitions assume that

25 See Charles Mills, *The Racial Contract* (Ithaca: Cornell University Press, 1997).
26 Rawls, *Political Liberalism*, 1996, 15.

the world is divided into separate, closed, self-sufficient systems of cooperation. But that just isn't so. There is social cooperation, but it takes place both within and across national boundaries. There is no self-sufficiency. We are interdependent, not just as individuals but also as groups, communities, and countries.'

'But surely a society is an ongoing system of cooperation, like Rawls says,' said **Temi**. 'What else could it be?'

'A society is not an ongoing system or scheme of cooperation,' **I** said. 'Social cooperation is ongoing, and it takes place within and across and among societies.'

'But what is a state if not a cooperative venture?' said **Antoine**.

'That's a good question,' **I** said, 'and one we struggled with a few weeks ago. There's no doubt that many cooperative ventures are initiated by governments, and political agents within the state, just as there are many others that involve states and other parties. These include economic ventures as well as political ones, not to mention cultural, scientific research, and humanitarian ventures. But these are all shifting involvements, and the state itself is often transformed in the process, some more regularly or dramatically than others.'

'Surely, you don't mean that,' said **Tracy**. 'We have to hold the state constant. It's the stable entity around which we think about all the questions we're trying to address. I think you're imagining the world to be more anarchic than it really is. Surely!'

'We don't have to see the world as anarchic,' **I** said, 'just in flux. But I don't want to deny the point you're making altogether. Constancy and change are matters of degree, and we understand some things to be stable or constant not because they never change but because the change takes place within limits we can understand or handle. The world is matter in motion. Everywhere, atoms are, as Professor Feynman would say, jiggling about at different rates depending on their interaction with others. But some form solids and others, gases.'

'Well, I think the state is a solid,' said **Tracy**.

'I think some states are more solid than others,' said **Diana**. 'I mean, if you look at southern Europe, we've seen some pretty serious boundary changes. And in Asia and in the Middle East.'

'Maybe things are settling down,' said **Antoine**. 'I mean, it's not so long since the end of colonialism and things have to work themselves out.'

'Yes, but how long will it take?' said **Temi**. 'I mean, was there ever a time that states were stable for a long time, even in Europe?'

'Stability or solidity is a matter of degree,' **I** said. 'On that much I hope we all agree.'

'Sure,' said **Temi**.

'Okay,' said **Tracy**, 'but now what? Do you agree that we hold the state as a constant and then address all other questions with the state as a given?'

'Let me put it this way,' **I** said. 'We have to take the existence of states into account when addressing the question of immigration, since what makes immigration *immigration* is the existence of political boundaries that distinguish and separate nations. But given that the boundaries of the state are subject to change, that the interests and indeed the very identities of people also change, and that some of this change is the outcome of conflicts over the desirability of immigration of one kind or another, or of all kinds, I don't think we must assume that the preservation of any or all states in their current forms is the only thing that matters or even the thing that matters most.'

'I'm not saying things don't change,' said **Tracy**, 'but I do think we should prioritise what the people think. We should operate on the people's terms.'

'Perhaps we should,' **I** said, 'but the people do not all agree. They do not agree on how many immigrants is too many, or on who should be excluded, or how much some should be given privileged access. Which voice is the people's voice?'

'That's a problem for all political questions,' said **Temi**, 'isn't it?'

'Yes,' said **Antoine**, 'that's why we try to address things democratically.'

'Tell me, Xandros,' said **Tracy** suddenly, 'or tell us, do you care about any state or country? Is there a country you think you belong to and whose passing you'd be unhappy about?'

'That's a very personal question, Trace,' said **Diana**, 'not a philosophical one.'

'Yes,' said **Antoine**, 'it sounds very personal. I think we need to talk about democracy, not about Xandros's allegiances.'

'It's okay,' **I** said. 'I'm not bothered by the question, though I agree we need to turn to the question of democracy Antoine has raised.'

'Alright,' said **Tracy**, 'to whom do you feel allegiance? To what country do you belong?'

'Let's get one thing straight,' **I** said, laughing. 'I belong to no one. No one owns me!'

'You don't own me,' **Diana** started to sing. 'I'm not just one of your many toys.'

'And don't tell me what to do,' **Astrid** sang, joining in.

'Don't tell me what to say,' **Diana** continued.

'And please, when I go out with you, don't put me on display,' **Astrid** and **Diana** continued in unison, before falling about in giggles.

'Very funny,' **I** said, 'but do keep looking for proper day jobs.'

'Harsh, Xandros,' said **Diana**, pretending to look hurt. 'Très harsh.'

'Okay,' **I** said, 'you want to know my allegiances, here they are in no particular order. Leeds United in football or soccer as you might call it, the Denver Broncos, the Australian cricket team except when they're cheating, the English football team, and whoever is the underdog anytime else.'

'But what about a country?' said **Tracy**.

'I've lived in a lot of countries, including Malaysia, Australia, Singapore, Britain, and the US, and I like them all,' **I** said, 'though I might not say that about all their governments.'

'Wouldn't you be sad if any of them disappeared?' said **Antoine**.

'Of all of them you could say that once upon a time they were not, then they were, and one day they will not be,' **I** said, 'and on that I am indifferent. If the people are free and happy, I think neither the name nor the boundary matters.'

'Epic!' said **Kaveh**, with a whistle.

'Xandros!' said **Diana**. 'You can't mean that!'

'He does,' said **Temi**. 'I think I sorta get it.'

'He's serious,' said **Tracy**, 'but somehow I find I'm not surprised.'

'Me neither,' said **Antoine**.

'Well, I'm a little shocked,' said **Astrid**. 'I mean, it's all very well in theory. How can you have a country without people who believe in it? Who want it to survive, to endure.'

'Yes,' said **Tracy**, 'to prevail!'

'For how long?' **I** asked.

'Forever!' said **Tracy**, her eyes flashing.

'Ooh,' said **Kaveh**, 'that's quite a long time.'

'It is,' **I** said. 'That's rather longer than even the dinosaurs prevailed.'

'You know what I mean,' said **Tracy**, with a shrug. 'Nothing is forever, but I don't think that's what we mean when we say "forever" or "in perpetuity".'

'Xandros will be making distinctions forever,' said **Diana**, 'once he's defined "forever".'

'Fair enough, Tracy,' **I** said. 'I won't take you to be making a literal claim. Unless they change the second law of thermodynamics, everything we know will come to an end sometime. You just mean a really, really, really long time.'

'Yes,' said **Tracy**.

'It's not that I'm unaware of the sentiment,' **I** said, 'since people everywhere have attachments to all kinds of things that they cannot bear to imagine might one day disappear. For some, it's the family, whose line they want to see continue indefinitely.'

'That matters,' said **Kaveh**, 'or at least it does patrilineally.'

'We're ignoring you, Kaveh,' said **Diana**.

'There are many Canadians who would be distraught if Québec seceded and Canada were diminished,' **I** continued, 'just as there are francophone Quebeckers who care more about the survival of their identity—about *la survivance*.'

'Jewish people want that too,' said **Antoine**, 'and we are really conscious of the challenge we face.'

'Not surprisingly,' **I** said, 'though we should also note that the desire for continuity is not related just to mere survival. Many Serbians want Kosovo returned because they think it's inherently part of Serbia, many Irish want a future that includes a united Ireland, and Venezuelans are taught that two-thirds of Guyana belongs to Venezuela.'

'Don't the Aussies want New Zealand?' said **Astrid**.

'The Australian Constitution has left it open for the Kiwis to join the federation, but I think they're taking their time mulling it over,' said **Kaveh**.

'Like I said,' **I** continued, 'I don't deny that people are attached to their lands and their identities and want to see them outlast them and live on far into the future, but I'm not one of those people.'

'Wouldn't you care if your race died out?' said **Tracy**, sounding a bit shocked.

'If you mean the race of Malaysian-born Australians of Sri Lankan Tamil descent, I don't think much of our chances,' **I** said.

'You're an outlier, Xandros,' said **Diana**.

'Thank you,' **I** said, 'but to go back to the point of all this, I do accept that we have states, that it's better for them to be reasonably stable, that at least some people should care about preserving them, and that they can't care without assuming that their state will continue in perpetuity, since it would make no sense to think of one's country as having a use-by date.'

'Thank you,' said **Tracy** triumphantly.

'Then again,' **I** continued, 'I'm not sure how many people you need to be self-consciously and determinedly vested in the perpetuation of the country for it to be stable and successful. After all, nearly 90% of the United Arab Emirates is made up of immigrants, and over 75% of Qatar.'

'They're not democracies,' said **Astrid**. 'I'm not sure they count.'

'We could consider that,' **I** said, 'but Singapore is a democracy and has over 40% of its population made up of immigrants.'

'Is it a real democracy?' said **Diana**.

'Almost a third of Australia and New Zealand are made up of foreign-born,' **I** said, 'and Canada and Germany around 20%. Do they count?'

'What's your point, Xandros?' said **Temi**. 'I'm not sure where this is going.'

'What I'm calling into question,' **I** said, 'is the idea that to have a stable state you need a population that is deeply committed to it and believes a particular narrative about its history, its purpose, or its future. There seem to be a lot of countries that are quite successful that are built on significant transient populations, some of whom may never settle permanently or become citizens. Is stability really dependent on a kind of social unity that embraces a society or a nation as a whole?'

'What you're imagining is a city without a soul, Xandros,' said **Tracy**, 'or a country without one. I don't think you can have such a thing. Why would anyone want that?'

'I think you can,' **I** said, 'and we have them all the time, if you have in mind what I think you do.'

'What does she have in mind,' said **Antoine**. 'I'm very curious. We're a long way from what I thought we'd be talking about.'

'I think what Tracy is thinking is not that far from Rawls,' **I** said.

'Oh dear,' said **Tracy**, 'can I take something back? Just tell me what.'

'Too late, I'm afraid,' **I** said, 'but let me try to put some more words in your mouth. The soul of the city, or country, is what's in the soul of the citizens. Its soul is its institutions, but what are institutions but what is in the minds of the people whose beliefs, whose thinking, makes them work. If the people don't think and behave how the institutions require, the institutions won't work or indeed exist. That's why people need to be educated, as you told us way back at our first meeting. How am I doing?'

'I think you're doing okay,' said **Tracy**, looking a bit shocked but not displeased.

'Now, I don't disagree that for any society to function you need some kind of shared understanding,' **I** said, 'and that goes even more for the workings of government. You can get only so far through the sheer use of force, though sometimes, and in some places, further than at others. Generally, though, the population needs to feel that compliance is less trouble. Governments go to a lot of trouble to ensure that compliance by whatever means they can, including argument, storytelling, fearmongering, bribery, and, of course, education. They try to shape the population, though they'd better do it in a way that's consistent with what the people think.'

'With the spirit of the people!' said **Kaveh**. 'Yes!'

'Pretty much,' **I** said, 'but the question is, which people? Or to put it differently, what is the people?'

'Not another conceptual question!' said **Diana**, trying to sound exasperated. 'Really, Xandros? I mean, seriously?'

'Secretly, you love it,' **I** said, smiling. 'That's why you keep coming back. So, here's the thing. Does "the people" mean all the people all the time, or most or some of the people most or some of the time, or some subset of the people who really matter regardless of what the rest of the people think? And does "all" mean only citizens, or citizens and settled residents, or anyone residing, or anyone within the boundaries of the state, or that and including others living abroad who have a connection to the country through descent or having a valid but unused residence permit? Who is the people?'

'I think you're making this harder than it needs to be,' said **Tracy**. 'Can't we just use some common sense?'

'Sure,' **I** said. 'What does common sense tell us?'

'The people is just, well, the people,' said **Tracy**.

'Nice one, Trace,' said **Kaveh**. 'Very convincing.'

'Shut up,' said **Tracy**, failing to suppress a giggle.

'Don't worry,' **I** said, 'it's a difficult question to answer because in political life, and in the life of any country for that matter, the issue of who belongs—who is the people?—is among the most contested of all questions. As much a subject of debate as the question of what the people *want*.'

'I get it,' said **Antoine**, 'I think. But where does this leave us? Apart from confused?'

'Well, you'll recall that we got into this because you thought I had a soulless understanding of the city or of a country,' **I** said, 'so let's return to that question.'

'Okay, boss,' said **Temi**, sounding very subdued, 'but I'm finding all this a bit troubling. If we don't know who the people are, where does that leave democracy.'

'We'll need to come to that,' **I** said, 'though no need to despair. You can still have democracy, but perhaps not everywhere, all the time, or all at once.'

'That's depressing,' said **Astrid**. 'Is there no hope, no progress?'

'There's always progress,' **I** said, 'but not everywhere, all the time, or all at once. On the bright side, the same goes for regress.'

'I'm not sure why you call that the bright side,' said **Temi**, now in a very disconsolate voice.

'Nil desperandum,' **I** said. 'Milk will be spilt till the end of time. Try not to worry too much about the clumsiness of others.'

'Very deep, Xandros,' said **Diana**, 'deeeeep!'

'I like it,' said **Kaveh**. 'No idea what it means, but I like it. It has soul.'

'Back to the city and the soul, then,' **I** said. 'What I'm trying to tell you, and I repeat myself, is it is wrong to think that to have a stable state you need a population that is deeply committed to it and believes a particular narrative about its history, its purpose, or its future. Most people, most of the time, are just busy with their own lives. They will take to the streets if you cheese them off, and different people are cheesed off by different things, so the trick is to keep things in the zone.'

'The zone of what?' said **Temi**. 'A bit of conceptual clarity, please, Xandros.'

'Just the zone,' **I** said. 'I reserve the right not to clarify further and leave it for you to work it out.'

'Seriously?' said **Temi**.

'I think I get it,' said **Astrid**, 'but it seems like a very bleak and uninspiring view of political life. There's no room for "we the people" moments.'

'Yes,' said **Antoine**, 'it sounds like a country is just a bunch of guys held together by nothing much at all. There's no glory.'

'Absolutely no glory,' **I** said. 'Completely correct. As to what holds a society or a country together, well, as I said, there has to be some shared understanding so that people accept and abide by the norms or the rules that govern them. The question is, how deep must this commitment to the norms be and how widely must they be shared? If you took the United Arab Emirates, my guess is that there's a fairly deep acceptance among the citizenry of the legitimacy of rule by the Emirati and of the privileges enjoyed by that class, but the other 88% of the population doesn't much care. In Singapore, the three-and-a-half million Singaporeans might buy the "Singapore Story" but the other two-and-a-half million residents are fairly indifferent, unless they're looking to become citizens.'

'But what about the content of the norms?' said **Antoine**. 'Doesn't that matter?'

'Yes,' said **Tracy**, 'shouldn't they be just?'

'No,' **I** said.

'What?!' said **Diana**. 'I mean, whaaat?'

'Let me clarify,' **I** said. 'No.'

'Are you against justice, Xandros?' said **Astrid**.

'Are you against democracy?' said **Antoine**.

'Are you a relativist?' said **Temi**.

'No, no, and it depends on what you mean,' **I** said.

'Okay, you really need to explain this,' said **Diana**.

'Of course,' **I** said, 'let's start with justice. I'm for it. But, as we've observed before, the tricky part is figuring out what justice requires, since people disagree on this all the time. So, we need institutions that dispense justice, absolutely, and they need to be more or less acceptable to most of the people most of the time so they can continue to function, but we can't expect them to deliver justice in the sense of the right outcome all the time, even if we could know what the right outcome might be.'

'And democracy?' said **Antoine** plaintively.

'Not against it,' **I** said, 'but wouldn't go out of my way to advocate it everywhere.'

'Why not?' said **Antoine**.

'Well, to start with, we should probably recognize that democratic institutions come in all kinds of shapes and sizes,' **I** said, 'so before advocating democracy, one should get clear on what one wants to see. What voting system shall we use? Who should be eligible to vote? Should immigrants get a vote, and if so, how soon after they arrive? What do we vote for: individuals, parties, policies? What powers should those who are voted for be given? How long should they keep them? What determines the outcome of a vote: the majority view, a supermajority view? And what is the scope of democracy, meaning which questions do we submit to democratic decision, and which are beyond democratic bounds?'

'Technicalities,' said **Temi**. 'I agree we need to adapt systems to conditions, but democracy is democracy. It's preferable to autocracy.'

'Generally, I agree,' **I** said, 'but I'd be very cautious about this. Moving to democratic rule might not be as benign an outcome as we'd like. And I wouldn't bet on immigrants doing well out of it.'

'But we can't just ignore the people,' said **Astrid**. 'What the people think has to be paramount.'

'Yes,' said **Antoine**, 'ultimately, the people should rule.'

'I agree,' said **Temi**, 'and different peoples will have different systems and different outcomes.'

'Are you a relativist, Temi?' **I** said. 'I didn't think you were, but now…'

'Oh, shut up,' said **Temi**, laughing. 'Sometimes you're just horrible!'

'Okay, Xandros,' said **Diana**, 'what do you stand for? I mean, what kind of society would you like to see? You've been swerving about, evading our questions, but not really putting up.'

'That's unfair,' **I** said. 'I've put up with all of you and your questions for five sessions now!'

'Very funny,' said **Diana**, 'but you're not getting away so easily. What does a good society look like?'

'And if you say it depends on what we mean by "good," we're going to pelt you with falafels,' said **Temi**.

'No, no,' said **Kaveh**, 'not the falafels, use something else. Anything.'

'Be calm, everyone,' **I** said. 'There'll be no falafel felling, absolutely none. And I will tell you what a good society looks like.

Though I have to warn you that it's more of an account of why this is as good as a society can get rather than a vision of some kind of utopia, realistic or otherwise.'

'That doesn't sound very inspiring,' said **Astrid**.

'It's not,' **I** said, 'but it has the virtue of being true.'

'You're feisty today, Xandros,' said **Diana**, 'but if you're actually going to advance a view of your own, I'm all for it.'

'Yes,' said **Antoine**, 'go Xandros.'

'Try to contain your excitement,' **I** said, 'and listen. Imagine, if you can, a space defined by two axes [Figure 5.1]. The vertical axis is the axis of *integration* and it describes a range of societies, or perhaps social policies, that extend from *prohibition* on people in the society integrating—that's at the bottom of the axis—to *requiring* or *forcing* people to integrate—at the top of the axis. In the middle of the axis, the policy is neither to prohibit nor to force people to integrate.'

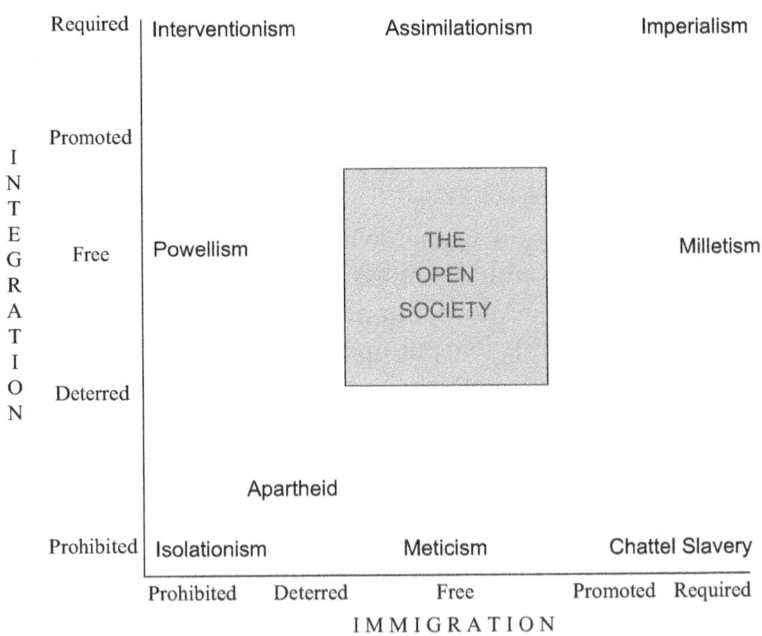

Figure 5.1 The Open Society.

'What do you mean by integration?' said **Temi**.

'Good question,' **I** said. 'So consider a society that excludes some people from participating in certain parts of social life. Under apartheid, South Africa prohibited black Africans from some areas of work, from having relationships with other races, and from entering areas reserved for whites. Something similar was true of the US in the Jim Crow era. But now consider the other extreme, in which everyone is required to conform to certain norms or practices. For example, everyone might be required to practice the same religion, under threat of punishment or expulsion. Now integration is not prohibited but required.'

'But surely there's a medium between the extremes,' said **Astrid**.

'Of course,' **I** said, 'I'm describing a range or a scale, and between these extremes integration is neither prohibited nor required. People are free to decide whether and to what degree to conform. They are not prevented, either by the laws or by the resistance of those around them, from associating with others and living as they wish.'

'So, a society has three standards,' said **Diana**. 'Either it prohibits or it requires or it permits, right?'

'Not quite,' **I** said, 'though not far off. A society could discourage or penalize some actions without prohibiting, and it could encourage some actions without requiring them. Sometimes governments, and other elements of society for that matter, try to nudge people in one direction or another. Control can be exercised with blunt force, but mostly the use of power is more subtle.'

'Nudge, nudge, wink, wink,' said **Kaveh**.

'Correct,' **I** said. 'Nudging and fudging is mostly the order of the day. That's how the world works.'

'Okay,' said **Temi**, 'but what about your other axis? You said there were two.'

'Yes,' **I** said, 'now imagine the horizontal axis, which I'm calling the axis of *immigration*. At one extreme, where the horizontal axis meets the bottom of the vertical axis, immigration into a society—and out of it, for that matter—is completely prohibited. No one is allowed in, and no one is allowed out. The closest example I can find to this condition is contemporary North Korea, though even there you'll find some movement of people, since there are imports of goods, some international tourism, the exchange of diplomats, and so on.'

'Why would tourists go there?' asked **Antoine**.

'Pyongyang Disney World,' said **Kaveh**.

'Really?' said **Antoine**.

'No,' said **Temi**, 'not yet. It's more the hermit kingdom than the magical kingdom. Try to ignore Kaveh.'

'Never mind, you all get the picture,' **I** said. 'So consider the other extreme of the horizontal axis, at which immigration is not prohibited but required.'

'How can immigration be required?' said **Diana**. 'That would be like slavery.'

'Exactly the example I was thinking of,' **I** said. 'Slavery, or at least some forms of it, could be regarded as involving forced migration. Slaves sent from Africa to North and South America and the Middle East didn't choose to go.'

'I don't think the convicts sent to Aussie-land did either,' said **Kaveh**.

'Yes,' **I** said, 'but between prohibited and forced migration, there is free migration, to the extent that movement is neither prevented nor mandated. Though again, there are gradations of freedom to the extent that societies might make immigration more difficult or, alternatively, actively encourage it through various schemes or incentives.'

'This is all very nice,' said **Temi**, 'but how does this help us understand what a good society might be?'

'Ah,' **I** said, 'here comes the killer move.'

'Seriously, Xandros?' said **Diana**. 'You're in a mood today!'

'You're welcome,' **I** said. 'So here's the thing. If you draw a line headed north from the middle of the horizontal axis, where immigration is tolerated or free, and draw another line headed east from the middle of the vertical axis, where integration is tolerated or free, the intersection of the two lines is where you'll find the good society.'

'I'm not sure I can quite see it,' said **Antoine**, 'though I really want to.'

'Not to worry,' **I** said. 'I just happen to have a graph I've drawn to help you. I thought you might need it.'

'Very sneaky, Xandros,' said **Diana**. 'You're full of surprises!'

'It's what I do,' **I** said.

'But what's this grey box in the middle?' said **Antoine**. 'We'll need more than just a surprise. What about an explanation?'

'A reasonable request,' **I** said, 'so allow me to elaborate. I think a good society is an open society. This is not a new idea. Karl Popper's famous book, *The Open Society and Its Enemies*, offers us the first account of the idea, which he develops in a critique of Plato, whom he criticizes for being an advocate of the closed society. He's a bit unfair on Plato, but I've always liked the idea of the open society. The way I want to conceptualize it, however, is a bit different. I want to think of it not as a kind of regime but as describing a world in which different regimes co-exist.'

'Whatever do you mean, Xandros?' said **Astrid**. 'This is getting more obscure by the minute.'

'Sorry,' **I** said. 'You wanted me to explain my thinking, but the picture I want to paint in words can't be seen in a single snapshot, so you'll have to bear with me.'

'Tell us more, Socrates,' said **Diana**. 'I mean, Xandros.'

'Very well,' **I** said, 'now listen closely. The open society is a realm within which people live freely in the sense that they may come and go more or less as they please and can live according to their own lights, pursue their own goals or ends, and act according to their own understandings of what is right and wrong.'

'Surely, that's impossible,' said **Tracy**, who'd been rather quiet. 'There have to be rules. Everyone can't just decide for themselves what's right and what's not. There'd be chaos.'

'The end of civilization as we know it,' said **Kaveh**.

'Completely correct,' **I** said. 'You're absolutely right, Tracy.'

'Whaaat?' said **Antoine**. 'But, I mean, it's not, you know, you just said, like...'

'Nice objection,' said **Kaveh**, 'very incisive.'

'Shut up, Kaveh,' said **Antoine**, laughing.

'Tracy's on the mark,' **I** said, 'but I can see why this needs explaining. I agree that there have to be rules, norms, laws, institutions, and all the constraints on action that tell us what we may and may not do, if only so that others know what we are likely to do and not do. We all depend on the certainty that knowing how others will probably act gives us. But we don't all agree on what those rules should be, and to that extent they limit our freedom. And as long as they don't limit us in ways we find onerous, we accept them. Indeed, we accept them even when they're onerous if the cost and risk of challenging them would be more onerous still.'

'We might accept them if the rules are just,' said **Diana**, 'mightn't we?'

'No,' **I** said, 'I don't think justice makes much difference. It's not a great motivator.'

'Really?' said **Temi**. 'I mean, do you think regimes can survive without justice?'

'Sure,' **I** said, 'they do all the time. This is not an original thought of mine. When Cicero suggested that political society was a form of association founded on justice, St Augustine observed that that would then exclude Rome and its empire, since it was founded on violence, theft, and murder. It lasted a while. How many societies in existence today would you say are more or less just societies?'

'Switzerland,' said **Antoine**.

'That's one,' **I** said.

'Except they don't like mosques,' said **Kaveh**, 'and they're getting stricter with refugees.'

'They had a referendum on mosques,' said **Tracy**. 'They didn't stop people worshipping.'

'It's still not just,' said **Kaveh**, 'is it?'

'It is just,' said **Tracy**, 'but even if it wasn't, it's a pretty just society overall. I mean, how high a standard of justice do you want.'

'That's really my point,' **I** said. 'There's a lot of ruin in a nation, as Adam Smith once observed, and a society can and will put up with a lot of injustice—much more than you'll find in Switzerland, which looks like a pretty nice place to live. Many Muslims would move there even without mosques if the alternatives they had were poorer in other respects.'

'Doesn't justice make any difference at all?' said **Astrid**. 'Surely, it contributes to making a society stable, and governments legitimate.'

'I'm not saying it doesn't matter at all,' **I** said, 'but you can still have a lot of injustice. The United States before the Civil Rights Act—and, some would say, since—was hardly a just society for African Americans, and native Americans have had at least a few legitimate grievances, yet it wasn't unstable and was pretty peaceful, with millions of people clamouring to immigrate and take up citizenship.'

'It wouldn't have lasted without reform,' said **Antoine**, 'would it?'

'Everything comes to an end,' **I** said, 'so it depends on how long you have in mind. It's now lasted almost 250 years with a lot of injustice.'

'How does all this fit in with your view,' said **Temi**, 'going back to your idea of the open society?'

'I'm so glad you asked,' **I** said. 'Allow me to finish the thought. As I noted before, people have different views about what kinds of rules or norms or laws they're prepared to live under, and will find themselves living under different kinds of systems of rules or regimes depending on where they're born or have moved to. Some regimes will require greater conformity and others less. Some regimes will be easier to enter and leave, others less. Some regimes will try to absorb others, some will try to compel others to adopt their ways but deny people much or any freedom to move. Some will allow people to move freely but require them to conform. To the extent that we find ourselves in a realm in which we can move freely and live without being required to conform or prohibited from associating with other like-minded people, we live in an open society.'

'How open would it have to be to count as an open society?' said **Temi**. 'I mean, what's more important, freedom not to conform or freedom to move? Is integration more significant than immigration when trying to judge whether a society is open? And what do these words like "Powellism" and "Milletism" mean?'

'Well,' I said, 'I've used the term "Powellism" to identify a position that holds that we should limit immigration but any immigrants we admit should have the same freedoms as existing citizens. This is the position of Enoch Powell, the famous British politician who worried about immigration to the UK in the 1960s. I've used the word "Milletism" to describe a position that favours allowing groups to live by their own traditions but forces them to be part of the empire. The Ottoman empire is the model for this idea, as it had separate "millets" that could make some of their own laws but were still ruled from afar. And I use the term "Meticism" to identify the position that accepts having foreigners as guest workers but won't give them the same rights as citizens. In ancient Greece, these people were the "Metics"—hence the term. As for the axes of integration and immigration, they're really two dimensions or aspects of a particular kind of freedom, which is the freedom to associate with others or to dissociate from others. Associating or living with others requires conforming to some degree, figuring which of your commitments are so important that you aren't prepared to give them up in order to conform. But if you can't move, the extent of that freedom diminishes inasmuch as you'll have to conform regardless of your wishes. But moving is hard at the best of times, so often people will just suck it up, so to speak, rather than leave their communities, let alone emigrate to another country.'[27]

'Suck it up, is that a technical term?' said **Kaveh**.

'Yes,' I said, 'most of life is about sucking it up, and I've graded enough student papers to say this with some authority.'

'I thought you liked marking our essays,' said **Diana**, trying to sound hurt.

'It's up there with having teeth pulled and going through US immigration control on a foreign passport,' I said.

27 See Chandran Kukathas, 'Liberalism's Essential Tension: on Jacob Levy on Rationalism, Pluralism and Freedom', *Online Library of Liberty: Liberty Matters*,2016.https://oll.libertyfund.org/publications/liberty-matters/jacob-levy-rationalism-pluralism-freedom#post_1300.

'Our essays are that good?' said **Kaveh**.

'Up there but not equivalent,' **I** said. 'Between going to the dentist and marking 50 essays, I'd take the dentist, but to choose going through immigration control I'd have to be relieved of at least 100 essays.'

'Why did you ever become a professor?' said **Astrid**.

'I've been trying to explain, life is about making trade-offs,' **I** said, 'and there's no regime in which everyone isn't making compromises all the time. We give up some freedom for other things, including other freedoms. And we put up with injustice. Overall, we tolerate a lot of injustice, whichever view of justice you happen to take.'

'Why care about the open society, then?' said **Tracy**. 'What's so great about it? Especially if you're such a relativist?'

'One way to think about it is to imagine the positions at the extremes on the graph I showed you,' **I** said. 'The southwest corner means no immigration and no freedom to associate with others of your choosing. The northeast corner means you're forcibly moved and incorporated into a regime to whose norms you must conform. The southeast corner means you're forced to move but forbidden to associate with the rest of society. And the northwest corner means you're made to conform to the norms of an invading power but have no freedom to escape. Moving away from these extremes means moving closer to a free society. You'd want to be living in a regime at the extremes only if you're in power and like exercising power over others. The less you like having power over others, the closer you'd want to move to the centre.'

'And you think most people would want to move to the centre because they don't want power over others,' said **Diana**, 'is that it?'

'No,' **I** said, 'I think most people who would want to move toward the centre do so because they don't like others having power over them, but they don't want to keep moving in that direction because they also want to be able to make others conform to their views. We like being right and like even better having others acknowledge it.'

'You're so right, Xandros,' said **Temi**, laughing.

'Yes, you are,' **Diana** said, piling on.

'Yes, totally,' said **Antoine**. 'You've never been more convincing.'

'Tell us more,' said **Astrid**, 'please, please.'

'Okay, okay,' **I** said, unable to keep myself from smiling broadly, 'shut up the lot of you, ungrateful wretches that you are.'

'I'd no idea you were such a relativist,' said **Tracy**. 'You're almost a nihilist, with a really pessimistic view of people. I don't see why you would care whether we live in an open society or if there's free immigration. What do you care?'

'Maybe Xandros is just a kind of quietist,' said **Astrid**, 'happy to stay above the fray, looking down on the rest of the world with a kind of studied indifference. All he wants is the freedom to observe and make a few distinctions, clarify a few concepts, you know, be a philosopher.'

'Ouch!' **I** said. 'Now who's being harsh?'

'Xandros walks softly but carries a big dictionary,' said **Kaveh**. 'That's not being quietistic. He's a truth warrior.'

'Thanks for the defence, Kaveh, I think,' **I** said.

'Welcome, boss,' said **Kaveh**.

'But to answer the charges,' **I** said, 'I wouldn't say I was a relativist if you mean by that that I have no moral convictions. I'm a relativist in the sense that I'm not an absolutist. I'm not convinced that there are moral values that hold no matter what. And I'm a relativist inasmuch as I'm not convinced there are any universal values in the sense that that everyone holds them to be so.'

'What about murdering innocents?' said **Tracy**. 'Surely, that's absolutely wrong and universally agreed upon.'

'Not a great example,' **I** said, 'since saying murder is wrong when murder means "wrongful killing" is a tautological statement. I agree that wrongful killing is wrong, but I'm not sure it helps. But it gets harder when we have to decide what counts as murder or who counts as innocent—civilians delivering food to munitions factories, foetuses, deserters in battle—or what counts as torture. I have views, but my level of confidence in them varies.'

'Then what are you for, Xandros,' said **Temi**, 'and why?'

'I'm for lots of things,' **I** said, 'but since the list is long, let me give you just a few examples. I'm for hospitality, for one thing.'

'You've got us there,' said **Tracy**. 'We've had a feast today. And you have given generously of your time too.'

'And wine,' said **Antoine**, 'seriously.'

'Yes, truly epic,' said **Kaveh**.

'I appreciate the appreciation,' **I** said, 'but the morality of hospitality is something I value highly in a more general way. A good society leaves people free to exercise their generosity. To show a bit of kindness. To be welcoming. Without requiring everyone to be so or to do it in the same way. That can't happen as much if people aren't free, to live as they wish or to move where there are some people ready to welcome them. What's most worrying, in my view, is how easy it is to make people wary of others, how easy it is to make people ready to differentiate some people from others, and how quickly they can be brought to be content with their own loss of freedom and indifferent to the fates of others. Controlling people diminishes all their best instincts. Or so I fear. So, I'm for whatever makes us better hosts but not confident of success or anything more than temporary victories.'

'Two steps forward, two steps back,' said **Kaveh**. 'The dance of mankind.'

'More or less,' **I** said, 'but throw in an occasional pirouette.'

'It still sounds to me like a very pessimistic outlook,' said **Astrid**, 'or maybe a kind of disengaged way of looking at things, all conceptual clarification and no action.'

'Well, I'll admit that I haven't scaled the heights that I did in my political activist youth,' **I** said, 'but I'm not for disengaging like some modern-day Chuang Tse, much as I admire his way of thought. I'm more with Mill. "Bad men need nothing more to compass their ends, than that good men should look on and do nothing."[28] I've never advocated doing nothing, even though, in public discussion, I wish there were more people ready to adopt

28 John Stuart Mill, *Inaugural Address delivered to the University of St Andrews, February 1st 1867* (Sothis Press, 2023).

the temper of a philosopher rather than an advocate or, worse, a catastrophist.'

'You were an activist?' said **Diana**. 'I don't believe it. Were you ever arrested?'

'Don't be ridiculous,' **I** said. 'Of course, I was never caught. Too smart. Too quick.'

'Or just too late to the protest march,' said **Tracy**, 'too many late nights reading Mill. Or Nietzsche. Or too glum!'

'Hey,' **I** said, 'I'll admit to being a bit of a pessimist, but I'm never glum. Seeing the world as it is doesn't mean you have to be morose.'

'Between Nietzsche and Pollyanna falls the shadow,' said **Kaveh**, with a smirk.

'Where does all this leave us?' said **Tracy**. 'I feel like we've reached the end but we're right back to where we started. Nothing's been settled.'

'You're right,' **I** said. 'We are. But is nothing clearer?'

'I'm not sure,' **Tracy** said. 'I feel like I've taken a series of detours, each one promising to get us somewhere but all leading us to more questions.'

'That's how we advertise philosophy seminars,' **I** said. 'Come for the answers, stay for the questions.'

'Maybe that's what's wrong,' said **Antoine**. 'We're doing philosophy, and philosophy doesn't grapple with reality, only with concepts.'

'Yes,' said **Astrid**, 'the reality is that people don't want immigrants or immigration. All this conceptual analysis isn't going to change that.'

'Perhaps,' **I** said, 'but who knows? The world changes for many reasons, and sometimes those reasons appear in words.'

'Fair enough,' said **Temi**, 'thanks, Xandros. I guess it's time for us to go. Kaveh's managed to eat everything.'

'You're welcome,' said **Kaveh**. 'It's important to be a good host, but you can't be one without good guests who appreciate what's on offer.'

'And I appreciate your appreciation,' **I** said. 'Before you all go, however I have something to share with you.'

'Oh?' said **Diana**. 'Something cool, like some nice gossip?'

'Almost,' **I** said, 'but not quite. No. The news is that I'm getting married and moving.'

'Whaaat!' said **Diana**. 'Seriously? I mean, seriously seriously?'

'You went on a date?' said **Temi**. 'I don't believe it. And you'll be an immigrant. Again. Is that right?'

'Yes,' **I** said. 'Yes to all your questions. I'm moving to Greece.'

'To teach?' said **Antoine**. 'Where?'

'Whisky, tango, et cetera!' said **Astrid**. 'I mean, what the Franz Fanon. How long have you known?'

'No, not to teach,' **I** said. 'I'm not sure just what I'll do. I have some savings. I'll figure it out. Nothing ventured, nothing gained. Drop me a note on my personal email, and I'll be glad to answer any conceptual queries you have. I leave in a month. And I'll be married to a Greek goddess who appreciates conceptual clarity a month after that.'

'We have to say goodbye,' said **Diana**, 'but not tonight. Can we come to the bus station? I assume you'll be taking the coach to the airport.'

'Yes, yes,' said **the others**, almost in unison.

'That would be very nice,' **I** said, 'very nice indeed.'

'Epic,' said **Kaveh**, 'totally epic.'

Epilogue

The students decided that the coach station wasn't a suitable place for a farewell, so I suggested that they visit me at home in the morning before my Uber came to fetch me. Since the larder would be bare, they offered to bring coffee, which they did, along with a large box of donuts.

'We know you love donuts,' said **Antoine**.

'Where did you hear that vicious rumour?' **I** said, biting into one that sent strawberry jelly squirting out onto my chin.

'There are no donuts in Greece,' said **Kaveh**, 'so enjoy.'

'We thought we'd bring you only ones with holes in them,' said **Temi**. 'You know, because of how you love finding holes in arguments. But none of those looked good.'

'I'm not sure it's really a donut if it doesn't have a hole,' said **Astrid**. 'What do you think, Xandros? Could you tell us what the concept of a donut requires of anything claiming to be a donut?'

'That's an interesting question,' **I** said, 'but the more intriguing puzzle is whether a donut hole exists. In one sense it does, obviously, at least on ring-shaped donuts, but donut purveyors sell donut holes, which aren't really holes, since there's nothing around them and the things being sold have no holes and certainly can't be holes in themselves.'

'Kant says we can never know things in themselves,' said **Kaveh** brightly, 'so I guess we can't know holes in themselves, only experience them.'

DOI: 10.4324/9781003629641-6

'Oh, for Hobbes's sake,' said **Temi**, 'I should have known this would happen. Do you guys understand the concept of a farewell? We've come to say goodbye, not to deconstruct morning coffee!'

'It's our homage to Xandros,' said **Diana**. 'Deconstruction is the sincerest form of flattery.'

'And I appreciate it,' **I** said, 'and I'll send you my forthcoming paper on the concept of the donut when it has come forth.'

'But first you'll have to finish your book on immigration,' said **Tracy**, 'right? Of course, you'll have to change your arguments after the philosophical beating we've given you.'

'What do you mean "we", Trace?' said **Temi**. 'Have you changed your mind?'

'Very funny,' said **Tracy**, 'but I guess arguments don't change minds in the end. Not the way reality does. Philosophy is for fun. Whether we're talking about donuts or deportation, philosophers don't change the world. They don't have the power.'

'Ideas can be powerful,' said **Antoine**, 'though I'm not sure the ideas Xandros shared with us are—sorry Xandros, I think they're cool, but I don't think you're going to change anyone's mind.'

'Xandros just wants to clear up a little rubbish,' said **Astrid**, 'isn't that right?'

'There's a lot of rubbish out there,' said **Temi**. 'We're going to need an army of janitors if we're to make any progress.'

'There's no hope,' said **Diana**. 'There's an even bigger rebel alliance of litterbugs out there. All the Jedi masters in the world won't be enough.'

'Um, the Jedi are on the side of the rebels,' said **Kaveh**.

'I'm not sure which is more confusing,' said **Astrid**, 'the politics of *Star Trek* or actual politics.'

'*Star Wars*,' said **Kaveh**, 'wars, not trek.'

'You're right,' said **Astrid**, 'Trek Wars is or are more confusing.'

'Are you going to clarify things, Xandros,' said **Diana**, 'come on, one last explanation?'

'Clarify I will,' **I** said, 'since ask you must.'

'Nice one!' said **Kaveh**. 'Epic!'

'We live in a world of words,' **I** said, 'of thoughts, if you like, but thoughts given expression and indeed existence through words. No words or sentences or paragraphs or even whole books are going change everything, but they all become part of the network of thoughts that structure our lives. So, yes, philosophy is for fun, but it's also a form of engagement. If you want to change the world, whether in small or more substantial ways, you'll have to do it with words. Bullets and bulldozers won't be enough.'

'Good answer for a job interview, Xandros,' said **Tracy**, 'but I'm not sure your papers on the concept of meaning and the meaning of concepts are going to do the trick.'

'No,' said **Antoine**, 'I guess not even a book on immigration is going to change anything. No matter how much you clarify everything.'

'Mao Zedong said a single spark can start a prairie fire,' said **Kaveh** helpfully.

'Not if it's winter,' said **Tracy**, 'and it's sleeting, and the prairie is blanketed in snow.'

'That's the thing,' said **Diana**, 'no matter what the arguments, it seems like the reality is that people—not all of them, but a lot—just don't want immigrants. What's the good of all the philosophical analysis and ethical jujitsu if the plain fact is that populations, and so their governments, just don't want more immigrants, let alone open borders. Will they want you in Greece? To us you're Xandros, but you're really Professor Prakash. The real world is a lot less friendly than we are.'

'Well,' **I** said, 'I have a good friend who is fond of a line of William the Silent: 'One need not have hope in order to undertake, nor succeed in order to persevere.'

'Doesn't sound very silent to me,' said **Tracy**.

'More like William the Stubborn,' said **Kaveh**, 'yeah?'

'I have undertaken to teach you all,' **I** said, 'and I persevere.'

'Harsh, Xandros,' said **Diana**. 'We're here to farewell you, we're nice! Well, some of us are.'

'Why do you persevere, Xandros?' said **Astrid**. 'I mean, all jokes aside, what motivates you? Do you want to save the world? Will philosophers change the world? Can they change immigration policy?'

'I'm content if I can sow a little confusion among you,' **I** said, 'and anything else is a bonus.'

'Well, mission accomplished,' said **Temi**. 'I mean, well done!'

'Not that well done,' said **Diana**. 'We were pretty confused already.'

'But now you know it,' **I** said. 'I peddle a higher-quality confusion.'

'Yeah,' said **Kaveh**, 'philosophical confusion, not just your everyday, garden variety confusion.'

'But seriously, Xandros,' said **Antoine**, 'don't you want to make a difference? Why teach? Why write books? What's the point if they don't make a difference?'

'I have made a difference,' **I** said. 'After all, you're all here to farewell me. Truly, I'm touched. But I suspect that's not the answer you're looking for. Do I want to change the world? Do I want to change the way more people think—perhaps about immigration and the open society? That's what you're asking, correct? How big a difference do I want to make?'

'Yes,' said **Astrid**, 'how ambitious are you?'

'Well, it all depends on what you mean by ambitious,' **I** said, 'wouldn't you say?'

'Oh, for the love of Hobbes, Locke, and Rousseau,' said **Temi**. 'I can't believe we gave you that opening. We're like Wile E. Coyote and you're the Roadrunner. You get us every time.'

'Beep, beep,' said **Kaveh**.

'We surrender, Xandros,' said **Diana**. 'We're waving a white flag and begging for mercy.'

'Okay, okay,' **I** said, 'I think I do know what you're asking, but old habits die hard, and I can't help asking for conceptual clarification whenever the opportunity arises. You want to know what my ambitions are, so let me share some of them. One is definitely helping students see things a bit more clearly, not because I supply the right answer but because I can usually ask better questions, or ask questions better, and point them to places to look. The rest is up to them. To you.'

'Is that it?' said **Diana**. 'Surely, there's more?'

'There is,' **I** said. 'I don't want to spend my whole life asking questions and pointing out places to look, not least because some of you aren't really listening and are more interested in lunch or the football or K-dramas or whatever it is you do.'

'Getting a little harsh, Xandros,' said **Astrid**. 'Please don't do the whole young-people-today thing.'

'Sorry,' **I** said. 'We people of advancing years do have a tendency to do that. Very bad habit. So, no, I would like to try answering some questions. About immigration, for example.'

'So do you think you'll come up with some answers?' said **Diana**. 'I mean, we've had five sessions with you, and the last one was, well, epic, as Kaveh would say. Are you any closer to knowing what you think?'

'I'm getting closer every day,' **I** said, 'but I'm not there yet.'

'Well, I thought you were going to tell us you were in favour of open borders,' said **Temi**, 'and the whole open society theory you laid out makes me think that that's where you'll end up.'

'Yes,' said **Tracy**, 'that's what I thought too, but you really pulled your punches in the end in my opinion.'

'Open borders for refugees and the rest pay cash—that's what Kaveh said, didn't he?' said **Diana**, 'and I thought that's where you'd go. Why didn't you?'

'Well,' **I** said, 'it really depends on what you mean by open borders.'

'No, no, no,' said **Antoine**, 'you can't make that move now. No tricks. We're farewelling you so you have to end on a more positive note, not with another "what do you mean?" question. It is not civilized.'

'I know you think I'm just trying to mess with you,' **I** said, 'and I'll admit that sometimes I pull out the "it all depends" line for the fun of it. But right now, I'm quite serious. There are numerous advocates of open borders, but none of them has, to the best of my knowledge, actually given much thought to what the concept of open borders means. Nor have the critics, for that matter. Equating open borders with a "free for all" isn't helpful. What are open borders?'

'It's not that difficult, surely?' said **Antoine**. 'We can look at the EU or, even better, the Schengen area, and say the borders are open across all those national boundaries. Anyone can cross them anytime they want.'

'Yes,' said **Astrid**, 'and you can also look at the US or Canada or Australia and their state or provincial boundaries which anyone can cross anytime they want once they're in the country. Open borders across the world would mean that you have as much right to cross a national boundary as you have to cross a domestic one. Moving from Mexico should be no different from moving from Texas to Florida or from South Australia to Victoria. Open borders. Simple.'

'You're both admirably clear,' **I** said, 'but I have a couple of questions.'

'Watch out, it's a trap!' said **Kaveh**. 'He's gonna get you.'

'No trap,' **I** said, 'just questions. When someone crosses from Mexico to Texas and it's supposed to be the same as crossing from Texas to Florida, does it mean that the Mexican or Guatemalan or Venezuelan or Chinese border crosser acquires the same rights as the American moving across state borders within the US?'

'What do you mean?' said **Tracy**. 'Of course not.'

'I'm not sure I understand the question,' said **Diana**. 'I mean, crossing the border doesn't give you rights.'

'What I'm trying to ascertain is whether open borders really could mean that there would be no difference between moving across a national boundary and moving across a state or provincial boundary,' **I** said. 'Is that all there is to open borders? Everyone is allowed to cross a boundary, is that it? I'll admit that would be a change, since most people in the world do not have the right to move to most countries. But is that it?'

'I think so,' said **Antoine**. 'I mean, that sounds right, or close, though I'm not sure.'

'Thanks for clarifying, Antoine,' said **Temi**. 'That was masterful.'

'Shut up,' said **Antoine**. 'Xandros has a way of tripping me up.'

'Sorry, Antoine,' **I** said, 'but I'm not sure that the freedom to cross a border is all there is to the idea of open borders. I think the advocates of open borders mean something more. Otherwise, the borders are open between a lot of countries. The borders between North America and Europe and Australia and Singapore and Japan are open as you don't need even to apply for a visa to travel across these countries. And you can easily get a visa if you have the right passport. Unless you want to work. Or study. Or open a business or buy a house or stay for a longer period or marry a native.'

'"Open borders" has to mean more than just crossing,' said **Temi**. 'I mean, for a lot of people, it's the opportunity to work that makes all the difference. So, yes, "open borders" has to mean those crossing them have the right to work.'

'And that means the right to stay,' said **Antoine**, 'because otherwise you'd have to quit your job.'

'Are there any other rights these boundary crossers would have?' **I** asked.

'Like what?' said **Astrid**.

'Like the right to get a driver's license,' **I** said, 'and the right to send their kids to school, and the right to use public services, and the right to vote, and the right to stand for public office—to name a few rights existing residents might have.'

'Giving foreigners the right to vote would be weird,' said **Tracy**. 'We can rule that one out.'

'Commonwealth citizens can vote in UK elections if they're resident in Britain,' said **Kaveh**, 'but yeah, totally weird.'

'EU citizens can vote in each other's elections,' said **Diana**, 'but just local ones, I think.'

'I think you'll find the matter more complicated than that,' **I** said, 'since the rights of foreigners—and I use this term advisedly—to vote varies not only across countries but also within them. In the UK, Wales and Scotland allow all resident foreign nationals to vote in local elections as well as elections for the Welsh and Scottish parliaments. In Switzerland, the voting rights of foreigners vary by canton. Spain has reciprocal voting rights through treaties with different countries. New Zealand gives national voting rights to all permanent residents. And so on and so on.'

'Will you be able to vote in Greece, Xandros?' said **Astrid**.

'I will indeed,' **I** said, 'but only in local elections. Not in European Parliament elections as I'm not from an EU country.'

'The world is not a tidy place,' said **Temi**. 'I thought there'd be a bit more consistency.'

'Yes,' said **Tracy**, 'I can't believe so many countries allow non-citizens to vote. And vote in national elections too.'

'The world is a crazy place,' said **Kaveh**, 'yeah?'

'*Eppur si muove*,' **I** said.

'Huh?' said **Antoine**.

'Galileo,' said **Kaveh**, 'believe it or not, however crazy it seems, the world keeps moving.'

'And what do we need in this crazy world?' **I** said, looking around at the blank faces around me. 'Conceptual clarity!'

'You never give up, do you Xandros?' said **Temi**.

'Nope,' **I** said. 'It's my job. It's my calling.'

'But what about the open society you described at our last meeting?' said **Diana**. 'Isn't an open society one with open borders?'

'Again, it depends on what you mean,' **I** said, 'but before you start groaning, let me explain. As I said before, the openness of a border can't just be a matter of the ease with which one can cross a boundary. What one can do after crossing is no less important. The more rights one has, the more open the border. So, if someone entering a society can work, or go to school, or rent or buy a home, he or she has found the borders more open than someone who could enter but do none of these things.'

'What if she had to get a visa first?' said **Antoine**.

'Good question,' **I** said, 'since the ease with which one acquires rights makes a difference to the openness of the border. If one has to jump through numerous hoops, or pay large fees, or wait for a long time to secure permission to enter, the border is less open. In that sense, the border's openness is a function of the number of rights one acquires on crossing and the ease with which one acquires them.'

'And the number of people to whom the border is open,' said **Diana**.

'Now you're getting the hang of it,' **I** said.

'It sounds like borders can't really be fully open as long as there are countries or states,' said **Astrid**.

'Borders mean borders,' said **Kaveh**, with a flourish.

'I'm afraid so,' **I** said, 'but as we've seen, some are more open than others. And it's not all that easy to say which are more open because openness has to be judged on a number of different dimensions. And that's before we even start asking how easy it is for people who cross borders to become citizens, whether or not they can pass on their status to their children, or bring in their relatives or loved ones, and whether the society is internally open to the movement of people between cities and provinces. Few, if any, societies are open all the way down.'

'We have to go deep,' said **Kaveh**.

'Indeed, we do,' **I** said, 'for we should also consider some other factors still. What difference will it make, for example, if a society's ethos is not welcoming or its institutions are riven with prejudices of all kinds? If the law permits easy entry but the population is anti-immigrant, that might make the society less open than one in which the law is hostile but the citizens are welcoming.'

'How could that be?' said **Tracy**. 'The laws reflect, or should reflect, the wishes of the citizens, surely.'

'Then why do we have sanctuary cities?' said **Diana**. 'I don't think we all agree on all the laws.'

'Quite so,' **I** said, 'and not least on the laws governing immigration. Disagreements and disputes over immigration are for the most part disagreements among citizens rather than between citizens and immigrants or would-be immigrants.'

'Well, most of them don't want immigration,' said **Tracy**, 'or at least they want it controlled. So surely you agree we should control it—as far as we can?'

'Well, herein lie several dilemmas,' **I** said, 'stemming mostly from the difficulty we face trying to control immigration. Or anything, for that matter, but let's stick to immigration.'

'How hard can it be?' said **Tracy**. 'I'm sure we can't stop everyone who wants to come in, but surely we can do a lot better than we're doing now in the US. And in Europe for that matter.'

'I don't think we can,' **I** said, 'or that anyone can—not at a price we're willing to pay.'

'You get what you pay for,' said **Kaveh**. 'That's for sure.'

'We're paying a lot,' said **Diana**. 'I remember from researching the economics of immigration.'

'Indeed, we are,' **I** said, 'but not just in money. Immigration control means paying a price not merely because it requires border checks, or a bureaucracy of civil servants to track people, or judges to hear cases and appeals, or detention centres to hold suspects, or police to apprehend people thought to be violating immigration law. We pay a price because all these institutions and regulations also limit or ensnare our own citizens and make us subject to surveillance. The more control we seek, the greater the risk of harming our fellow countrymen. So, the question is, how high a price are you willing to pay in that respect?'

'How high is the risk?' said **Tracy**. 'Maybe we should settle that question first?'

'What's the price of control?' said **Kaveh**. 'Brilliant! Can we model it?'

'Anything can be modelled,' **I** said, 'though I fear that most models are useful only to the modellers, who have a very nice time playing with them.'

'Calm down, Xandros,' said **Diana**. 'Kaveh was just raising a question. And I can't believe I'm defending Kaveh.'

'Ta, Diana,' said **Kaveh**, 'happy to be rescued.'

'Okay, okay,' **I** said, 'let me put it more politely. I think it will be difficult to assess the price of immigration control for several reasons. First, and most obviously, the price paid is different for different people and may be highest for those who want more or some particular, immigrants.'

'How could that be?' said **Antoine**.

'Take the case of employers who can't find workers,' **I** said, 'whether at a higher, a lower, or at any wage. The burden falls hard on them and perhaps indirectly on their industries, their customers, or even on their workers if they lose their jobs because the business goes bust for want of workers, low-cost or otherwise.'

'It might still work out overall,' said **Tracy**, 'especially if workers' wages rise more generally.'

'Perhaps,' **I** said, 'though that might mean a price rise if goods become more expensive to produce. But even before we consider whether we can make such a calculation of the overall benefit of immigration control, the truth is that some people bear higher burdens.'

'So what?' said **Tracy**. 'If there's no control, some bear higher burdens and others lower.'

'I agree,' **I** said, 'but that's really my point. It's not as if there's a kind of natural level at which all these burdens rest, such that we are just left to decide where the overall burden should lie. Alleviating the burdens on some citizens might just place burdens on others. I make this point because I think it should be understood that there is a price to be paid for immigration control. But I'd be wary of those who think we can measure or model the outcomes when people have different preferences. We can draw attention to the costs and benefits of policy but must recognize that we can't always make fine-grained calculations. All the more so because some advocates will talk up the costs and others will talk up the benefits.'

'What else?' said **Diana**.

'Another reason the price of immigration control is difficult to assess is that people adapt,' **I** said, 'and here I mean not just immigrants but everyone who is affected by the controls, whether these are employers, or educational institutions, or workers, or traders in the market, or parents, or partners, or citizens more generally. Rules and human beings aren't fixed. Human beings make rules and rules make human beings.'

'I don't understand,' said **Temi**. 'It sounds like a bit of an exaggeration. I mean, I understand adaptive preferences as an idea, but

I don't see why it's a problem. Surely, we can still assess whether or not controls work and whether they're worthwhile?'

'Let me try out an example,' **I** said, 'maybe using the case of an American medical practitioner who moved to Britain with his British wife to take a position in the NHS but discovered that of their three children, the two adopted ones were not eligible to enter as immigrants because their mother, although British, was not British-born. The ten- and twelve-year-old boys had their passports confiscated, were put in detention, and scheduled to be deported without their parents to a city in the US.'

'Are you making this up?' said **Astrid**.

'It was a mistake, surely,' said **Tracy**.

'That's terrible,' said **Antoine**, 'but they must have resolved it sensibly. And I'm not sure what this has to do with adaptation.'

'The parents found a lawyer who got the boys out of detention and prevented them from being deported,' **I** said, 'but the family spent ten months trying unsuccessfully to regularize the children's status before being told that they could apply for the children to be given residency only by returning to the US since they could not legally do so while in the UK. During this time, the children had no right of access to medical services or any right to travel as their passports remained confiscated. Several thousand pounds of application fees later they had no choice but to return to the US to re-apply for admission, in a process they were told would take eighteen months and another several thousand pounds. Either the family would be separated or the husband would lose his NHS job to return, unemployed, to the US with his wife and children.'

'It is terrible,' said **Tracy**, 'but I don't know how much should be made of such cases. Surely, they're the exception.'

'But what does this have to do with adaptation?' said **Antoine**. 'I'm still confused.'

'Sadly, they are all too common,' **I** said, 'but what struck me most when I read about the case were the behaviour and advice of the immigration officials. First, they placed two minors in detention, then proposed to deport them unaccompanied to a random city in the US with no one to receive them, and finally, when telling the family that they would have to separate for eighteen months while the British mother applied to return to the UK with her adopted sons, they said they could not see a problem as the family could stay in touch using Skype and email. The adaptation I have in mind here is not that of the family but that of the public officials, who have so thoroughly internalized the rules that decisions all of you find terrible are viewed as quite reasonable or normal.'

'This has to be an isolated case,' said **Tracy**. 'It's just too weird.'

'I don't think it is,' **I** said, 'but to go back to my main point, if we want to consider the price of immigration control, or any form of control for that matter, I think we have to enter into the calculus the way in which it transforms us. The tricky question here, however, is this: if our preferences are satisfied once they've been transformed, are we better off? If the public becomes less and less bothered by such cases, and becomes hardened or indifferent to the suffering of others, does that mean that the price of control goes down? Or does it go up?'

'This is depressing,' said **Diana**. 'We came to farewell you and were feeling a bit sad, but now we're truly disheartened.'

'Oh dear,' **I** said, 'maybe I can cheer you up.'

'That would be good,' said **Kaveh**. 'That last example was a real downer.'

'I'm not sure how much this will help,' **I** said, 'and maybe not at all, but perhaps you'll be heartened to know that, in the end, immigration control just doesn't work.'

'What do you mean?' said **Temi**. 'Surely, immigration policy has some effect. There are borders, with guards, there are police, there are visa requirements, people are deported all the time. If there was no immigration control, things would be very different.'

'You're undoubtedly right,' **I** said, 'and maybe I've overstated things a little for effect. My point, however, is fairly straightforward. Immigration control doesn't really work in the way we think it does. Or the general public and even the educated public and political leaders think.'

'Really, Xandros?' said **Diana**. 'And you're going to enlighten us? How come you know so much?'

'I'm smart, I read a lot of books,' **I** said to a chorus of groans.

'Okay,' **I** continued, 'let me explain. Have you noticed that in countries like the US and the UK and Europe immigration is continuing to rise even as immigration controls are getting tougher?'

'Not tough enough,' said **Tracy**.

'We need a wall!' said **Kaveh**. 'A beautiful wall.'

'Thanks, Kaveh,' said **Tracy**, 'thanks a bunch. But seriously, if immigration is increasing, it means that not enough resources have been put into limiting illegal migration and not enough has been done to restrict legal migration. What's missing is the political will to control both kinds of movement. I'm not against all immigration, but limits should be set and if they are they should be enforced.'

'Why do you think that's not happened?' said **Antoine**. 'I mean, that sounds pretty straightforward.'

'Political will,' said **Tracy**.

'Do you mean that governments have tried and failed or that they've not tried?' said **Astrid**.

'I think they've not tried hard enough,' said **Tracy**. 'Political will.'

'Is that it, Xandros?' said **Diana**. 'Is there any other explanation? Or why is the will lacking?'

'Disease is relative, but medicine is absolute,' **I** said, smiling.

'That's a tad cryptic, Xandros,' said **Diana**, 'if you don't mind my saying. What are you trying to say? Exactly. And a bit of your beloved conceptual clarity here, please.'

'Yes,' said **Kaveh**, 'or no more donuts for you. Ever.'

'I don't negotiate with terrorists,' **I** said, 'but since I've always bought my own donuts, I'll explain out of the goodness of my heart.'

'Curses,' said **Diana**, 'but go ahead.'

'There are two things we have to consider,' **I** said. 'First, why do immigrants keep coming?'

'Lots of reasons,' said **Temi**. 'There are push factors and pull factors, obviously. People move to where there are opportunities and if they are trying to get away from bad situations.'

'Nicely put,' **I** said. 'So what are the pull factors exactly?'

'Again, there are lots,' said **Temi**. 'Jobs, family reunion, I'm guessing those would be the most common pull factors.'

'Again, perfectly correct,' **I** said, 'and indeed, when unemployment is high, immigration goes down, and when it's low, immigration goes up.'

'Really?' said **Astrid**.

'Pretty much,' **I** said. 'When there are no jobs, fewer people move looking for them, since moving is risky and expensive and the incentive decreases. When labour is scarce, however, not only do immigrants come looking for employers but employers go looking for workers. Immigrants come because we want them. We want workers. You can build all the walls you want, but the people on our side of them will help those on the other find their way through, under, over, or around them.'

'Are you sure?' said **Tracy**, looking a little downcast. 'I'm sure it's more that politicians haven't gotten their acts together to do what's needed. Political will.'

'I'm afraid the reality is that they will talk a good game to appease those who don't want immigrants, or at least more immigrants,' **I** said, 'but they won't act on it because employers are pressuring them from the other direction. They'll take a few measures, but nothing of any great consequence. They're largely powerless.'

'I don't think that's right,' said **Tracy**. 'I think they could do a lot more.'

'Well,' **I** said, 'that then brings me to the other thing we need to consider: the effects of the controls themselves. Do controls discouraging immigration actually reduce immigration?'

'I'm guessing the answer is "no",' said **Diana**.

'Quite right,' **I** said, 'though we need to be a little cautious here since a precise answer would have to account for time and circumstance. I'm as wary of sweeping generalizations as are all of you.'

'Oh, totally, Xandros,' said **Temi** and **Antoine** in unison, and I heard vigorous mutterings of 'right' and 'absolutely'.

'Good,' **I** said, 'but why might regulations discouraging immigration or making it more difficult have some other effect?'

'Just tell us,' said **Diana**. 'Don't keep us on tenterhooks.'

'Sorry,' **I** said. 'I didn't mean to make you so nervous with excitement. It's not that complicated really. Most so-called illegal immigrants come in legally and overstay but can't risk leaving if they want to come back again because it would now be difficult if the regulations penalize them. Those who enter legally at great cost or risk also don't want to leave if they hope to return, because they may not get the chance to come back under tougher rules. So cyclical migration is replaced by one-way migration, and immigrant numbers swell.'

'Surely, that's not how things work,' said **Tracy**, 'and I'll bet if political leaders and administrators put their minds to it, they could fix this.'

'Perhaps they could,' **I** said, 'but the evidence suggests otherwise. My guess is that in the years to come in Europe and the United States, immigration numbers will continue to rise unless economic growth goes into decline and that we will continue to enjoy the fulminations of commentators bemoaning the incompetence of governments, the fecklessness of those they blame, and the way in which the country is going to the dogs.'

'Xandros!' **Diana** exclaimed. 'You're getting a little worked up. Some philosophical self-control, please!'

'My apologies,' **I** said. 'I've always prided myself on being able to conduct myself with a certain amount of grace and self-command. The truth is, self-control is all one can really achieve, and that with some difficulty. Controlling others is another matter altogether, as anyone trying to conduct a class will tell you. You can lead students to the university, but you can't make them think.'

'Starting to lose it again, Xandros,' said **Temi**. 'Just take a deep breath.'

'I think I get what you're saying,' said **Antoine**. 'It has to be difficult to control a society and get the outcomes you want. People are not very cooperative in my experience.'

'Yeah,' said **Kaveh**, 'they look like pieces on a chessboard, but they don't move as they're supposed to or like you want.'

'I think you're all wrong,' said **Tracy**. 'I mean, it's not as if we're powerless, even if we're not omnipotent and things don't always go according to plan. There's been public policy since the dawn of time!'

'First the big bang, then public policy!' said **Kaveh** with a flourish.

'Oh, shut up!' said **Tracy**, laughing.

'Policy will surely have some absolute effects,' **I** said, 'but the outcome will be uncertain because the conditions it addresses are complex. Society is a bit of a mystery, isn't it?'

'Do you have a plan, Xandros?', said **Diana**. 'It looks like you do, getting married, moving to Greece, starting a new life. You look like you're in control, even if you're sceptical about controlling others.'

'No,' **I** said, 'I'm drifting.'

'Whaaat?' said **Astrid**. 'You're kidding, right? Don't you want to have some control? Isn't that the whole point of getting clarity? Isn't that the point of philosophy?'

'Yes,' said **Temi**, 'you said it was all about asking questions about how one should live, didn't you? What's the point of asking these questions if they don't have a bearing on the decisions we take, whether individually or collectively.'

'Clarity is good,' **I** said, 'but control is a limited possibility. We live in two worlds—of theory and practice. Under the sun but also in the darkness. Maybe because we need shelter. Ignorance limits us and knowledge cannot save us, even if it helps. So, I'm going with the flow.'

'I can't believe it,' said **Diana**. 'You've discovered your inner hippie!'

'Could be,' **I** said, 'or maybe, like so many people in the world, I've just grown a little restless. But I can move. So I shall.'

'Is that it?' said **Antoine**. 'Is that all there is?'

'I'm afraid so,' **I** said, 'and time's winged Uber is hurrying near, so it really is goodbye now. Thank you for coming by with the donuts. You've been among the least poor students I've ever had.'

'What do you mean?' said **Temi**, grinning. 'I think you need to explain what you mean by poor.'

'Ah,' **I** said, 'a topic for another day. But now, I'm leaving on a jet plane—for Greece. I hate to go, but the Uber's waiting, it's blowing its horn.'

'But we have more questions,' said **Diana**. 'So annoying. So, so annoying!'

'There are always more questions,' **I** said. 'Always.'

Works Cited

Abizadeh, Arash, 'Democratic Theory and Border Coercion: No Right to Unilaterally Control Your Own Borders', *Political Theory*, 36 (1), 2008, 37–65.

Abizadeh, Arash, 'Democratic Legitimacy and State Coercion: A reply to David Miller', *Political Theory*, 38 (1), 2010, 121–130.

Aristotle, *Politics*, translated by T.A. Sinclair, revised and edited by Trevor J Saunders, London: Penguin, 1981.

Augustine of Hippo, *City of God*, translated by Henry Bettenson, with an introduction by R.G. Evans. London: Penguin Classics, 2003.

Bansak, Cynthia, Nicole B. Simpson and Madeleine Zavodny, *The Economics of Immigration*, second edition, New York: Routledge, 2021.

Borjas, George, *Immigration Economics*, Cambridge, MA: Harvard University Press, 2014.

Borjas, George, *We Wanted Workers: Unravelling the Immigration Narrative*, New York: Norton, 2016.

Brimelow, Peter, *Alien Nation: Common Sense About America's Immigration Disaster*, New York: Random House, 1995.

Brock, Gillian, *Justice for People on the Move: Migration in Challenging Times*, Cambridge, UK: Cambridge University Press, 2020.

Brown, Peter, *St Augustine of Hippo: A Biography*, Los Angeles: University of California Press, 2013.

Cafaro, Phillip, *How Many is Too Many: The Progressive Argument for Reducing Immigration to the United States*, Chicago: Chicago University Press, 2015.

Callan, Eamonn, *Creating Citizens: Political Education and Liberal Democracy*, Oxford: Oxford University Press, 2004.

Caplan, Bryan, *Open Borders: The Science and Ethics of Immigration*, New York: First Second, 2019.

Carens, Joseph, *Equality, Moral Incentives, and the Market: An Essay in Utopian Politico-economic theory*, Chicago: Chicago University Press, 1981.

Carens, Joseph 'Aliens and Citizens: The Case for Open Borders', *Review of Politics*, 49 (2), 1987, 251–273.

Carens, Joseph, *The Ethics of Immigration*, Oxford: Oxford University Press, 2013.

Clemens, Michael A., 'Economics and Emigration: Trillion-dollar Bills on the Sidewalk', *Journal of Economic Perspectives*, 25 (3), 2011, 83–106.

Clemens, Michael A., *Migration on the Rise, a Paradigm in Decline: the Last Half-Century of Global Mobility*, London: Centre for Research and Analysis of Migration, 2022. https://www.cream-migration.org/publ_uploads/CDP_02_22_1.pdf

Clemens, Michael A., and Lant Pritchett, 'The New Economic Case for Migration Restrictions: An Assessment', *Journal of Development Economics*, 138, 2019, 153–164.

Cohen, G.A., *If You're an Egalitarian How Come You're So Rich*, Cambridge, UK: Cambridge University Press, 2000.

Cohen, G.A., *Rescuing Justice and Equality*, Cambridge, MA: Harvard University Press, 2008.

Dauvergne, Catherine, *Making People Illegal: What Globalization Means for Migration and Law*, Cambridge, UK: Cambridge University Press, 2009.

Deaton, Angus, and Anne Case, *Deaths of Despair and the Future of Capitalism*, Princeton: Princeton University Press, 2021.

Fine, Sarah, 'Freedom of Association is not the Answer', *Ethics*, 120 (1), 2010, 338–356.

Frum, David, 'Enforce the Border – Humanely', *The Atlantic*, June 20, 2018. https://www.theatlantic.com/ideas/archive/2018/06/need-for-immigration-control/563261/

Frum, David, 'If Liberals Don't Enforce Borders, Fascists Will', *The Atlantic Monthly*, April 2019, https://www.theatlantic.com/magazine/archive/2019/04/david-frum-how-much-immigration-is-too-much/583252/

Gandhi, M.K., *Hind Swaraj and Other Writings*, edited by Anthony J. Parel. Cambridge, UK: Cambridge University Press, 2010.

Gest, Justin, *The New Minority: White Working Class Politics in an Age of Immigration and Inequality*, Oxford: Oxford University Press, 2016.

Goodhart, David, *The British Dream: Successes and Failures of Postwar Immigration*, London: Atlantic Books, 2013.

Goodhart, David, *The Road to Somewhere*, Harmondsworth: Penguin, 2017.

Goodin, Robert E., 'What is So Special about Our Fellow Countrymen?', *Ethics*, 98 (4), 1988, 663–686.

Goodin, Robert E., 'Enfranchising All Affected Interests, and Its Alternatives', *Philosophy and Public Affairs*, 35 (1), 2007, 40–68

Goodin, Robert E., 'Enfranchising All Subjected, Worldwide', *International Theory*, 8 (3), 2016, 365–389.

Haas, Helen de, *How Immigration Really Works: The Facts About the Most Divisive Issue in Politics*, New York: Basic Books, 2023.

Hayek, F.A., *The Constitution of Liberty*, London: Routledge, 1960.

Hayek, F.A., *Law, Legislation and Liberty*, London: Routledge, 1979.

Hayton, Bill, *The Invention of China*, New Haven and London: Yale University Press, 2020.

Hidalgo, Javier, 'The Ethics of People Smuggling', *Journal of Global Ethics*, 12 (3), 2016, 311–326.

Hobbes, Thomas, *Leviathan* [1651], edited by Richard Tuck, New York: Cambridge University Press, 1991.

Hochschild, Arlie, *Strangers in Their Own Land: Anger and Mourning on the American Right*, New York: The New Press, 2016.

Huemer, Michael, 'Is There a Right Immigrate?', *Social Theory and Practice*, 36 (3), 2010, 429–461.

Huntington, Samuel P., *Who Are We? The Challenges to American National Identity*, New York: Simon and Schuster, 2005

Kaldor Centre for International Refugee Law, https://www.kaldorcentre.unsw.edu.au/publication/cost-australias-asylum-policy

Kaufmann, Eric, *Whiteshift: Populism, Immigration and the Future of White Majorities*, London: Penguin, 2019.

Kukathas, Chandran, 'In Praise of the Strange Virtue of People Smuggling', *Quadrant*, 47 (9), 2003, 40–41.

Kukathas, Chandran, 'The Case for Open Immigration', in Andrew I. Cohen and Christopher Heath Wellman, *Contemporary Debates in Applied Ethics*, Malden MA: Wiley-Blackwell, 2005, 207–220.

Kukathas, Chandran, 'Why Open Borders?', *Ethical Perspectives*, 19 (4), 2012, 650–675.

Kukathas, Chandran, 'On Sen on Comparative Justice', *Critical Review of International Social and Political Philosophy*, 16 (2), 2013, 196–204.

Kukathas, Chandran, 'The Labour Theory of Justice', in Alexander Kaufmann (ed.), *Distributive Justice and Access to Advantage: G.A. Cohen's Egalitarianism*, Cambridge, UK: Cambridge University Press, 2014, 235–248.

Kukathas, Chandran, 'Are Refugees Special?', in Sarah Fine and Lea Ypi (eds.), *Migration in Political Theory: The Ethics of Movement and Membership*, Oxford: Oxford University Press, 2016, 249–268.

Kukathas, Chandran, 'Liberalism's Essential Tension: on Jacob Levy on Rationalism, Pluralism and Freedom', *Online Library of Liberty: Liberty Matters*, 2016. https://oll.libertyfund.org/publications/liberty-matters/jacob-levy-rationalism-pluralism-freedom#post_1300

Kukathas, Chandran, 'Immigration and Freedom', in Johannes Knolle and James Poskett (eds.), *Migration*, Cambridge, UK: Cambridge University Press, 2020, 18–49.

Kukathas, Chandran, *Immigration and Freedom*, Princeton: Princeton University Press, 2021.

Kukathas, Chandran, 'Immigration and Liberal Freedom', in Duncan Ivison (ed.), *Research Handbook on Liberalism*, Cheltenham: Edward Elgar, 2024, 210–224.

Kunz, E.F., 'The Refugee in Flight: Kinetic Models and Forms of Displacement', *International Migration Review*, 7 Summer 1977, 125–146.

Lebland, David, and Benjamin Helms, *The Ties that Bind: Immigration and the Global Political Economy*, Cambridge, UK: Cambridge University Press, 2023.

Macedo, Stephen, *Diversity and Distrust: Civic Education in a Multicultural Democracy*, Cambridge, MA: Harvard University Press, 2000.

Macedo, Stephen, 'Why Can't We all Just Move Around? *Mind*, 132 (526), 2023, 595–604.

Maley, William, *What is a Refugee?*, London: Hurst, 2016.

Mann, Michael, *The Sources of Social Power, Volume 1: A History of Power from the Beginning to AD 1760*, Cambridge, UK: Cambridge University Press, 2012.

McCabe, David, *Modus Vivendi Liberalism: Theory and Practice*, Cambridge, UK: Cambridge University Press, 2010.

Melzer, Arthur, *The Natural Goodness of Man: On the System of Rousseau's Thought*, Chicago: University of Chicago Press, 1990.

Mill, John Stuart, *Inaugural Address Delivered to the University of St Andrews, February 1st 1867*, London: Sothis Press, 2023.
Miller, David, 'The Ethical Significance of Nationality', *Ethics*, 98 (4), 1988, 647–662.
Miller, David, 'Immigration: The Case for Limits', in Andrew I. Cohen and Christopher Heath Wellman, *Contemporary Debates in Applied Ethics*, Malden MA: Wiley-Blackwell, 2005, 193–206.
Miller, David, 'Why Immigration Controls Are Not Coercive', *Political Theory*, 38 (1), 2009, 111–120.
Miller, David, 'Is There a Human Right to Immigrate?', in Sarah Fine and Lea Ypi (eds.), *Migration in Political Theory: The Ethics of Movement and Membership*, Oxford: Oxford University Press, 2016, 11–31.
Miller, David, *Strangers in Our Midst: The Political Philosophy of Immigration*, Cambridge, MA: Harvard University Press, 2016b.
Moore, Margaret, *A Political Theory of Territory*, Oxford: Oxford University Press, 2017.
Mulhall, Stephen, and Adam Swift, *Liberals and Communitarians*, revised edition, Oxford: Wiley, 1996.
Murray, Douglas, *The Strange Death of Europe: Immigration, Identity, Islam*, London: Bloomsbury, 2017.
Nietzsche, Friedrich, *Thus Spoke Zarathustra: A Book for All and None*, edited by Adrian Del Caro and Robert Pippin, translated by Adrian Del Caro, Cambridge, UK: Cambridge University Press, [1883-85] 2006.
Nixey, Catherine, *Heresy: Jesus Christ and Other Sons of God*, New York: Picador, 2024.
Nozick, Robert, *Anarchy, State and Utopia*, Oxford: Blackwell, 1974.
O'Neill, Onora, 'Ethical Reasoning and Ideological Pluralism', *Ethics*, 98 (4), 1988, 705–722.
Obama, Barack, *The Audacity of Hope*, New York: Crown Publishing, 2006, 263.
Oberman, Kieran, 'Can Brain Drain Justify Immigration Restrictions', *Ethics*, 123 (3), 2013, 427–455.
Oberman, Kieran, 'Poverty and Immigration Policy', *American Political Science Review*, 109 (2), 2015, 239–251
Oberman, Kieran, 'Immigration as a Human Right', in Sarah Fine and Lea Ypi (eds.), *Migration in Political Theory: The Ethics of Movement and Membership*, Oxford: Oxford University Press, 2016, 32–56.
Owen, David, *What Do We Owe to Refugees?*, Oxford: Polity, 2020.
Parker, Kunal M., *Making Foreigners: Immigration and Citizenship Law in America 1600-2000*, Cambridge, UK: Cambridge University Press, 2015.
Quinn, Josephine, *How the World Made the West: A 4,000-Year History*, London: Bloomsbury, 2024.
Rawls, John, 'Justice as Fairness: Political Not Metaphysical', *Philosophy and Public Affairs*, 14 (3), 1985, 223–251.
Rawls, John, *A Theory of Justice* [1971], Revised Edition, Cambridge, MA: Belknapp Harvard University Press, 1999.
Rawls, John, *Political Liberalism* [1993], Revised Edition, New York: Columbia University Press, 1999.
Rawls, John, *Justice as Fairness: A Restatement*, edited by Erin Kelly, Cambridge, MA: Belknapp Press of Harvard University Press, 2001.

Rawls, John, *The Law of Peoples with "The Idea of Public Reason Revisited"*, Cambridge, MA: Harvard University Press, 2002.
Reus-Smit, Christian, *The Moral Purpose of the State: Social Identity and Institutional Rationality in International Relations*, Princeton: Princeton University Press, 1999.
Rousseau, Jean-Jacques, 'Discourse on the Origin and Foundations of Inequality Among Mankind', in J.J. Rousseau, *The Social Contract and the First and Second Discourses*, edited by Susan Dunn, New Haven: Yale University Press, 2002.
Sager, Alex, 'Methodological Nationalism, Immigration and Political Theory', *Political Studies*, 64 (1), 2016, 42–59.
Sager, Alex, 'Political Philosophy Beyond Methodological Nationalism', *Philosophy Compass*, 16 (2), 2021, e 12726.
Sen, Amartya, *The Idea of Justice*, Cambridge, MA: Harvard University Press, 2009.
Shachar, Ayelet, *The Birthright Lottery: Citizenship and Global Inequality*, Cambridge, MA: Harvard University Press, 2009.
Shacknove, Andrew E., 'Who is a Refugee?', *Ethics*, 95 (2), 1985, 274–284.
Shariatmadari, David, *Don't Believe a Word: The Surprising Truth About Language*, London: Weidenfield and Nicholson, 2020.
Shumsky, Neil Larry, 'Noah Webster and the Invention of Immigration', *The New England Quarterly*, March 2008, 81 (1), 126–135.
Sugden, Robert, *The Community of Advantage: A Behavioural Economist's Defence of the Market*, Oxford: Oxford University Press, 2018.
Tinti, Peter, and Tuesday Reitano, *Migrant, Refugee, Smuggler, Saviour*, Oxford: Oxford University Press, 2017.
United Nations High Commissioner for Refugees website: https://www.unhcr.org/sites/default/files/legacy-pdf/4ca34be29.pdf
Walzer, Michael, *Spheres of Justice: A Defense of Pluralism and Equality*, New York: Basic Books, 1983.
Watson, Tara, and Kalee Thompson, *The Border Within: The Economics of Immigration in an Age of Fear*, Chicago: Chicago University Press, 2022.
Wellman, Christopher Heath, "Immigration and Freedom of Association." *Ethics*, 119 (1), 2008, 109–141.
Wellman, Christopher Heath, and Phillip Cole, *Debating the Ethics of Immigration: Is There a Right to Exclude?*, New York: Oxford University Press, 2011.
Wenar, Leif, 'Rights', *Stanford Encyclopedia of Philosophy* (Spring 2023 edition), Edward N. Zalta and Uri Nodelman (eds.), URL: https://plato.stanford.edu/archives/spr2023/entry/rights
Yglesias, Matthew, 'The Deaths of Despair Narrative is Wrong', *Slow Boring* blog: https://www.slowboring.com/p/the-deaths-of-despair-narrative-is
Ypi, Lea, 'Justice in Migration: A Closed Borders Utopia', *Journal of Political Philosophy*, 16 (4), 2008, 391–418.
Ypi, Lea, 'Irregular migration, historical injustice, and the right to exclude', *Royal Institute of Philosophy Supplements, Volume 91: A Philosophers' Manifesto: Ideas to Change the World*, May 2022, 169–183.

Index

Pages followed by "n" refer to notes.

For Product Safety Concerns and Information please contact our EU representative GPSR@taylorandfrancis.com Taylor & Francis Verlag GmbH, Kaufingerstraße 24, 80331 München, Germany

Printed and bound by CPI Group (UK) Ltd, Croydon, CR0 4YY

27/05/2025

01884449-0001